Agile Architecture for Service Oriented Component Driven Enterprises

Encouraging Rapid Application Development

AF800945

DataThunder

Ray Harvick

DataThunder Publishing

Kissimmee, FL www.datathunder.com

Publisher: Data Thunder Publishing

DataThunder has been a consulting and publishing company for more than 10 years.

www.datathunder.com

Ordering information:

Quantity sales: Special discounts are available on quantity purchases by corporations, associations, and others. For details, contact the publisher/author at e-mail address above.

Printed in the United States of America

Library of Congress Cataloging Publication data

Agile Architecture of Service Oriented Component Driven Enterprises

ISBN-13: 978-0615596433 (DataThunder Publishing)

ISBN-10: 0615596436

1. The main category of the book: Information Technology
2. Another Subject category: Software Development
3. Another Subject category: Agile Development
4. Another Subject category: Service Oriented Architecture
5. Another Subject category: Component Driven Architecture

First Edition

14 13 12 11 10 / 10 9 8 7 6 5 4 3 2 1

Dedicated to my wife Lee without her encouragement, this would not have been possible.

In memory of my father Joe Harvick, who I deeply miss: Who once told me son, if you reach for the stars and jump for the moon and you only get one foot off the ground that is one foot more than had you never tried.

Table of Contents

Preface

This book was written for those who desire to go beyond the object oriented programming, Design Patterns, and basic Architecture Patterns. There are many who believe all you need to do to start a new project is to start writing code. Some have described this as code and fix which usually results in what is called in technical terms, the the big blob of mud. For those of us who have seen the good, the bad, and the ugly of project development, they instinctively know that long term software development requires up front planning and coordination. Projects that fail to plan, plan to fail. Some believe you can create a project starting with a prototype, but prototypes tend to never go away once adopted.

Software for the most part has common Architecture patterns that are illustrated in this book. While there have been many books that have given high level concepts on how to layer software, many are so abstract that they tend leave a lot to interpretation. One of the most important features of Architecture is its ability to break down software into components. In order to easily transverse from component to component so type of facade and Meta data is required. Facades are important so that each layer and component can utilize common features such as exception handling. Meta data is required so that once a component is entered, the right block of code can be executed.

The Architecture present here has been developed over a number of years utilizing lessons learned and information from a number of articles and publications. While there is always room to grow, I believe the architecture presented here will work for almost any type of application.

While it may be possible to use other technologies to create the architectural patterns presented here, Java is the language used in this book as well as other Technoligies such as Spring, Hibernate, JSF, and IceFaces. Java is a very powerfull and flexible language that allows for greater deal of control. But with power also comes the potential for pitfalls. Java is also a great language for creating components and Service Oriented Architectures. Since Java is a robust technology it used to accomplish many advanced types of processing such as Component Based Architectures as well as Service Oriented Services.

Complexity exist and is part of the nature of software development. It can not be eliminated or destroyed, it exists regardless. Complexity can be mitigated or it can be exacerbated. One way of mitigating complexity is to use well defined Architectures and Frameworks. They issolate the complexity from the developer so that it does not have to be solved repeatedly.

About This Book

Written for Advanced Java Developers and Architects

This book is for those who love to write Java Code and Architects who want to be successful. This book is written around a successful architecture that has been developed for a number of companies over a number of years. There are an extensive number of java code example that can be examined and imitated.

Written for Managers and Executive who want results

Writing Java code is complex, good Architectures make is simplier. Component Based Architectures make it easier to manage java projects. Component Based Architecture makes it possible to do Rapid Application Development.

Knowledge of advanced technologies is assumed

This book assumes you have advanced knowledge of software development technologies including Java, J2EE, Spring, Hibernate, JSF, and IceFaces.

About the Author

Ray C. Harvick

Ray Harvick first started writing software in high school back in 1973 writing business basic. Later he switched to C, then C++, SmallTalk, and then Java.

He has a Master Degree in Computer Science and a Bachelor of Education in Computer Science. Since the early stages of his career Ray has had an interest in Software Architecture and his knowledge and understanding has grown over the years. The author has also been an instructor at several colleges teaching principles of Java, object oriented programming, and C++.

The author has worked on a number of software systems ranging from Banking and Finance, to Telecommunications, Military applications, to Shipping companies, to Health Care.

In all of these types of application each had one thing in common to their success, software architecture. After working with and studying different kinds of Architecture, the Author has developed detail understanding of many types of Architectures and Software Patterns.

Definitions

Agile Architecture: Is a Software Architecture that promotes Agile Development. There are key factors that are required for Architecture to be Agile. First, it must be adaptable to change. In other words, if a software element changes in one part of the system, the architecture must be able to quickly adapt to that change. Second, it must allow for dependency injection. When Architecture is built on the concept of dependency injection, then only the interface needs to be predefined, the implementation can change at will without the need for other software elements to change. Third, it must allow for pattern driven development, or in other words, each software element must follow a similar pattern to other similar software elements.

Aggregation: Represents a whole that comprises various parts; A Committee is an aggregate of its Members. A Meeting is an aggregation of an Agenda, Room, and the attendees.

Annotations: In Java, annotations are a way of facilitating Meta programming (see Meta Programming below). Annotations themselves do not affect execution of the software, but are rather tags that can be used by application with the use of Meta programming to perform runtime activities by on values in the Annotation tags.

Architecture: The structural coordination and representation of a system that provides the foundation of the overall pattern of implementation and execution of a software system.

Cohesion: Is a measure of how modules work together to accomplish a task or function activity.

Communication Latency: Latency is the time difference between a call to a method or a service and then return to the original execution flow, communication latency is the overhead caused by the communication protocol and the time to move information from one location to another.

Command Message Object (CmdMsg): Is a software component for passing information between tiers and layers of an application. The Command Message

Object holds a collection of objects for processing logic. These may include Request Object, Response Object, Session Object, and collection of Errors.

Common coupling: When two modules utilize the same global data.

Component: A deployable independent unit of work that exposes its behavior through a set of well-defined interfaces or methods. A component is based on a set of standards and definitions that are universal in scope for a software system and are defined by a specification and is implemented in a self-contained software unit. Components can usually other components through integration patterns to form a more course grain software unit. For purposes of this document, is any class that implements the Component interface.

Component Injection: Is the process for injecting a component into another component or architecture so that when all components are injected they form a working Software Application.

Composition: Tight coupling between its parts. If a class of objects (container) is composed of other objects (elements) and the elements live only as long as the container lives. Example: A Customers name and address cannot live without the customer itself.

Component Architecture: Is the coordination and structure for internal software system that process the interaction between individual and collection of software components.

Component Driven Architecture (CDA): An architecture that supports well defined components using dependency injection.

Component Granularity: The amount of work and size of a component in context to the overall system; the lower the level the Component in the Hierarchy, the less the Granularity. For instance an Exchange/Data Access Object is by definition is less granular than the Domain that calls it. As we move up the stack the Granularity of the Solution that calls the Domain has a much larger Granularity. Once at the Service Proxy level, the Granularity is considered high.

Component Adapter: Converts a Software Unit defined without the predefined Component Interfaces of the Architecture into a Component that can be injected into the architecture. This can be accomplished by wrapping the Software unit internally with a newly created Component that allows the adapted software unit to work as if it was constructed as part of the defined architecture. This allows software units that would not normally be compatible with the architecture to work as if it had been designed as part of the overall system application.

Content Coupling: Occurs when one module access the internal workings of another module, required less if it is read only or modifies the data. This produces highly coupled modules.

Control Coupling: When one module passes information to another module that controls its flow or execution path.

Controller: Is the bridge between the Model and the View. Its main responsibility is to be a go between the two tiers. In a MVC2 Pattern design the View receives initial interaction from the user, and then passes control to the Controller. The Controller performance translation process between the View and the Model and then passes a request to the Model. The Model returns a set of data which is then formatted by the Controller and passed to the View. Controllers can also use Mediators.

Controller Tier: Consist of a number of layers, including the Dispatcher, Mediator, and the Delegate layers. The Controller Tier is the bridge between the View and the Model.

Create, Read, Update, or Delete (CRUD): Used primarily in connection with a data storage technology such as a Database for data persistence.

Data: Information representing business datum or record that is maintained and manipulated by the component that is responsible for processing the information.

Data Access Object (DAO): An object used to perform CRUD operations on external data. Most often this data is in a database but could also be in a JMS Queue or a flat for file or any other storage mechanism.

Data Coupling: When one or more modules pass parameters or data elements such as a passing an integer to compute a value.

Data Transfer Object (DTO): Is a design pattern used to transfer data between software application modules.

Data Value Object (DVO): a java bean used to store results from a dynamic query in hibernate.

Declared Query: In a Declared Query, the query is declared using annotations. During processing Meta Programming is used to process the query by passing the annotation information to the DAO for processing.

Delegate: Is a classification of software elements that is used to delegate/transfer control from the current thread of execution to another software unit. This is can be either be a local object such as a Proxy class or it can call a Remote Service Object to send a request to a Service Oriented Object (such as a web service). The Delegate forms half of the requirement of a Service Oriented Architecture. It is the pitcher of a request for service. The other half of the Service Oriented Architecture, the receiver, receives the request, processes it, and returns a response to the caller.

Delegate Component: A Delegate Component is a Delegate that is a pluggable component or software unit that can be injected into a software unit using a named value for identification purposes. When injected into a Delegate Manager, the Delegate Component can be referenced by named and execution flow transferred to the object for processing.

Delegate Layer: The Delegate Layer is part of the Controller tier. It is the starting point of a Service call to the Model Tier or a web service. For this document it consists of the Delegate Manager and the Delegate Components.

Delegate Manager: Is a manager of Delegate Components. The Delegate components are injected into the delegate manager by name and are stored in the Delegate Manager. When a unit of work (Mediator) calls the Delegate Manager it does so by use of the name of the Delegate Component along with a Message object.

Dependency Injection: This is the process where Objects/Components are not fully aware of the underlying Objects, but are only aware of the interface definition of the Object or in other words, it only knows about the methods it can call, but knows nothing about how the class/object is implemented. This allows the class implementation to be injected from an external source (such as Spring Configuration File). This allows different objects to behave differently depending on how the underlying class implementation behaves based on the interface definition.

Dispatcher Layer: This is the top layer of the Controller Tier and it receives request from the view to take some type of action. This action may be as simple as storing data from the view or it may consist of a set of logic that is to be processed which could eventually return data to the calling view, or cause another view to be displayed with a set of new data elements.

Domain: a Component Object that represent the entities in the business domain that the system is designed to support. An example may be package tracking information.

Domain Component: Is an autonomous representation of a business concept, business logic, or a business process. It is the organization element that implements the logic based on business rules. The Domain component is small grained set of business logic or rules designed for reuse throughout the software system(s).

Domain Layer: Is part of the Model Tier and lies between the Solution Layer and the Exchange/Data Access Layer. It consists of Domain Components that define well defined business domain logic.

DRY Principle: Stands for Don't Repeat Yourself or in other words, common logic should always remain in one location and should never be duplicated. See also Single Source of Truth.

Encapsulation: The hiding or wrapping of information details such as the component is not dependent of the properties of the data but rather the behavior of the component.

Exception Handler: Is a software unit for handling specific types of exceptions. The Exception Handler is injected into the Exception manager and is designed to know what types of exceptions it can handle and what to do with that exception. It may be as simple as re-throwing the exception or it may consist of interpreting the exception, converting it into an error message that can be easily interpreted by up the stack software components. An exception handler can even redirect process logic to another execution flow for further processing.

Exception Management: This software unit of work is ever present in the architecture and crosses layer/tier boundaries. When an exception occurs, the Exception Manager catches it and uses the Exception Handlers that were injected into the Exception Manager for processing.;

Exchange: a Component Object that represents an exchange of data from external systems. An exchange is a wrapper around a Data Access Object (DAO) and isolates the framework from the technology that is used to process the Data Access Object. For instance, a DAO may be an access to a database table or it may be a set of code to write to a JMS queue. In either case, the Exchange is unaware how the DAO works, it only cares that it can request some action and it will receive results (even it is a success or a failure).

Exchange Component: An Exchange Component is an exchange that is designed to be injected into the architecture at the Exchange layer for processing of low level information exchange such as accessing a database.

Exchange Layer: The Exchange Layer is the lowest level of the Model Tier and is injected with Exchange Components for processing. The Exchange Layer resides under the Domain Layer.

External Coupling: When two modules share external source of data, regardless if it is communication protocol, data format, or device interface. This coupling is imposed by external devices or software applications.

Generic DAO: Is a Pattern for creating DAOs. Using the Java Generics, the DAO is built using a set of well-defined object types that control the execution of the DAO. These types may consist of Data Transfer Object, a Named Query and Value Object.

Hierarchical Foundation: The Tiers and Layers that form the foundation of the overall system architecture.

Hibernate: Is an Object Relational Mapper open source tool. It provides a layer between the Application Software and the database. Along with Hibernate Value Objects and Named Queries, it is capable of doing all of the Database work and returning results.

Hibernate Value Object (HVO): a Java bean consisting of Hibernate Annotations.

Infrastructure Component: A software module or element that supports application functionality not directly associated to any business logic such Exception Handlers, Command Message Object, etc.

Inversion of Control (IoC): is an abstract principle in which the flow of execution is modified depending upon the type of object that is injected into the system (see dependency injection). In traditional programming, process is tightly coupled to the object implementation In IoC processing is loosely coupled to the object implementation so that reusable generic code controls the execution of the problem specific code based on the object injected.

Java Bean: Any java object with a collection of private attributes and a set of public getters and setters for the set of attributes.

Layer: Is a separation of code where each layer has a well-defined separation of concern.

Layer Component: Is a component that consists of any implementation of a Solution, Domain, or an Exchange class. Each Component is responsible for a separate SoC.

Mediator: Is a pattern that used in conjunction with the controller can further the formatting of data received by the controller such as when a controller may want to output different types of outputs such as a JSP page or an Excel Spread Sheet or a PDF. In each of these cases the output of the data is similar but formatted for each particular technology.

Mediator Layer: Is part of the Controller Tier and lies between the Dispatcher Layer and the Delegate Layer. It used to process information received from the View and when appropriate passing it to a Delegate Component using the Delegate Manager. Once the Delegate is completed, it receives information from the Service Call and process the data for use by the Dispatcher which in turn passes the information to the View.

Message Coupling: This very low coupling is achieved by passing messages instead of parameters. This creates a decentralized module components where each component retrieves or sets only the data elements they are concerned with.

Meta Programming: Is a process of using the Object definition to process activities such as moving data from one object another using Java Reflection. It may also be used to direct execution flow using annotations contained in an object. In short, Meta Programming is the process of executing action based on the definition of one or more objects. Meta is information about data structures.

Model: is responsible for all business logic and storing and retrieving data. The Model is typically divided into a set of layers or SoC. In this document, the Model is divided into three layers (Solution, Domain, and Exchange/DAO).

Model Tier: The Model Tier is used to process business logic based on a set of Components and Layers. The Layers/Component consists of the Solution, Domain, and Exchange/Data Access Objects.

Model View Controller Pattern (MVC). Is way of dividing a program into General unique features or SoC.

Model View Controller Pattern 2 (MVC2): The original MVC pattern was designed for a software program that controlled the entire processing including how to display information to the User. The MVC2 Pattern is designed with the Web in Mind. It acknowledges the presence of a Server such as JBoss and uses web technology such as a Servlet.

Named Query: Is a hibernate protocol for passing Query definition to hibernate. It is based on a set of annotation defined in Hibernate and placed in a class whose structured is predefined by hibernate.

Page Transfer Object (PTO): Is a similar to a DTO except instead of being used to transfer data between layers in system; it is used to transfer data between a Controller and a View.

Presentation Tier (or View): Is the tier that presents information to the user. This usually consists of JSP/Html and tag libraries that are defined by an application to present data to the user.

Persistent Tier: Not actually part of the overall system architecture, the Persistent Tier is the external data access service such as a database.

Rapid Application Development (RAD): Is set of tools and/or process for rapidly creating applications. It may consist of anything that can help a software development team rapidly create and maintain software.

Reflection Programming: (See Meta Programming)

Remote Procedure Call (RPC): Is a process of calling a software unit of code from another unit of code indirectly using a communication protocol such as SOAP, TCP Sockets, etc.

Request Object: A Request object in this document is any Data Transfer Object that is stored in the Request repository of the Command Message Object to assist in further.

Response Object: Is any Data Transfer Object stored in the Response repository of the Command Message Object and represents the results of processing from any Component in the system.

Separation of concerns (SoC): is the process of separating computer program software into distinct features that overlap as little as possible. SoC is often achieved through layering and modularity of the program to encapsulate (black box/information hiding) unique features of the software.

Service Oriented Architecture (SOA): Is any Architecture that supports the Service Requests. In a SOA, there are usually two parts, the requestor of a service and the service provider. SOA does not define how that requestor communicates with the service provider nor does it define how the service provider receives a request.

Service Oriented Component: Is a top level component which acts as both a component and an entry point to a set of components forming a service.

Service Oriented Component Driven Architecture (SOCDA): Is an Architecture that combines Service Oriented Architecture with Component Driven Architecture . In SOCDA, the software is divided into tiers (usually the View, Controller, and the Model). The Controller and the Model software units are composed of a set of injected components that define the execution of logic in a well-defined separation of concern layers. The communication between the Controller and the Model is defined by a set of Service Calls (Delegates) and Service Providers (Service Proxies). This communication may consist of intra-tier communication (java to java calls) or may consist of inter-tier communication (Remote Processing calls such as web service calls).

Service Proxy: Is the entry point to a Service/Solution. The Service Proxy creates an interface that allows different types of inter and intra communication protocols to communicate with the overall service without the need to change or extend the service. The Service Proxy represents the actually service which is supplemented by a set of components that make up the logic required to complete the service request.

Servlet: is a Java Class in J2EE that conforms to the Java Servlet API protocol. It is specifically designed with Web Servers in mind and utilizes the web technologies to interact with the Web Server (such as JBoss).

Simple Object Access Protocol (SOAP): is a protocol specification for exchanging predefined information data packets used to interface exchange information with the requestor. Using XML for its data structure and relies on communication protocol defined by Http and SMTP to transmit message details to the service provider and to receive response transmitted back to the requestor.

Single Source of Truth: Is a concept where one and only one software component is responsible for providing information that is unique to the system such as the same logic exists one place and one place only.

Software Component: Is any software unit that is defined to work as an injectable software unit and that implements the interface Component.

Solution: a software unit that is used to solve one or more set of business logic. A Solution can either call one or more Domain objects or another Solution. While a Solution could be standalone, that is very rare.

Solution Component: Is a Component that implements a Solution and is an injectable component used in the Solution Layer.

Solution Layer: Is the layer that exists between the Service Proxy and the Domain Layer. It is the top layer of the Model Tier and is composed of a set of injected Solution Components.

Software Tiers: Is a set of Software Layers that make a well-defined layered structure. In the MVC pattern, there are four defined Tiers: View (or Presentation) Tier, the Model Tier, the Controller Tier, and the Persistent Tier (Database or other external system). In order for a collection of Software Units to be a tier, they have defined boundaries such as a Service Requestor (Delegate) or a Service Provider (Service Proxy).

Software Layers: Is division of a Software Tier such as when collected to gather form a Service Tier. An example of a set of Software Layers or those that make up the Model Tier; The Model Tier is made up of a set of Software Layers (Service Proxy, Solution, Domain, Exchange/Data Access Object).

Spring: Is an open source set of software units that provide a set of utilities used to build an application, primarily using dependency injection. Spring brings a lot to the table and the full scope of Spring is beyond the scope of this book.

Structure (Data) Coupling: Occurs when a structure data is passed from one module to another even if the receiving module only needs one field from the structure.

View (Presentation): is responsible for display logic of the software. In a web system, the View is often a JSP using such technologies such as JSF or ICEfaces.

Web Service: Is a defined method of communication between two software units over the internet. The W3C defines a "Web service" as "a software system designed to support interoperable machine-to-machine interaction over a network".

Web Service Definition Language (WSDL): A formatted XML structure used to define a set of message end points operating on a message describe abstractly and bound to a message format and a communication protocol forming a Service Resquest end point and a Service Response end point.

Chapter 1 Agile Application Principles

1.1 Defining what is a Software Architecture

Software Architecture is a system wide software pattern. The intent of Software Architecture is to enforce collaborative rules for the project. It is a set of significant decisions about the structure and organization of the system. The Architecture defines the behavior and interfaces by which the system is constructed.

Most often, Software Architectures are layered with well-defined roles for each layer. The intent of the Software Architecture is to decompose complex software rules into manageable segments.

While Software Architecture and Software Patterns are sometimes used interchangeably, they are not synonymous. While a Software Architecture is made up of a collection of Software Patterns, Software Patterns do not necessarily form a Software Architecture, they are holistically different.

One of the earliest and most successful Software Architecture is the Model-View-Controller, brought into promise by a programming language called Smalltalk. The basic idea was to divide the way that data was displayed (The View) from the way that data logic (The Model). The Controller was used to bond the two together. The Mediator, which is often over looked in the pattern, was used to mediate the difference between the business/logic data from the display data. This allowed a Model or a View to be reused while not tightly coupling the two together.

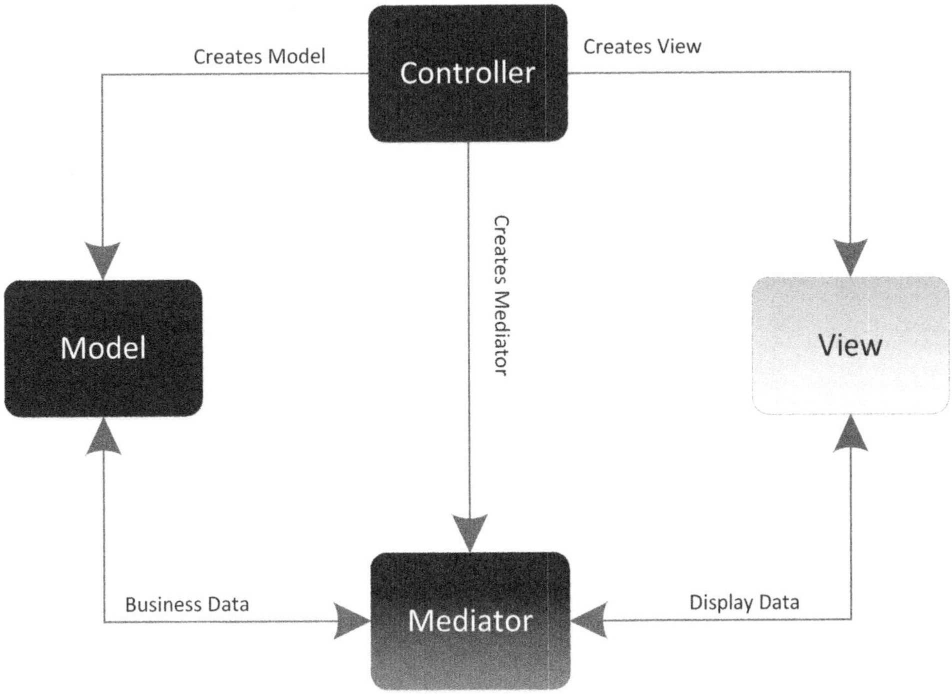

This pattern was later adapted to fit the web model known as MVC2. In the MVC2 Pattern, no longer could the data pass Omni-directional, it now had to pass vertically. This was due mainly to the differences in the technology. In the standard MVC pattern, all the code could reside on one computer using one base language such as SmallTalk where the MVC pattern originated. While there are still many systems where the software does reside on one computer, they can still use the basic MVC pattern.

But with the introduction of web technology, things had to change. No longer could we expect the code to reside on one computer, but rather it is more likely to reside on more than one computer system. To make an even greater difference, the technology or language of one tier/layer was likely to be different than that of the other. While the View was likely written in HTML or JSP, the Controller was likely written in java.

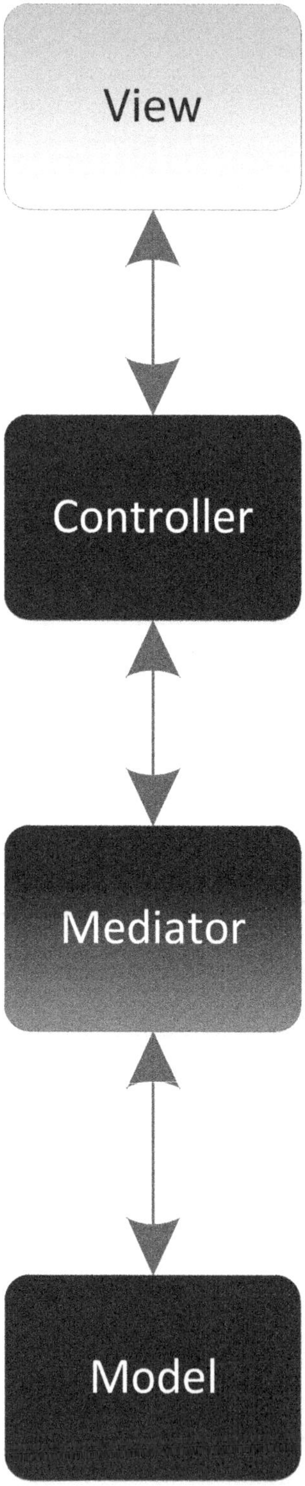

Data is passed between the controller and the view to present information to the user and receive their imput

Controller controls the flow of data between the View and the rest of the architecture.

The mediator is a translator that translate the data from a format that the controller receives or passes to the view into or from a format that the back end system can understand.

1.2 Family of Architectural Patterns

The families of Architectural Patterns are a very important concept in Agile Architecture development. By viewing the types of Architectural Patterns, we can get a better understanding of how to develop Architectural Patterns for an Agile Development effort.

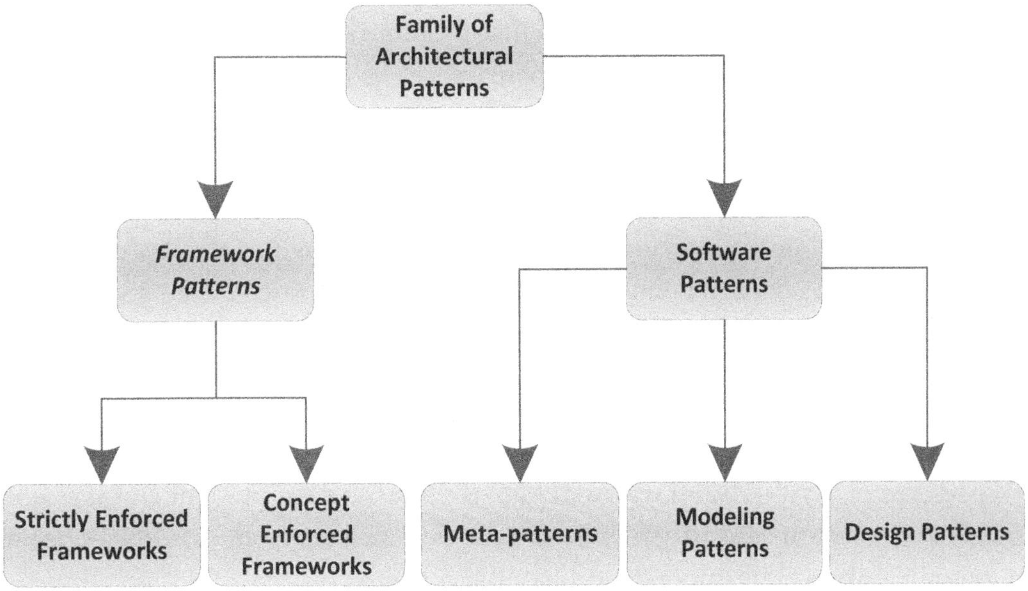

The first thing we must look at is the types of Architectural Patterns. Generally, speaking, Architectural Patterns can be divided into two sub groups, Framework Patterns and Software Patterns.

Framework Patterns describe how an Enterprise Application functions in the entire life cycle of an event, while Software Patterns are used on case by case bases.

Strictly enforced frameworks are exactly what they describe, they strictly enforce how Enterprise Application Architecture functions, and there is little or no deviation in the overall actions. They are enforced by the use interfaces, abstract classes, and procedural code used to combine the activities of the different parts of the system. Strictly enforced frameworks tend to create a greater cohesion between the elements of the system as developers are forced to follow strict guidelines enforced by interfaces and abstract elements.

Concept Enforced Frameworks provide only a suggestion of how a system interacts and can only be enforced by self-discipline of the developers. Concept Enforced frameworks tend to lose their cohesion over time as developers tend to get off the reservation and go their own way.

Software Patterns are a design pattern that promote an idea of a concept to solve a reoccurring problem in a given domain space. A design pattern in of itself is not a complete design that can be implemented into code. Rather it is a concept, description, or template that describes how to solve for a given situation. The design patterns describe how classes interact with each other and their relationship without specifying the final software elements, classes, or objects. Software Patterns tend to be more applicable in the Object-Oriented space rather than in procedural languages, although they can be adaptation is possible.

Meta-Patterns are a pattern for patterns. They provide a mechanism for designers to provide an even more abstract level of knowledge than other types of patterns. They can be an important concept in the development and usage of frameworks as a means of passing on design principles from one developer to another to enhance the understanding of the concepts.

Modeling Patterns are used mainly in the analysis and design phases of a project and do not focus so much on the technical design or the implementation. While design patterns and Modeling Patterns have similarities, they serve different purposes. Modeling Patterns deal with how to describe how the system not how to implement the solution. Modeling Patterns are useful when performing domain specific analysis in using concept abstraction. Modeling Patterns are useful in identifying concepts and do not elaborate on the implementation of the software.

Design Patterns in software development are reusable pattern for solving reoccurring problem common to software systems. Design Patterns are a templates or descriptions of how to solve problems for similar situations that can be converted into software. Typically design patterns represent the interaction and relationships between software elements. Most Design patterns are described in terms of object orientation but can be used in procedural languages using structures and functions that interact with these structures.

1.3 Software Complexity and Architectures

Software Complexity cannot be destroyed and it cannot be eliminated, but it can be controlled. Software Complexity is controlled by abstracting the complexity into well managed and well defined elements or components.

These Software Components are based on less complex logic. This allows the developers to think at a lower level of complexity without having to deal with the entire problem at once. When less complex components are combined together, they begin to form a more complex element. This can continue until the entire complexity of the system is contained.

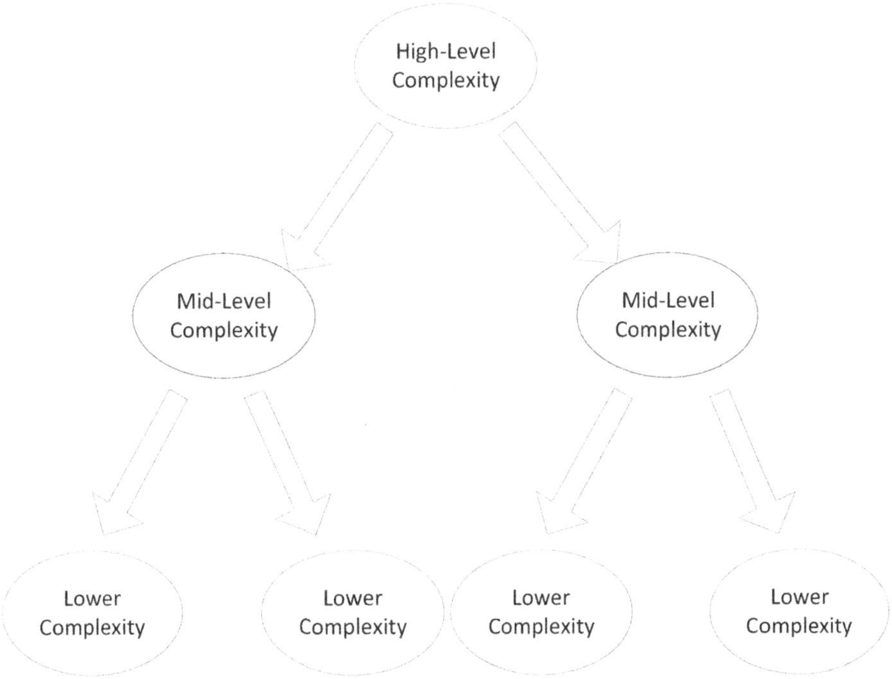

While this works in theory, there is no free lunch. In order to accomplish the idea of decomposing complexity, there will be some added overhead. To divide the complexity in reusable components common behavior will need to be abstracted out to promote shared logic.

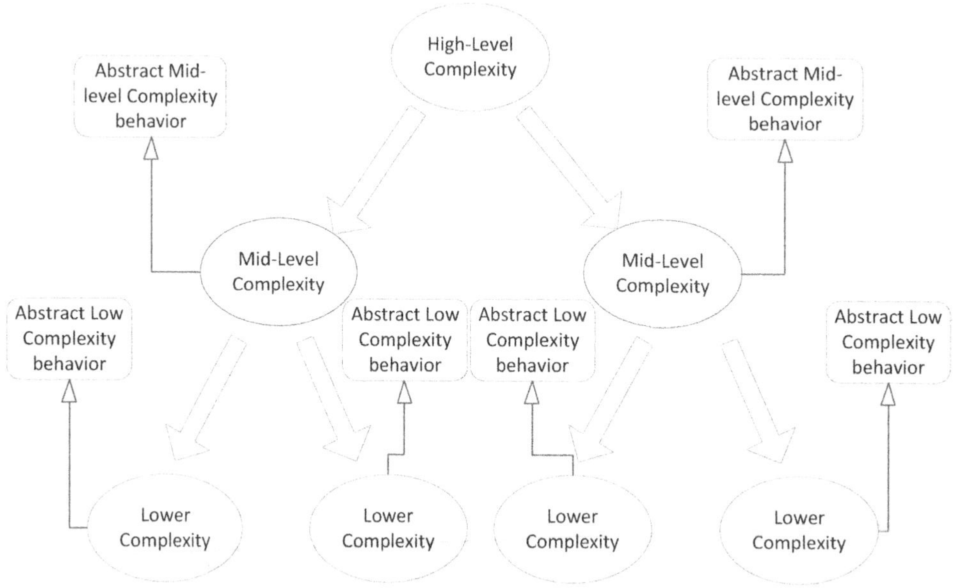

As is demonstrated in the diagram above, reducing complexity can in itself add extra complexity, a necessary evil. By creating abstract complexity behavior, we can create a family of similar software components. For example, we can have a family of components that deal with basic behavior such as data CRUD (Create, Read, Update, and Delete). At a higher level of complexity we can create a family of software component behavior such as components that handle business (Domain) logic. These higher levels of complex components can then utilize the lower complex components to process data while reserving the higher form of behavior for themselves. This process of dividing (layering) complex behavior can continue up the complexity ladder until the entire system is defined.

While the abstraction of complex logic will add overhead, it provides a myriad of advantages.

- It makes it possible to write complex logic once and then reuse it over and over again.
- Provides the ability to create families of complex logic that can follow a consistent pattern allowing the development of code in well-defined structure.
- Abstract highly complex system logic from the developer so they can concentrate on the business logic and not system logic such as how to connect to a database.
- Allows for loosely coupled complex logic making it easier for complex logic to change in one component without affecting the logic in another component.

1.4 Productivity and the impact of Architectures

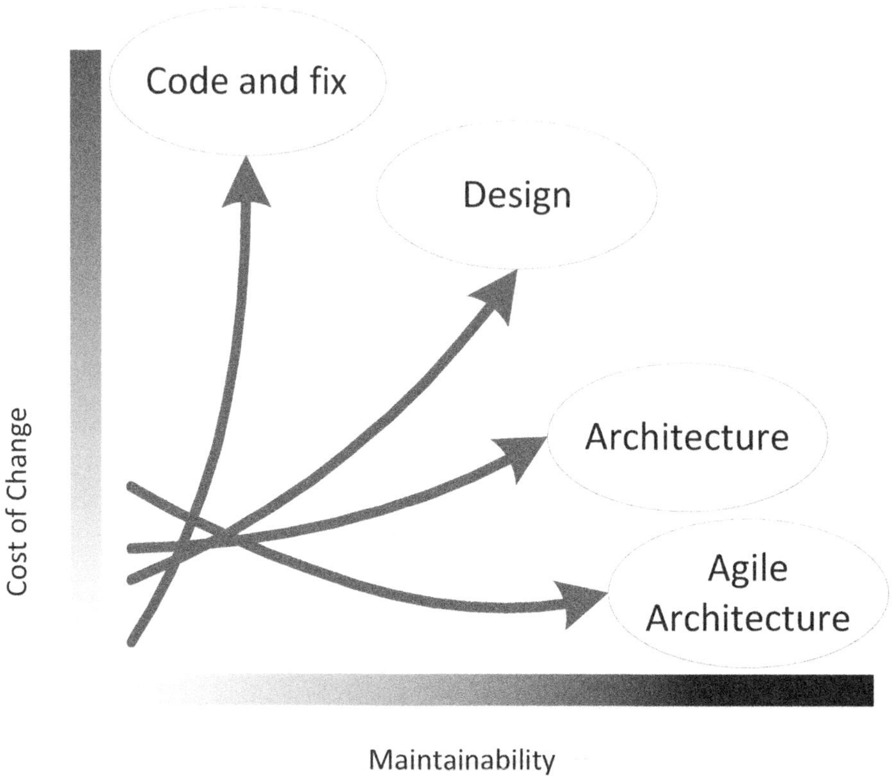

As demonstrated by the diagram above, software systems are greatly affected by the use of Software Decomposition. The initially a system without design or architecture produces greater results in a faster time, however as time goes on this type of development leads a project into a collision course with reality. As the cost of change increases, maintainability decreases where at some point progress comes to a near standstill as great amount of effort must be expended to make changes to the system.

Some years ago, I remember a commercial on oil changes for a car. The basic premise is that you can regular change your oil now, or wait and for the car engine to break down requiring much higher cost of maintenance including the possibility of having to replace the entire car. Software systems are no different, development can start at a rapid pace and a great deal of progress can occur at the beginning of project without an adequate framework, but in the end, progress begins to slow and eventually all but stops as developers have to spend enormous amount of effort to repair and maintain the system.

Some reduction in the cost of change and increase maintainability can occur with a good system design, but it too will eventually falter as the system becomes more complex over time.

1.5 IT Infrastructure and Business Domains

The business application development can be a very risky process. In order to reduce the risk, concentration on how software is developed is important. If a team of agile developers just start to attempt to write software without considering how the software correlates with each other a disaster may be waiting for that team. The history of IT development is full of teams that started with the best intentions only to be placed on the heap of failed projects.

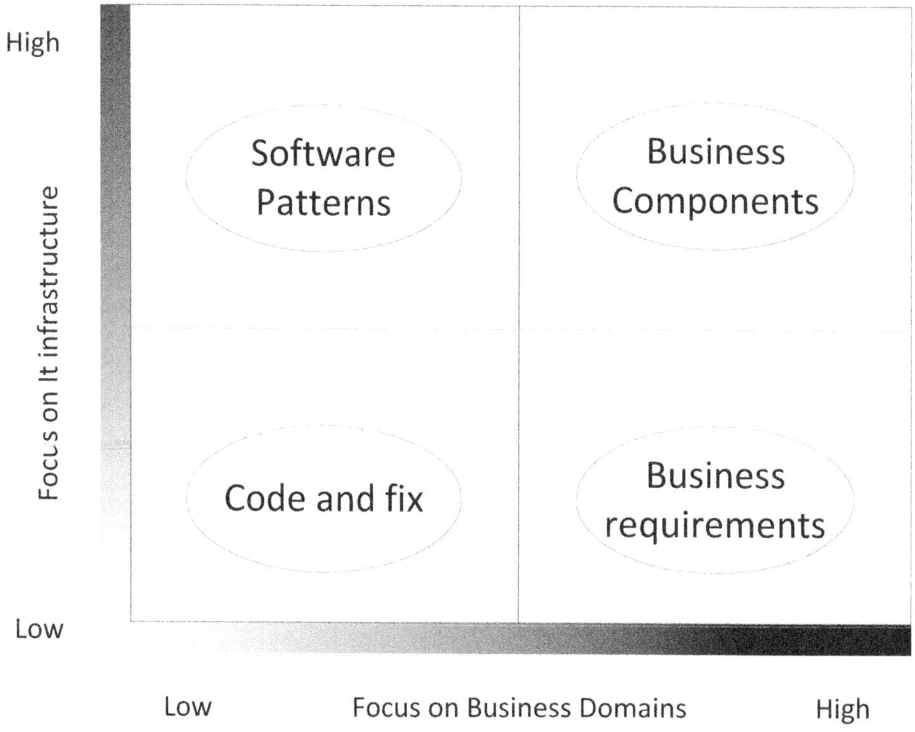

Development efforts must be conscious of the focus of the team. A team who is focused mainly on Software Patterns is likely to build something, they just don't know what. A team that is focused on what the business needs is more likely to build something the customer wants, but have a hard time maintaining speed of development as the structural integrity of the system begins to wane. By focusing on both at the same time by concentrating on the business component, the development effort has greater chance of success.

Chapter 2 Agile Framework Concepts

2.1 Why Frameworks allow for Agile Development

Frameworks help development build simpler systems that work, but also encourage software re-use. They increase productivity by creating well defined boundaries and repeatable processes.

One of the greatest examples of frameworks comes from the Ford Company and the Model T. At the beginning of the 20th century the automobile was custom built and complicated to drive. Henry Ford decided to build a simple, reliable and affordable car. Out of this came Model T. The concept was simple. Divide the car into components and at each assembly step, the individual components where assembled.

Creating software is no different. Either software can be built one class at a time, or they can be assembled by components. Frameworks make it possible for software to be created as a set of components.

2.2 Architecture versus Framework

Architectures are generally thought of as a concept and frameworks are the implementation of that concept. One typical example is the well-known the Model-View-Controller or the MVC pattern. In the MVC pattern, the Model controls the Domain Logic; the View is responsible for displaying output to the user; and the Controller works as an intermediary between the View and the Model.

These concepts can be implemented in a variety of technologies and frameworks. For instance, the View in a Web Based system is typically done using HTML or JSP while a non-Web View would use some technology such as Java Swing.

Even within a topology such as Web, the concepts can vary, such as synchronous versus asynchronous loading of web pages. In the Java web world, most web pages where loaded synchronously until the introduction of AJAX which then allowed for asynchronous loading of web page data.

2.3 Strictly enforced interfaces vs. concept

When adopting an Architecture concept, one of the most important decisions the Architect(s) must decide is how to enforce interface rules. Are the rules to be enforced by design concept or are they to be enforced by abstraction.

In determining the type of enforcement, the Architect must make a tradeoff between flexibility of the system and maintainability, between tightly coupled components and loosely coupled components. The main determination of this is the entry point to a component. If two components can call each other directly using free form methods, then the system becomes tightly coupled as the signature of entry points of components cannot change without affecting the calling component. This can be exacerbated as the depth of the layers increase. Take for instance a three layer architecture divided by Data Access Logic (DAO), and Business Unit Logic Layer (Domain), and a Business Process Layer (Solution). In a concept enforced interfaces, the access to the DAO would use a free form method and signature, the same would go for the Domain and the Solution. Consider the following pseudo code.

Solution:

Domain:

DAO:

List<AccountRecord> readAccountRecords(using account number)

- Create an empty list for account records
- Open database
- Select records by account number
- Store record in list
- Return list

In a Strictly Enforced Architecture, the Facade Pattern can come into play or some other method of enforcing compliance. This can be enforced using an Interface, Annotations or an Abstract class or a combination of any of them. These Facades define the entry point into the Components of the Application. In a Strictly Enforced Architecture the enforcement mechanism are designed to provide access to the components only when these components adhere to the Enforcement Rules. This may be as simply as implementation of an Interface Method, Implementing an Abstract Method, Overwriting a Method in an inherited class or providing annotations that indicate where the Component Entry point resides.

In a Concept Enforced Architecture, Modules, Classes, or other software Elements are not forced to follow any pattern by the Architecture, but rather compliance is by developer team agreement. If any developer does not follow the agreed upon Architecture Pattern, the only way to enforce compliance is by review of the software. Overtime, the Conception Enforced Architecture may lose compliance because team members are either under pressure to deliver software or the turnover on the team has changed so much that the original concepts are lost.

2.4 Differentiating between tiers and layers

The Multi-Tier Architecture (or N-Tier Architecture) is the physical structure of the Architecture while the framework layers are the logical makeup of the tiers. A typical example in a web application you will usually find a three tier architecture made up of the presentation tier, the controller tier, and the business logic tier. While a tier does not have to have a physical boundary, there needs only be the possibility of a boundary.

Each tier can then be sub-divided into layers. Each layer focused on a particular task.

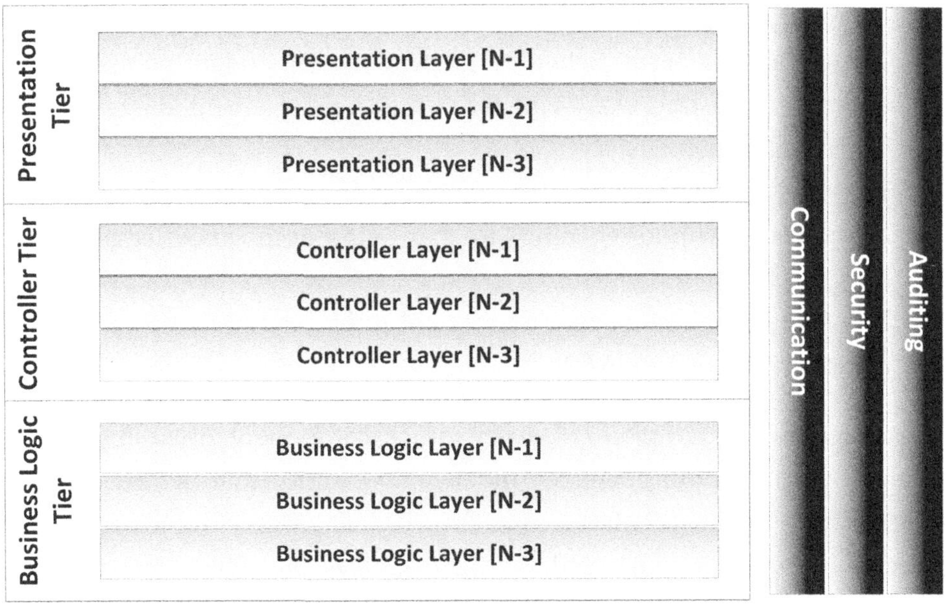

In the diagram above, there are presented three tiers with each tier having three layers. While this is an example of what the tiers may look like it is not definitive. Each tier will have its own make up and its only selection of layers. The controller is may have more or less layers than the business logic. Additionally, there are software units that span tiers and layers [crosscutting work units].

2.5 Agile Framework Cohesion and Coupling

An important concept in Agile Architectures Frameworks is enforcing loose coupling and high cohesion between the components in the tiers and layers.

In Frameworks, coupling is the linking between components in a tier/layer to the next tier/layer. If the components in the tiers/layers are too closely linked together they are called tightly coupled.

- Coupling refers to the degree of direct knowledge that one component has with another.
- Strong coupling occurs when a code points directly to a concrete component to provide the desired behavior.
- Loose coupling occurs when the dependent component points only to an interface or abstract class, which can then be implemented by one or more concrete components.
- Loose coupling increases the ability of developers to understand one component without having to have in-depth knowledge of other components in the system.
- Loose coupling allows one component to be modified without adversely affecting other components.

If every component is linked to every other component, then there is tight coupling. Tight coupling create undesirable results that which makes the software brittle and difficult to maintain and enhance. In loosely coupled software, components work independently of each other creating a more desirable outcome.

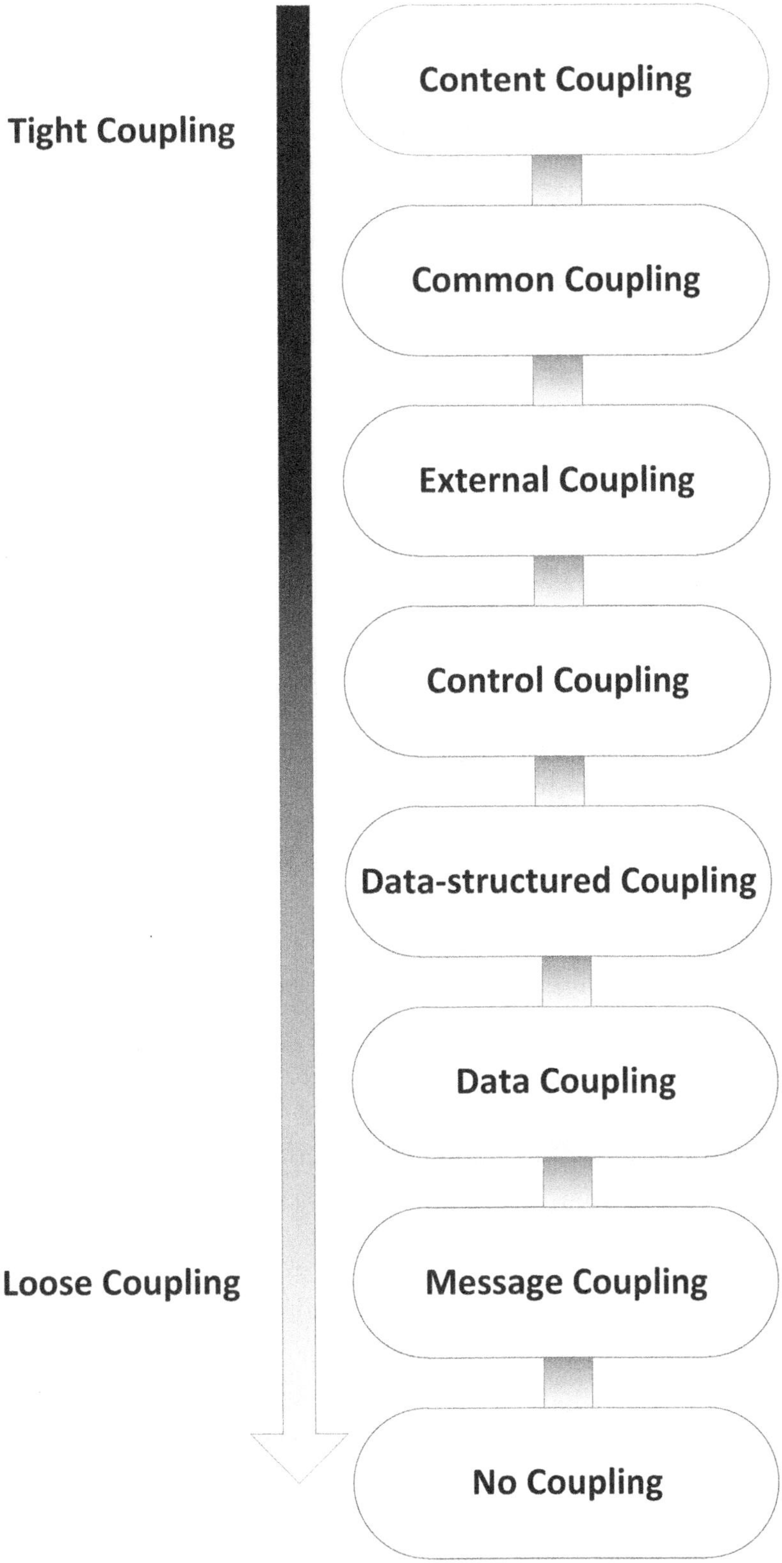
Tight Coupling
Loose Coupling
Content Coupling
Common Coupling
External Coupling
Control Coupling
Data-structured Coupling
Data Coupling
Message Coupling
No Coupling

High Coupling

Content Coupling	When component is linked to the internal properties
Common Coupling	When two or more components utilize a common set of properties where when one component changes the property, it affects the other components using it.
External Coupling	When two or more components utilize an external service that dictates a data format, protocol, and other interface used to communicate with external systems.
Control Coupling	When one component controls the process flow of another component by passing command information.
Data Structure Coupling	When one component shares a common data structure with another component regardless of the amount of information actually needed.
Message Coupling	When one component passes to another component a message object that is generic enough so that data in the message can be added or removed without directly effecting the operation of the component except as required by the receiving component.

Loose Coupling

Coupling and Cohesion are integral issues effecting Application Software including Agile Architecture Frameworks. These two terms are used to refer to the quality of a component to component interface. While Coupling deals with the dependency between components, Cohesion refers to the relationship between components.

High Cohesion indicates there is a deep relationship between the components while low Cohesion represents a distance or no relationship at all. As the Application becomes larger and more complex the Cohesion will reflect the difficulty in maintain the software where the Cohesion is low or will enhance maintainability when Cohesion is high. Some of the factors that can be used to determine the level of Cohesion are:

- When one component accesses the behavior or properties of another component directly and where they have little in common, Cohesion is considered low.
- When components perform logic using coarsely grained unrelated data sets, Cohesion is considered low.

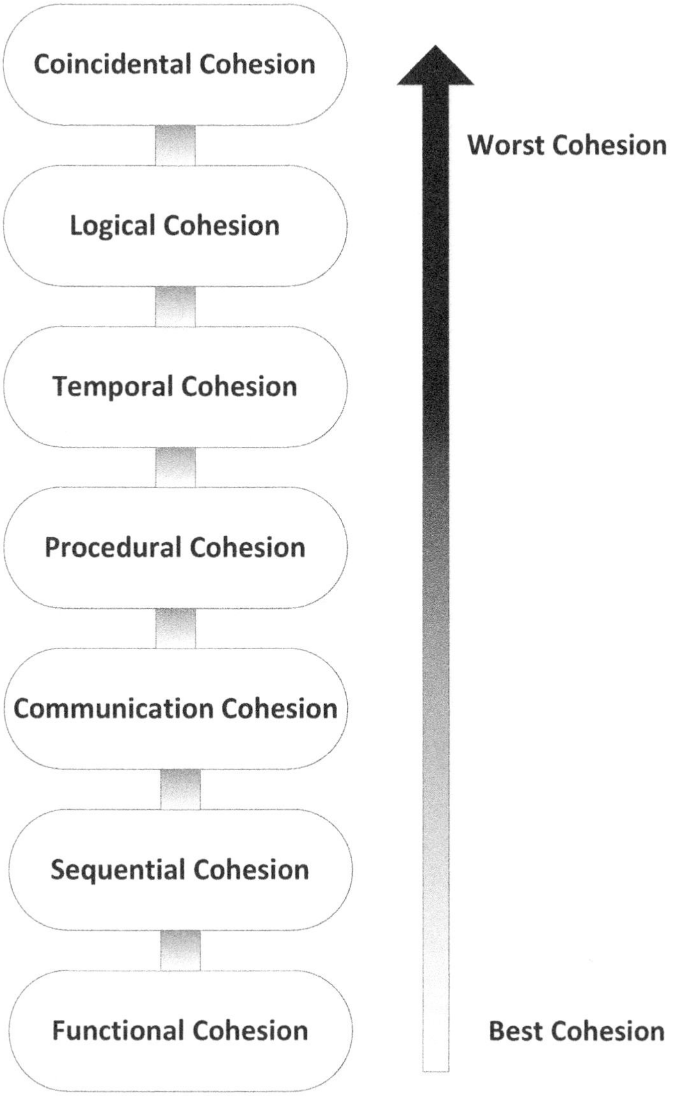

Low Cohesion

Coincidental Cohesion	When components are intertwined together for no other reason than they have been grouped together such as utility components.
Logical Cohesion	When components are organized together because they fit a particular category even if they are not related in functionally. Example might be a teacher and a manager of a company. They may be both people, but have very little else in common.
Temporal Cohesion	When components are organized together by the order in which they are processed in a time frame.
Procedural Cohesion	When components are organized sequence of events.
Communication Cohesion	When components are organized based on the fact they utilize the same data set.
Sequential Cohesion	When components are organized based on the data flow from one component to another.
Functional Cohesion	When components are organized because they are partners in a execution flow of a defined task.

High Cohesion

2.6 Service Oriented - Component Driven

While there are Service Oriented Architectures and there is Component Driven Architecture, a Service Oriented Component Driven Architecture combines the best of both worlds.

- Reusable components are encouraged
- Plug and Play development
- Encourages low level testing.
- Highly maintainable
- Encourages Rapid Development
- Ease of Development
- Cohesion of Components provide durable logic blocks
- Low Coupling of Service provide Enterprise reusability
- Dynamic Service interaction for Distributed Course Grain Components
- Service Elasticity provides mobility for components
- Decomposition of functionality provides Software agility.
- Extensibility of Services provided by Components
- Runtime replacement for Course Grain Services
- Compile time replacement for fine grain components
- Service Tiers and Component Layering
- High return on investment (ROI).
- Service Expansion and Contraction provided by components
- Functional decomposition of modularity provides stack of components from coarse grain to fine grain.

Service Oriented Architecture (SOA) provides a set of services where each service is autonomous of each other and applications are built using services as building blocks. In a Service Oriented Architecture, Services are orchestrated into business processes using and are loosely coupled together to meet a set of use cases. When the Services are all remote, there can be a danger of service crawl based on the latency caused by the Inter-Service communication stream. This is due to the fact that a communication stream such as SOAP is slower in nature than an internal call inside of a block of code. While Service Oriented Architectures are highly reusable with low coupling and high cohesion, performance can be a major issue. In addition to the latency problem, each Service must provide for its own security.

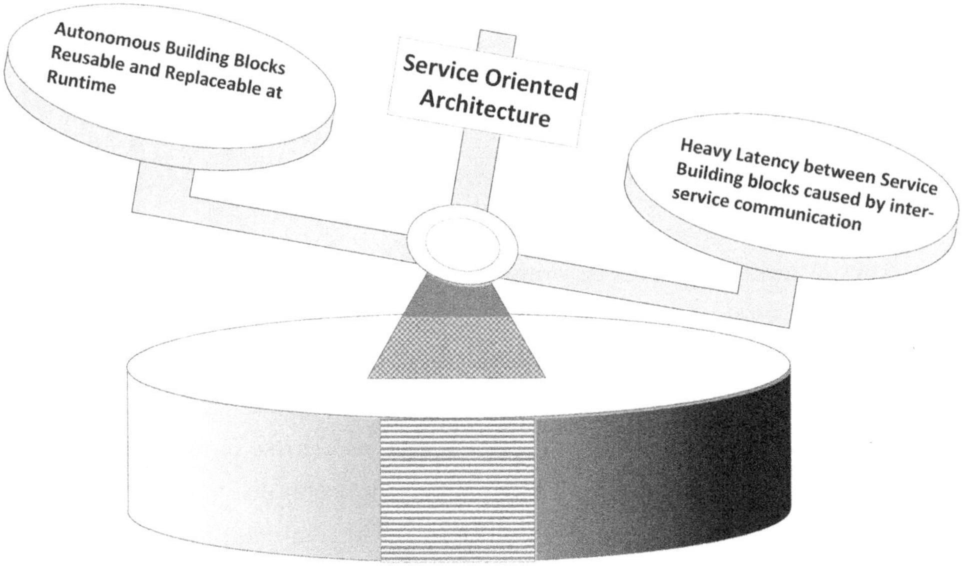

Component Based Architecture (CBA) is when the application is built using a set of components coupled together. A well designed Component Based Architecture will use loosely coupled highly cohesive components following the Facade Pattern. Component Based Architectures do not have nearly the problem with latency since the components are glued together in a local block of code and use Intra-Component communications.

A well designed Component Based Architecture will have a well-defined message driven intra-component communication methodology while not quite as fast as basic method calling, the latency is of such minor difference as to be of little importance. Unless the Architecture is supporting a system where every millisecond is of great importance such as might be seen in a medical device, the latency in a Component Based Architecture is negligible. Component Based Architectures are built of differently levels or stack of components starting with Course Grained Components and moving down the stack until we reach the bottom of the stack which comprises fine grained components.

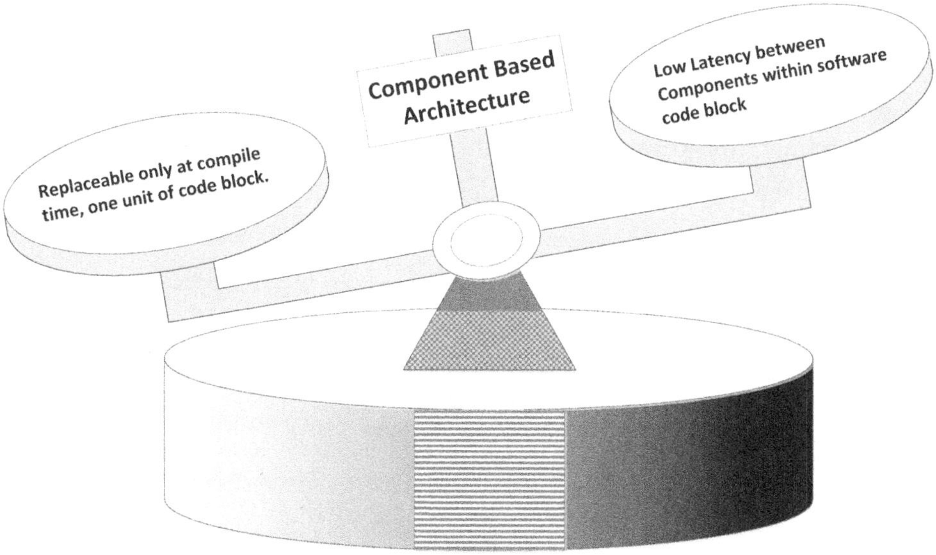

Each Component in a well-designed Component based Architecture is pluggable and Reusable. By using a combination of components a series of business processes can be created. In large scale systems, Component Based Architectures the system provides a set of course grained components that are reusable maintainable units of work which provides implementation for multiple business processes that are integrated together to form a monolithic system.

25 Agile Architecture for Service Oriented Component Driven Enterprises

By combining Service Oriented Architecture with Component Based Architecture a synergistic system can be built. The Service Oriented Architecture provides the flexibility of Services while the Component Based Architecture provides reusability without the inter-communication latency. The Service Oriented Architecture provides the interface to the outside world while the Component based Architecture provides low latency building blocks for the Service.

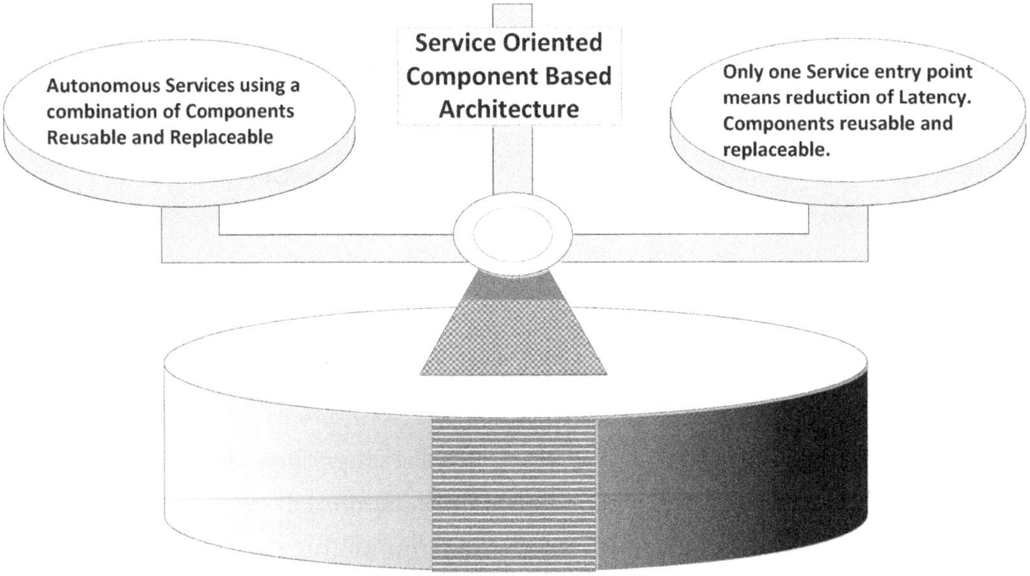

2.7 Separation of Concerns [SOC]

Separation of Concern [SoC] is a concept where complexity of a software system is delineated by packaging the software based on functionality type and granularity to solve a set of problems using loose-coupling concepts. By separating the complexity of the system into sub problems, highly complex problems can be reduced in complexity until they create a robust, simply to use elements. When the sub problem elements are combined they form an answer to the complex problem, but when looked at separately, they become easier to manage.

Separation of Concerns requires well defined boundaries with defined rolls and responsibilities for each concern or element. These concerns or elements are often designed to be vertical and composed of a stack of layers and/or tiers. From the bottom of the stack, the layers are usually fine grained with very specific types of functionality such as access a database. As we move up the stack, the granularity increases until we get to the top of the stack and highly complex system is solved.

The basic Principles of Separation of Concern is that the each software layer should have a distinct purpose with exclusive role and restricted only to that layer. In other words, the roles and responsibility of one layer should not overlap with another and the characteristic of the layer should not encompass any other purpose except for the designated roles and responsibilities assigned to that layer. The boundaries of each layer should be well defined and be designed to use loose coupling.

The establishment of boundaries in Separation of Concerns is achieved by creating constraints using either a logical or physical barrier based on a set of given responsibilities that delineate one Concern from another. To illustrate this proposition, consider the difference between the need to interface with an external resource and utilizing the information from that source in processing business logic. While the process of dividing the logical process into separate concerns based on a set of responsibilities, the goal is to insure that there is cohesion between the concerns and to avoid dividing the system into overlapping responsibilities. Separation of Concern is about bringing order to the system architecture. The main intent of Separation of Concerns is to define and establish an orderly system were roles and responsibilities are well organized while maximizing the rapid development of software with the ability to adapt to changes in requirements.

The benefits of utilizing Separation of Concerns principles can produce numerous benefits to an Agile Architecture.

- Reduction of redundancy of functionality
- Identifiable scope of layer
- Singularity of Responsibility and Roles
- Establishment of boundaries
- Increase maintainability
- Software Stability
- Reduces software brittleness
- Division of Labor simplified
- Cohesion of Responsibilities
- Extension points identification clarity
- Decoupling of Components

Separation of Concerns can be viewed both horizontally as well as vertically. When considered horizontally, Separation of Concern the software is logically divided into Tiers and Layers based on responsibilities and roles. When viewed in terms of the MVC Pattern, the tiers can be divided into a stack of three different tiers, each tier can also be sub divided into separate layers.

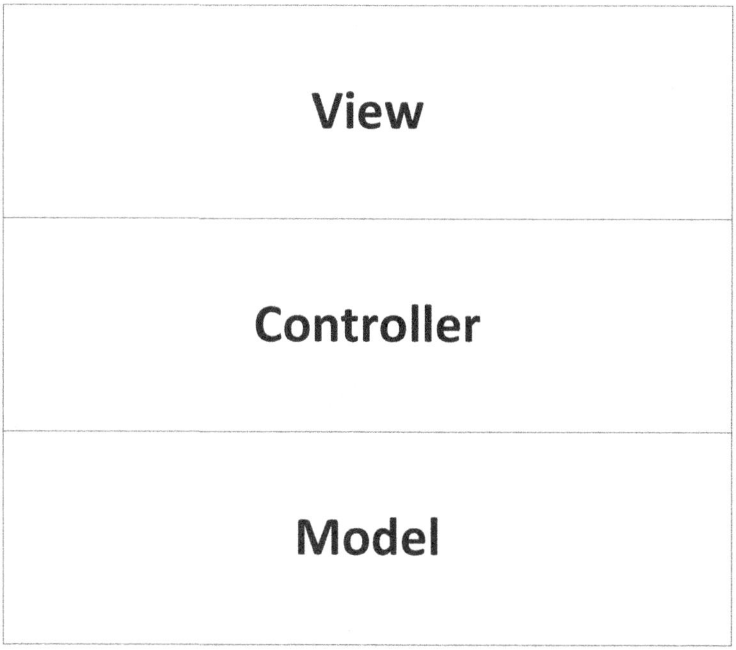

The stack of the Separation of concern holds that the View is only concerned with how to display information from a user and to allow user to enter information. At some point, the user will indicate that they are ready to proceed to the next set of business logic by causing an event to occur (such as pressing a submit button). Once the event occurs, user information is passed to the Controller which in turn decides the top level of business logic to process and passing the information to the Model tier in a format that the business logic in the Model can understand. Once the business logic in the Model has completed, it returns information to the Controller who in turn translates it into information that the next View (page) can understand and then passes control to that View.

When considered vertically, Separation of Concerns divides the application based on logical flow of the system from one tier/layer to the next and together provides a complete business use case.

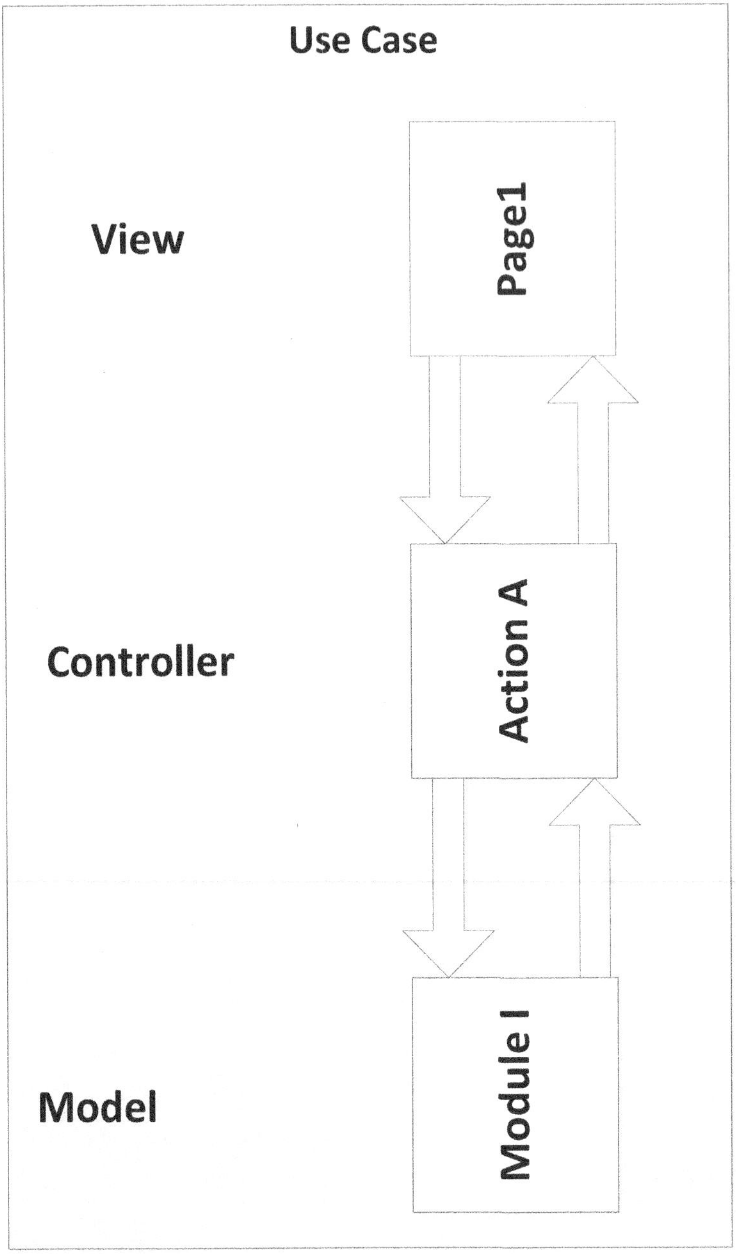

In the vertical Separation of Concern, only one use case is considered even though it may be made up of individual elements. Consider the use case of adding a test score to a student's grade report. The user would enter the new grade into the system and press the submit button. The information from the page (View) would be passed to the action event (Controller) which in turn would pass the information to the business logic module (Model).

The vertical and horizontal Separation of Concerns form a Matrix Separation of Concerns where components need to be viewed in both directions.

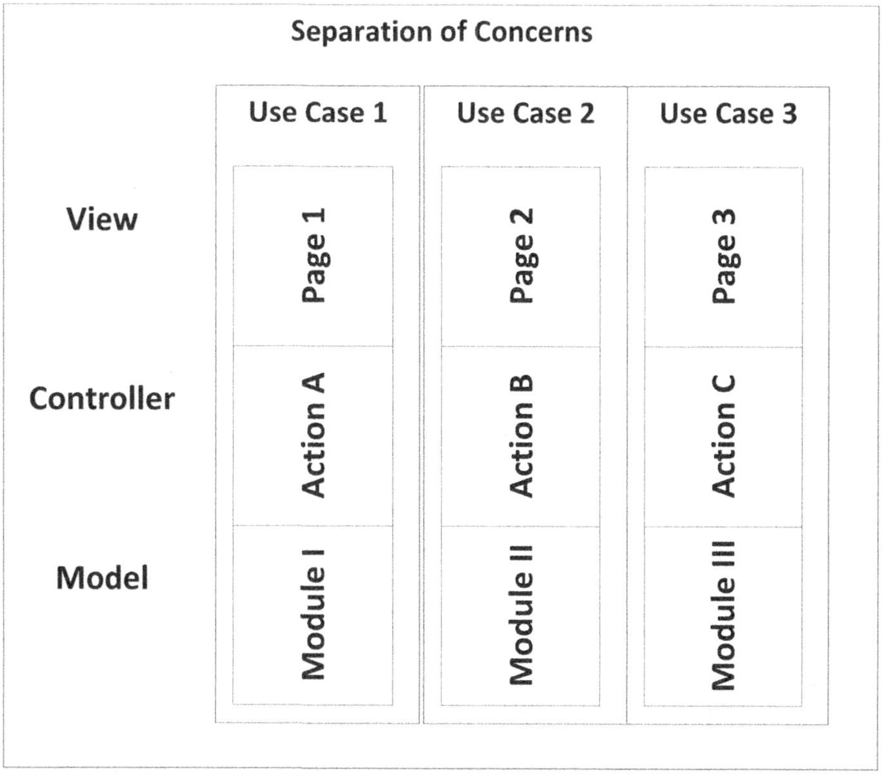

While the benefits of the Matrix of Separation of Concerns are numerous, it does have its draw back. When considering Cross Cutting Concerns such as message passing, transaction management, security, auditing, and logging to name a few, the Matrix of Separation of concern can be challenging. One way to meet these challenges is to consider the concept of Intra-Layer and Inter-Tier communication. To meet these challenges, the use of the Facade Pattern is useful, where all message received and return meet a consistent look and feel. To facilitate this, the use of Command Message Pattern can solve many of the components (concern) issues.

2.8 Inversion of Control

Inversion of Control is where software components are generalized in behavior and the flow of execution is inverted. In a standard execution of flow, applications have well defined modules that are tightly coupled together. In Inversion of Control the application framework uses abstract components which for the most part are black boxes to the application. The application doesn't know or really care what these components do. All they are aware of is that they perform so type of functionality and will be made available to the application at runtime and they are aware of how to interface with them. True Inversion of Control requires a Facade type pattern so that the application is aware of how to execute them but not what they do. Unlike standard execution flow of an application, the use of Inversion of Control produces loosely coupled components.

Consider a parent of a large family of children; she must create lunches for the children every day. The parent first grabs a brown paper bag for each child which they will use to carry to school [The Abstract Interface]. The parent writes the child's name on the bag and puts in there different items such as cookies and sandwiches. Each may vary slightly one from the other in content [Implementation], but from the outside they look the same except for the name written on the outside of the bag. In this instance, the parent [configuration] is in control of what goes into the lunches and what is inside is hidden from the children [application] all they are aware of is that their name is on the bag and that they need the lunch and will later open the bag [execute the interface] and retract the items from inside [The implementation]

In Inversion of Control, the application is provided with a place to retrieve the component either by name or by a defined location. It is said to be decoupled from the content of the component and is unaware of its properties or its behavior except for the entry point into the component. By designing application frameworks to utilize Inversion of Control application behavior can be changes simply by providing a different component implementation for the same block of logic.

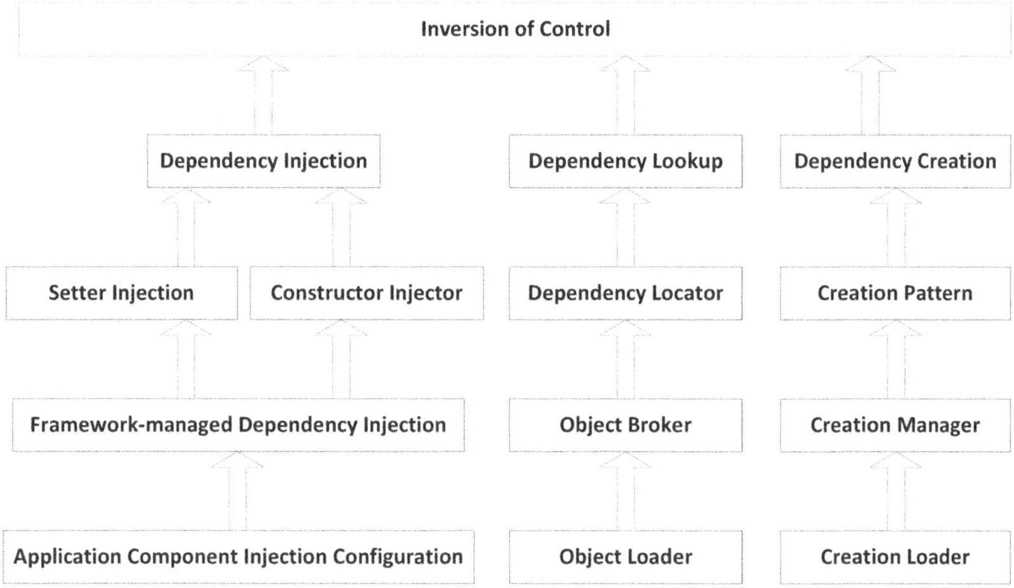

Inversion of Control can be accomplished in a number of ways. The Application Framework can use Dependency injection, it can use Dependency lookup or it can use Dependency Creation.

In Dependency Creation, objects do not exist until needed. When an application needs to run a module, it will request the creation of the module from the framework using information passed from the application. The framework will look at the information passed, determine what Object is to be created and return the Object to the application. In this instance, the usual method of implementing Dependency Creation is by use of Creation Patterns. When the application receives the created Object back, it is unaware of its properties and behavior except for the interface to the object. The interface itself is defined by an Interface or Abstract class.

In Dependency Lookup, Objects are created during startup of the application and are then placed inside some type of pool or repository [Object Broker]. When an application needs to run a module, it will do a Dependency Lookup through the application framework passing information used to delineate which type of Object is required. The application will be assigned an Object from the Object Broker and can use it for the duration of the execution flow. The Object can be stateful or stateless. If the Object is stateful then the object will carry with it properties containing valuable information. Generally speaking, a stateful object used in Inversion of Control cannot be used by any other execution path until the current path is completed or in other words, the stateful object is locked until released by the current execution flow. If the Object is stateless, then the Object can be used by multiple execution flow at the same time. In some cases it is possible to have a combination of both. Where the Object is consider generally stateless except when it passes through certain segments of the execution flow. When this occurs, the Object will need to lock that segment of the execution flow until the current flow is completed and it then can release that segment for use by other execution flows. Partial statefullness is general useful when accessing a resource or performing an execution where certain properties [static variables] are required for the execution to continue.

Dependency Injection is where the application or the framework has a placeholder for the Object to be injected and is defined abstractly. When the application starts up, the required objects are injected into various portions of the application defined by sometime of configuration information defined internally or externally. When the application execution reaches the location where the injected object is required, it retrieves it from its placeholder and executes its interface as defined by the abstract definition.

Inversion of Control has many advantages, the following are some:

- Business knowledge is encapsulated into Components.
- Decoupling of Execution of certain tasks from implementation
- Every component can focus on what it was designed for.
- The components make no assumption about what other components do or should do.
- Replacing component will have no side effect on other components.
- Single Source for managing dependencies

2.9 Dependency injection

Inversion of Control is an important concept in Framework development. How to implement various as described above. One of the ways of doing Inversion of Control that many well-constructed frameworks use is Dependency Injection. Dependency Injection is a design pattern whose purpose is to reduce coupling between components in an application.

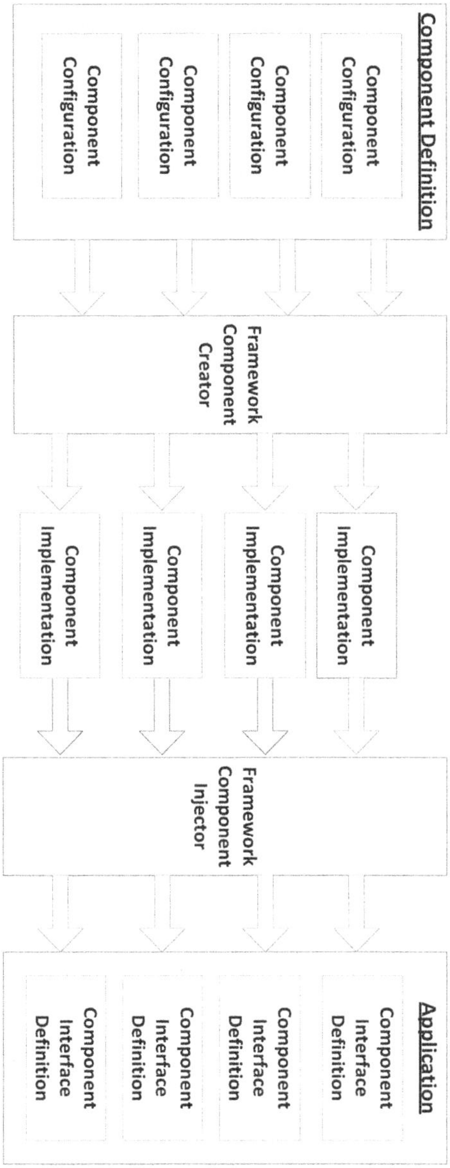

Dependency injection inserts the objects into the application the same way, but the initiation of the properties of the objects inserted can be accomplished by two different processes (or combination of processes). One form is by use of the constructor of the Component and the other is by using setters interfaces for the component.

With dependency injection, Objects go through a set of steps before they are injected into the application.

Step 1:	Construct Object [Use either the default constructor or use settings based on configuration]
Step 2:	Call setters based on configuration
Step 3:	Inject new Object into receiver
	Use Constructor settings
	Use Setter configuration
	Repeat Step 1 above for next object.

There are many advantages to using Dependency Injection including:

- Encourages code reuse
- Eases replacing of components implementation with another
- Reduces coupling between components
- Reduces need for one component to carry information for another
- New components render a service for one or more other components
- Increases maintainability
- Configuration Flexibility
- Code easier to read and understand
- Code is easier to test

2.10 Component and Service Oriented Components

Components as previously stated are built up of a stack of components starting with coarse grained Service Oriented Components which provided an interface to the outside world, followed by a slightly less coarse grained component that process the logic for the service (process component). The Process Component is a stateless and provides a full functional use case implementation. The Process Component is built up using either other process component(s) or one or more business components.

The business components provide functionality for a particular set of related business cases, for instance Inventory Items. In this instance, all the functionality for an inventory are provided for in the business component. When called by the Process component, the business component will provide a particular type of function such as increasing the count of an item in the inventor. The business component uses fine grained resource components to finalize its work such as updating the database with the new inventory count.

The resource component provides low level fine grained services dedicated to a particular resource such as database. Resource components provide such low level functionality such as CRUD operations (Create, Read, Update, and Delete).

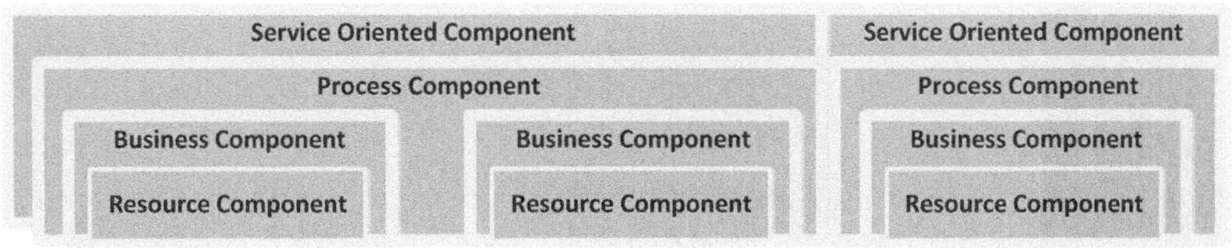

Components are boundary centric and provide rules for combining components to fulfill a business use case. Service Oriented Components provide an entry point into the system and provide limited capabilities. Their main function is to receive a request from the outside world and translate it and pass it to the Process Component for action.

Process Components form a logical block of work and provide a complete solution for a business use case. Process Components can be stand alone, they can call other process components or they can call business components or a combination of process and business components in order to compose a full set of business requirements implementation. Process components rules provide that they cannot link into anything lower in the stack of components than the Business Component.

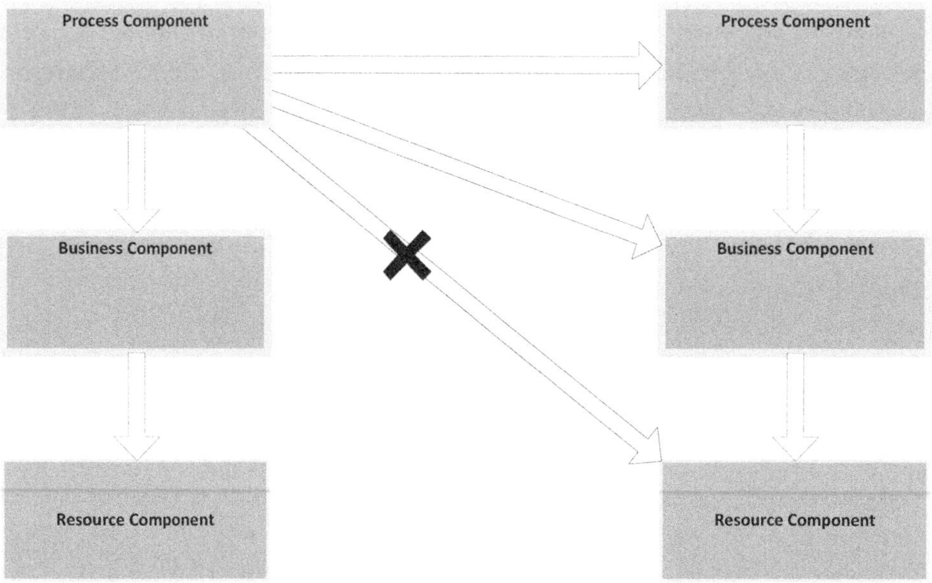

Likewise, the business component provides a set of functionality grouped by the domain of a business set. For instance, an Inventory Item business component would provide all the functionality that would be required by the software to process the business logic for Inventory Items. Similar to the Process Component, the Business Component can call other Business Components, is stand alone or Resource Components down or across the Component Stack but may not call components up the stack.

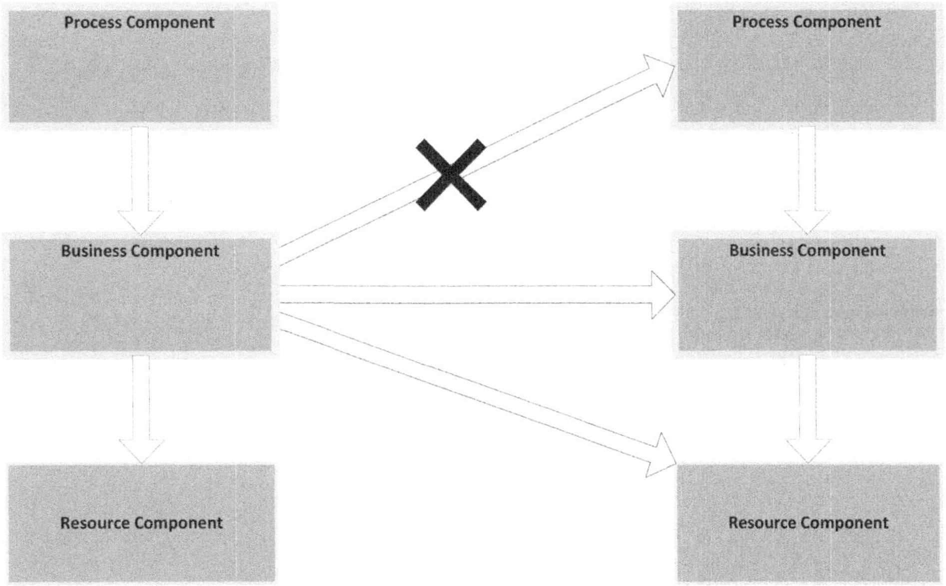

The Resource Component is the lowest level of the stack and can only call other Resource Components but usually they are stand alone. Resource Components provide fine grained low level services for access resources in the software such as database interaction.

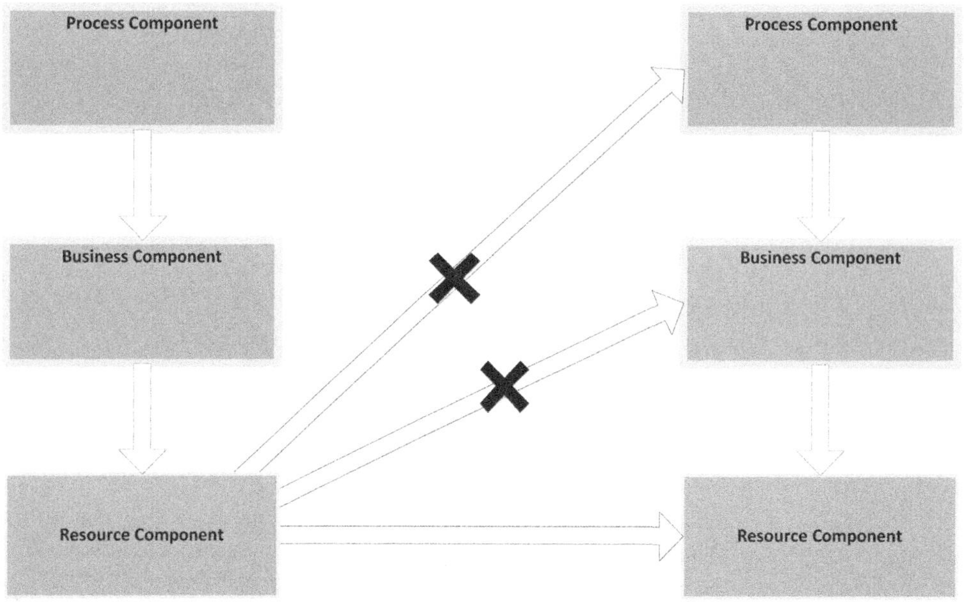

In addition to the Stack of Components, there are intra-component entities that are components that can be passed between the components to facilitate such functionality such as transferring data between components or storing session state and making it available to the different components.

2.11 Intra-layer Communication

While often overlooked when discussing Architectures and Frameworks, the way the parts communicate can be as important as or more so than the way the software is logically divided.

The majority of software use method signatures as the form of intra-communications, that is calling a class by method name, where a number of tightly coupled variables are passed and a tightly coupled data type is returned. Consider the following:

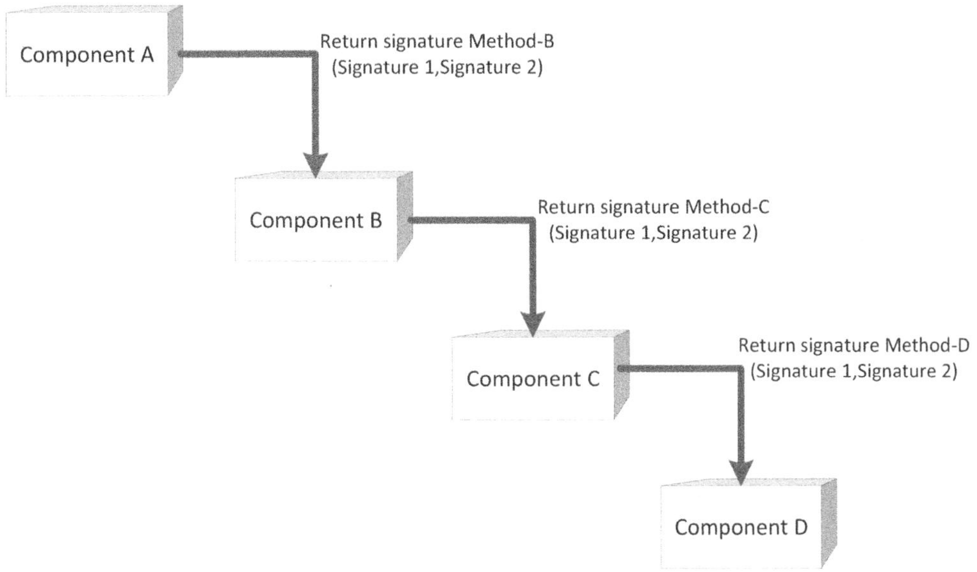

This type of intra-component-communication works fine until one of the signature needs to be changed. In the example above, if Component D method requires another variable and that variable exists initially in Component A, the all the components between A and D method signatures must be changed so that the variable can be received by component D.

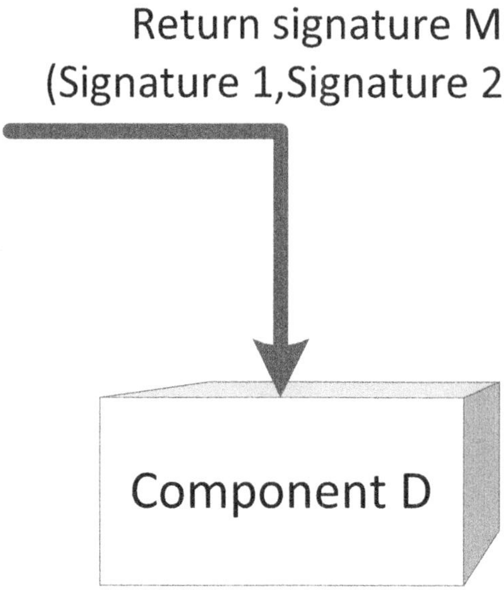

In a large software application, the ripple effect can cause a maintenance nightmare. In order to solve the intra-component-communication ripple effect, instead of using a method signature that can change as the requirements change, consider a Component Architecture that passes a single message object that contains all the information each component needs to process its logic flow.

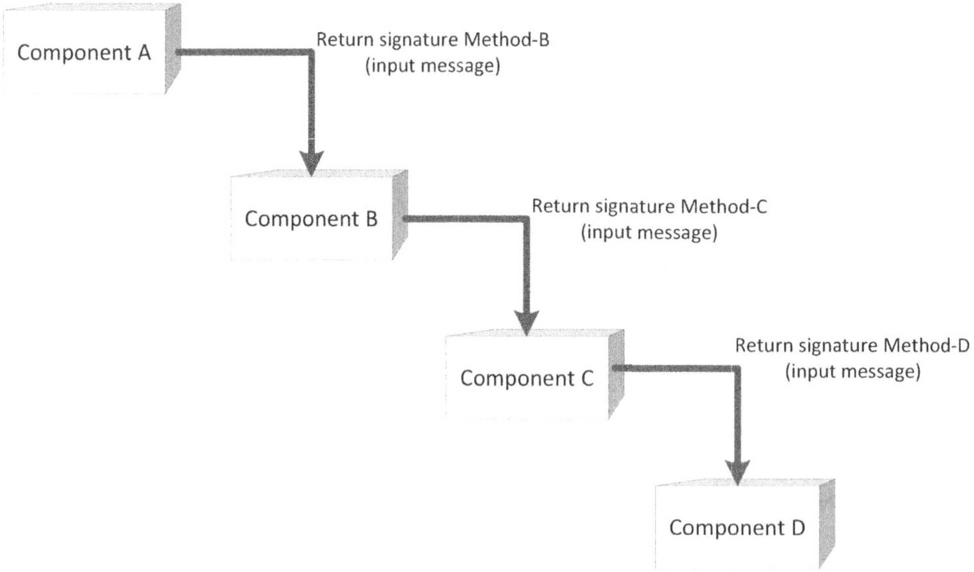

When component A starts up, it creates an input message and insert the message into the object in order to supply the data input required by component D. Then each proceeding components needs not to be concerned about the data input required by component D nor should they care. This works fine for input parameters, but still only allows for one return type at a time. If we change our signature again to allow for output data information, we can now have a component with the following signature.

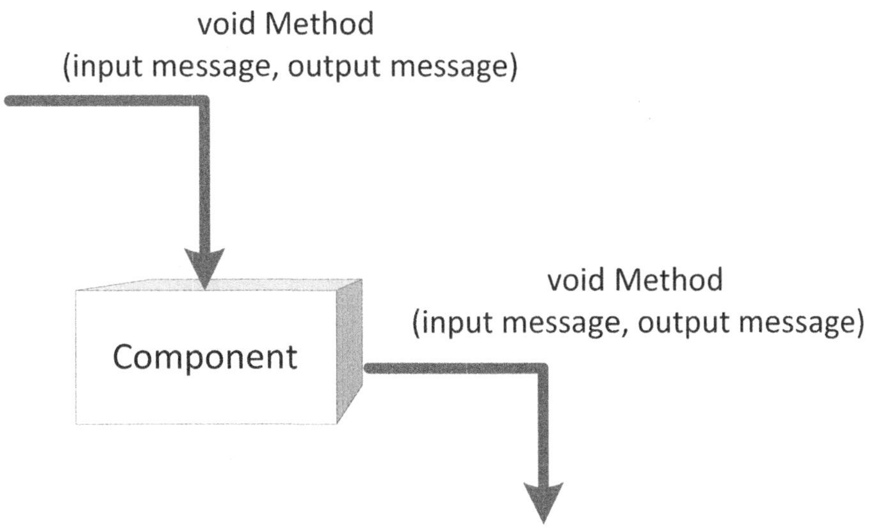

Because the output message is sent by reference, a change to the message at any level would affect the message at all levels. However, there is certain information that lives throughout the flow of the message. Consider such things as Session information like Transaction Management; additionally, what if we wanted to send logic information from one component to another [Command Pattern]. Instead of having a separate object for each of these, we can combine these into one message object.

Consider a message object that contains request information, response information, session information, error information, and command information. We would then have a command message object.

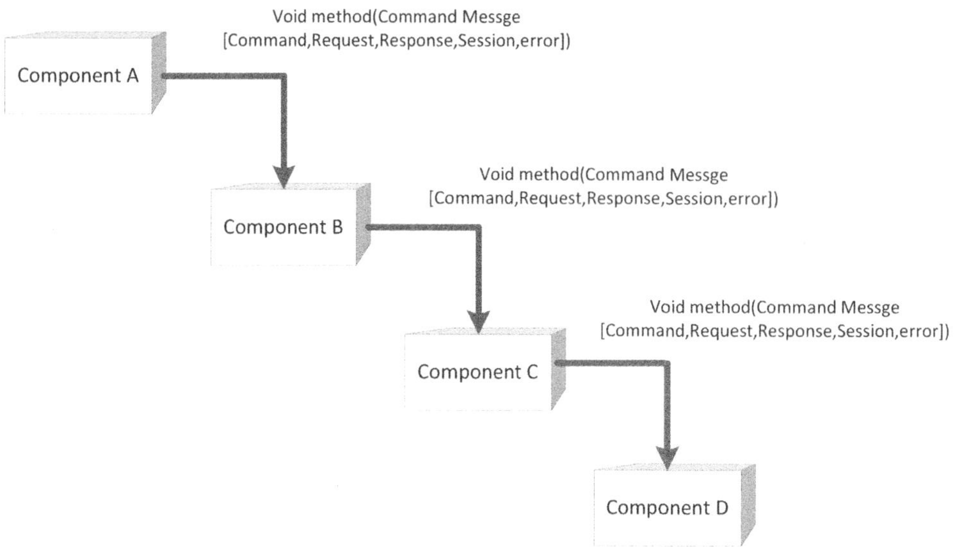

Not only does this solve the ripple effect going down the call stack, it also provides a mechanism for returning multiple data elements from each component on the call stack. This also has the additional effect of creating a pattern for every component which simplifies the dependency inject and Inversion of Control. Now, each component can put on or take off messages on the stack only the information they are responsible for. Otherwise they can treat each component they call as a black box.

2.12 Single Source of Truth (SSOT)

Information inconsistency can lead to software execution path deviations with the possibility of presenting to the user conflicting information. Worse is the possibility of report inaccurate data. Single Source of Truth is the principle that only one component or module is responsible for that truth. This source can be directed by a database row or some external interface. Internal to the Application, the system must be aware of the component that is the single source of truth and be able to cascade this truth to other parts of the system when the element changes. Propagation of the truth or data correctness is essential to the over health of the software.

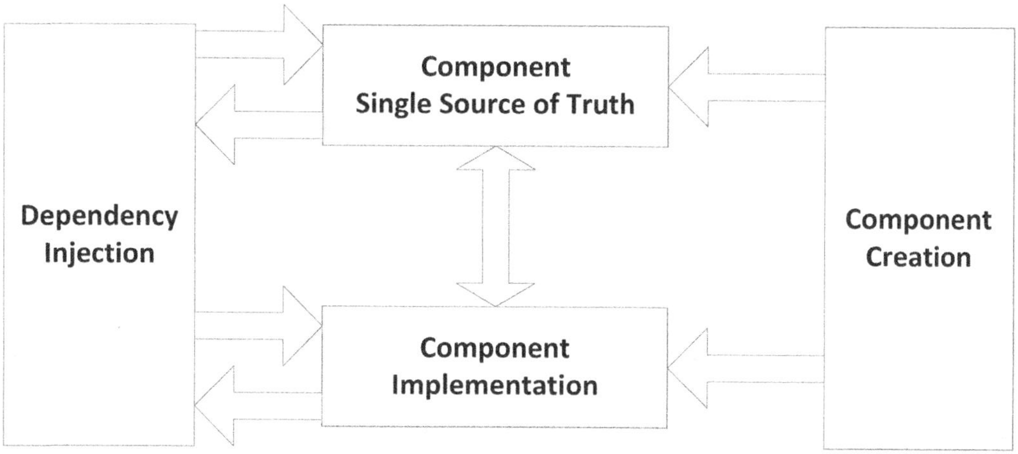

In an application system, when there is a single source of truth for a data element, one component is designated as that single source of truth. Other component implementations can have access to the information but must rely on the Single Source of Truth for Accuracy. In order for this to function correctly, the Single Source of Truth must have a reference to components that require updates to this truth when it occurs. Consequentially, a Component Implementation who requires this truth must have a reference to the Single Source of Truth as well. When data is changed on the Single Source of Truth component, the component will call all the other components and send the update. When a component changes it properties, it will do a callback to the Single Source of Truth component to update its values, which in turn will filter down to the other components these changes.

2.13 DRY Principle [Don't Repeat Yourself]

With the growing importance of architecture duplication of logic is increasing and data is often de-normalized, the risk to the logic is every increasing. When there is duplication of logic throughout the software, correcting logic error have become major tasks, this can get exasperated when the logic is cut and pasted throughout the system. Duplication of logic regardless of intentional or inadvertent will cause and usually does cause maintenance overhead to be far worse than necessary. Like Single Source of Truth, Dry Principle rule of thumb is that code for the same purpose should exist only in one place as much as possible. With conflict and contradiction of duplication enviable in large systems that are maintained over long period of time unpredictability can pop up in the least expected places. Overtime the effect can cause code to be implemented poorly or with unexpected results, confusion, where eventually the only way to cure the problem is toss the software away and start over. Many software projects fail due to duplication of code and poor planning especially when requirements change in mid-stream and all the duplicated code needs to be located and modified.

Part of the problem domain is determining what is duplicated and where the proper place to put the code so that it can be reused by other components. The principle of DRY, (Don't Repeat Yourself is: Every unit of logic must be located in a single location, be unambiguous, be accessible to other components that require that unit of logic, and have dominion over the logic representation within the system.

- Discourage cut and paste coding
- Every set of logic will have one and only one, location to represent the logic in an unambiguous representation within the system.
- Generic Components and abstract classes help keep software DRY.
- Business Logic, math formulas, and Meta Data should always be DRY.
- Structural units can be WET such as HTML Pages, test data.

Chapter 3 Application Framework Scaffolding

3.1 Introduction

In order for an Architecture to be Agile it must be able to be aligned with the principles of Agile development.

- It is imperative that user involment must be acive
- Empowerment of the team to make decisions
- Timescale is fixed, but requirement will evolve
- Requirements are captured at a high level are light weight.
- Incremental and Iterative development of small software units.
- Frequent delivery of incremental software units.

In order to accomplish this, the Application Framework must meet the needs of the agile team. In order to do this, the Application must:

- Be adaptive to changes in user requirements
- Encourage the team members to implement decisions
- Adjust to evolving requirements on a fixed time scale
- Allow for incremental and iterative development in small units
- Allow for frequent deliver of increamental code updates.
- Allow units of work to be developed independental.
- Allow for black box testing.

In order to accomplish Agile Development, the Agile Architecture must support all the principles of agile development. To do this, the Agile Architecture decomposes the units of work into separate areas of concern. First the Archtecture breaks the framework into three standard tiers [Model, View, Controller]. Each of these tiers are further decomposed into individual layers. Each individual layer is then formulated to allow for dependency injection. The agile application framework is also responsible for taking care of rudeamentry tasks such as transaction management, exception handling, validation and glueing the components together.

3.2 Architecture Overview

The agile archtecture framework provides the scaffolding for the construction of the software. It provides the method of dependency injection and the basic application logic flow. It implements inversion of control allowing the agile team members to concentraite of the tasks of implement the software logic rather than worring about how the system is wired together.

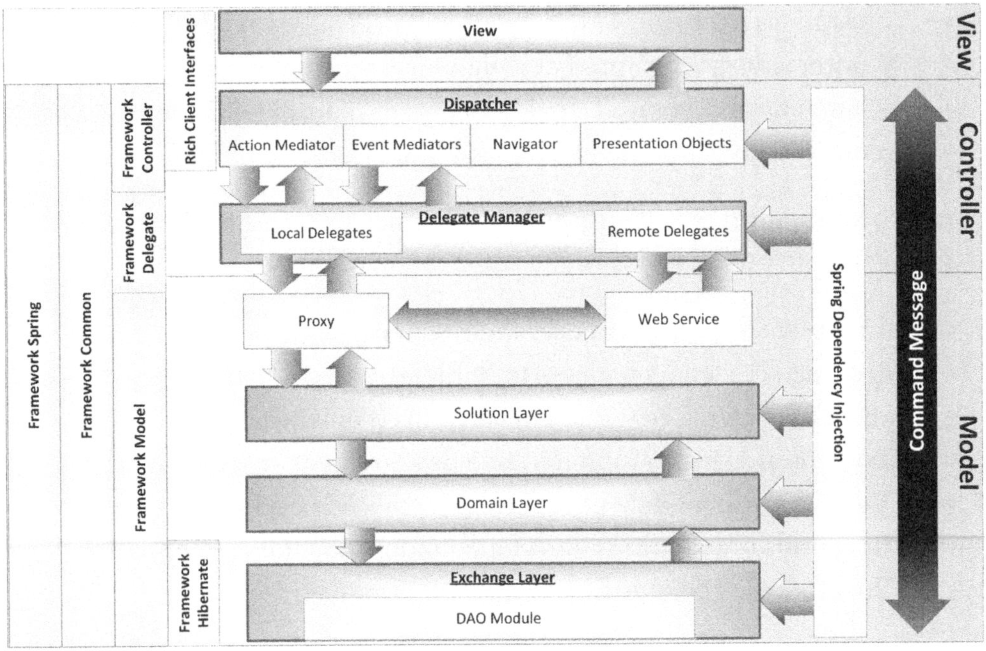

While the Architecture above may seem complex, the actual implementation is manageable. The basic principle of Software Architecture is to push complexity up into the framework so that the implementers (developers) need only worry about the implementation logic.

Other areas that the agile architecture must concern itself with are the organization of the code into projects, how components communicate with each other. The agile architecture must provide means for inter-communications as well as intra-communication within the system. The architecture must also allow for external systems to integrate with it.

3.3 Framework Patterns

Framework Patterns have existed since almost the dawn of computer software. Many frameworks deal with specific problems such as the TCP/IP architecture framework. We have already talked about the MVC framework pattern originated in Smalltalk.

In more modern recent times, there have been many good frameworks that have come forward. We will discuss a few.

Martin Fowlers Patterns of Enterprise Application Architecture

Martin Fowlers Architecture framework is really a collection of architectural patterns rather than one coherent layered system. Fowler presentations would fall mostly in the concept enforced type of framework(s). While he presents a basic set of principle layers, his book represents a choice of different types of patterns for each layer.

Fowler book has in many ways been the inspiration for this book, and he has many valuable concepts that this book will not go into. If the reader has not already done so, he would be well advised to read his concepts.

Fowler presents the following three principle layers.

- Presentation Logic
- Domain Logic
- Data Source

Other important concepts that Fowler presents are Unit of Work and Service Layer. In one of my earlier projects, the architecture I choose to use was a hybrid of Fowlers concepts.

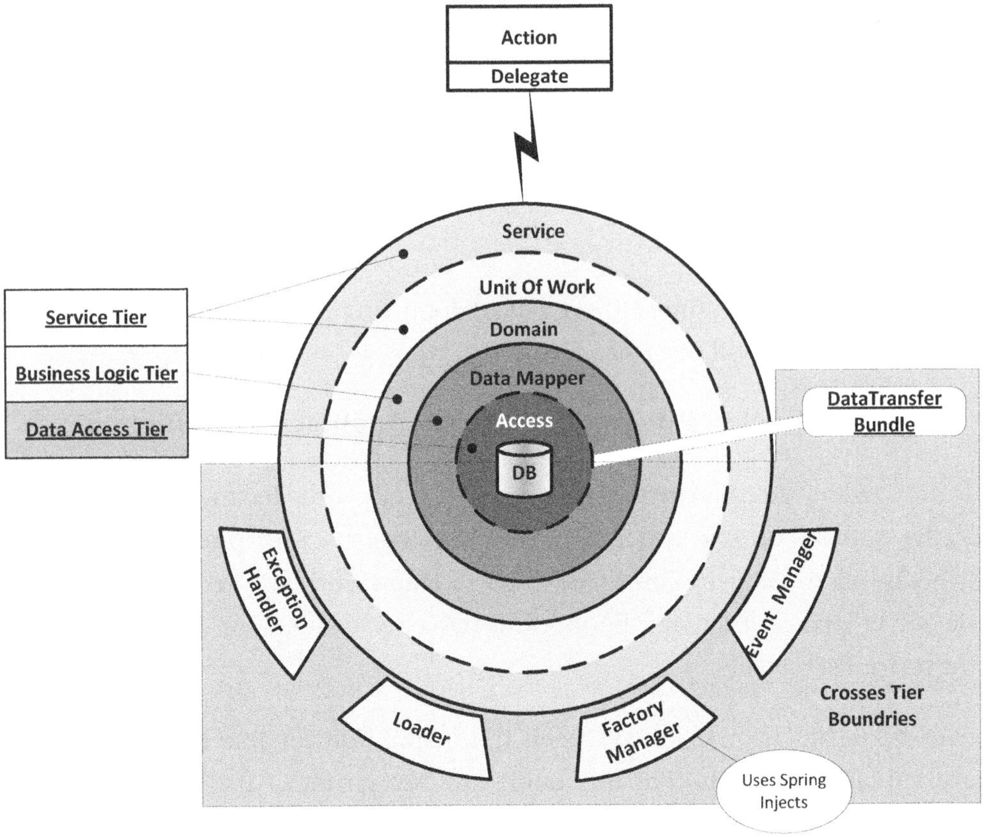
Action
Delegate
Service
Unit Of Work
Domain
Data Mapper
Access
DB
Service Tier
Business Logic Tier
Data Access Tier
DataTransfer Bundle
Exception Handler
Loader
Factory Manager
Event Manager
Crosses Tier Boundries
Uses Spring Injects

J2EE Blueprint patterns

For a while Sun's Java Blueprint pattern was all the rage. While their pattern was overly complex, it was possible to pick and choose pieces that made sense. Before discovering Fowler, I created several projects using a hybrid of the J2EE Blueprint pattern:

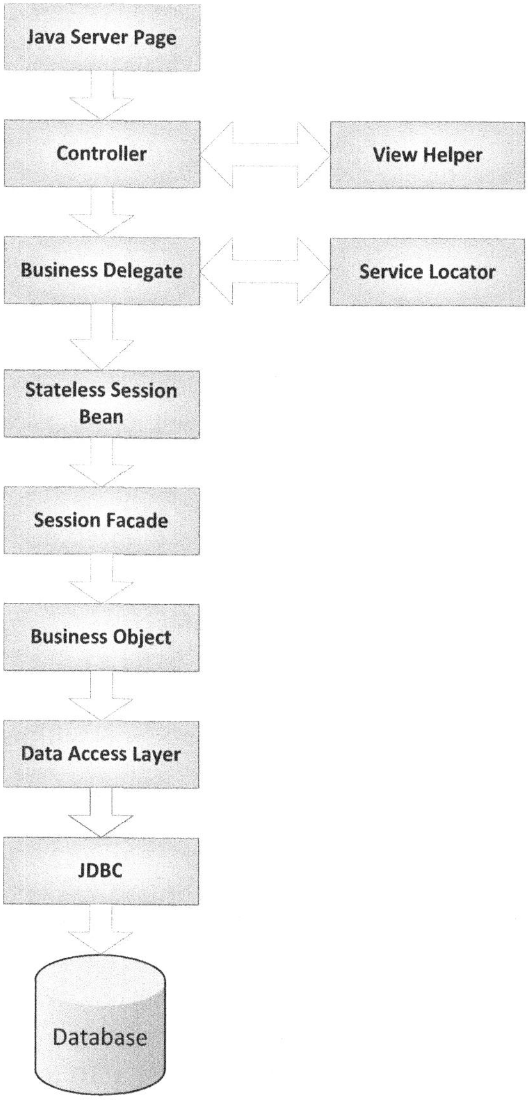

While there are a large segment of other frameworks out there, these are the major ones that have influence the writer.

3.4 Auxiliary Frameworks

3.4.1 Spring

What is Spring and why use it: In a nut shell, Spring is an open source auxiliary framework or more that is used to enhance productivity in the Java Development world. While Spring provides many useful features, its most useful features are its ability to do dependency injection and providing consistent ways of configuring your other auxiliary frameworks such as hibernate.

Organizes your software components and provides the plumbing to seamlessly injects objects into an application system providing value to any Architecture layer or tier.

Spring allows for the reuse of objects throughout the system without having to pass those objects by way of method calls. Spring can reduce the dependencies on Singletons.

Consolidates the property files into a single well defined format and allows for hierarchy of properties.

Encourages Inversion of Control and dependency injection; Family of classes can be created with a single interface. With Spring you don't have to know what the original class is, you simple need to know the interface.

Spring provides a means by which a component driven system can be implemented allowing for ease of sharing components within a system.

Spring for the most part, does not dictate how your application runs, but simply facilities good development practices.

Spring solve many problems that would be difficult when developing code from scratch.

Spring delivers easy services for data source connections regardless if you are accessing a database directly with JDBC or using an O/R mapper like hibernate.

Spring provides many more features that the developer can choose to use or not to use such as AOP, JMS, JavaMail, JNDI, etc.

3.4.2 Hibernate

Hibernate is an open source Java library object-relationship mapper (ORM) used to provide communication between the Persistent Layer (database) and the Application Software. Hibernate provides a set of functions that are necessary for a well-defined database application such as Connection Pooling and Transaction Management.

The Hibernate framework provides integrations tools to solve and provide assistant in database processing such as mapping data elements retrieved from or sent to the database into or from a Value object reducing the effort and maintenance required to provide such required integration with the Software Application.

While Hibernate's primary function is to map data from database tables to java classes and from SQL data types to Java data types, it also provides high level query tools to assist the developer in processing persistent data. Hibernate uses both standard and specific Database dialects to perform the processing of handling result data sets and conversion in order to keep the application portable and maintainable with little performance overhead. This relieves the developer from making changes to the software system when trivial changes are made to a database table such as when a column is added or removed. Instead of worrying about the order in which each column data is generated, the developer relies on Hibernate to perform the task of mapping data elements into java objects.

Additional information about Hibernate is beyond the scope of this book and readers should find other online and other books for a more detail look and the properties and behavior Hibernate provides.

3.4.3 Icefaces and JSF

JSF (JavaServer Faces is a Web application framework based on java intended to provide developers with a simple way of integrating presentation tier with backend processes.

A request-driven web based architecture framework based on the concept of component driven user interfaces using templates or Facelets based on XML and stored in files on a web server. The FacesServlet receives request to be processed which then loads the required template and builds component hierarchy or tree to process events and to render responses using web protocol such as HTML. At the end of each event, the state of the UI components and other objects are preserved after the completion of each request and made available when the next presentation or view is constructed.

JavaServer Faces or JSF is divided into several parts:

- Component definition that allows third party vendors such as Icefaces to provide additional components.
- An Event Driven Model allowing for greater interoperability with back in java classes.
- Predefined set of User Interfaces (UI) components used to build visual display.

ICEfaces is an implementation of JSF which provides an open source AJAX framework which enables developers to construct Rich Internet Application based on the Java Language and the JSF interface.

Further information on JavaServer Pages or Icefaces is beyond the scope of this book and the reader should look for more detail information either online or through other books.

3.4.4 Message Driven Beans

To understand the Message Driven bean, it is important to have a fundamental understanding of the Java Messaging Service (JMS). JMS is a layer over top of some other technology such as IBM MQueue. Messaging systems provide protocols for event driven data exchanges asynchronously.

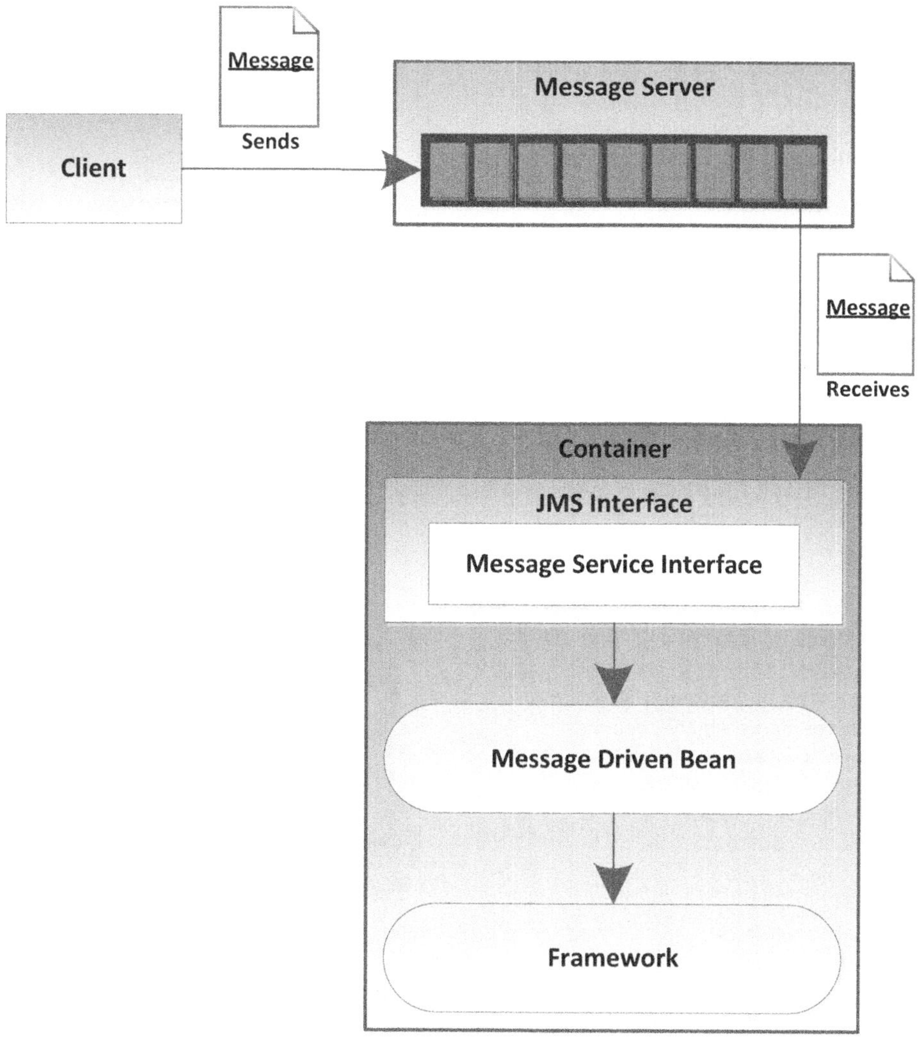

3.5 The Principle tiers

The successful Agile Architecture will promote the use of component architecture in order to reduce large complex logic units into smaller, easier to manage small simpler logic units.

External Interface Tier

This tier is used to translation information from external sources such as a web page or a message driven bean and when appropriate, back again. This tier is often referred to as the View Tier when dealing with user interfaces

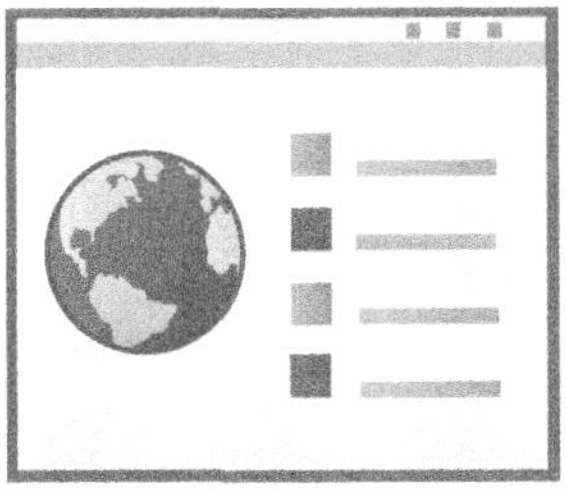

Controller Tier

This tier is like the traffic cop. It is responsible for directing traffic (Data) between the model and the Interface Tier.

Model Tier

Is the Engine of the system. It is responsible for doing all the heavy lifting. This is where the business logic resides as well as interface to storage mediums like databases.

3.6 Web Based Architecture tiers and layers

The Web Based Architecture is built on your classic MVC pattern. In this architecture, the External interface is the View.

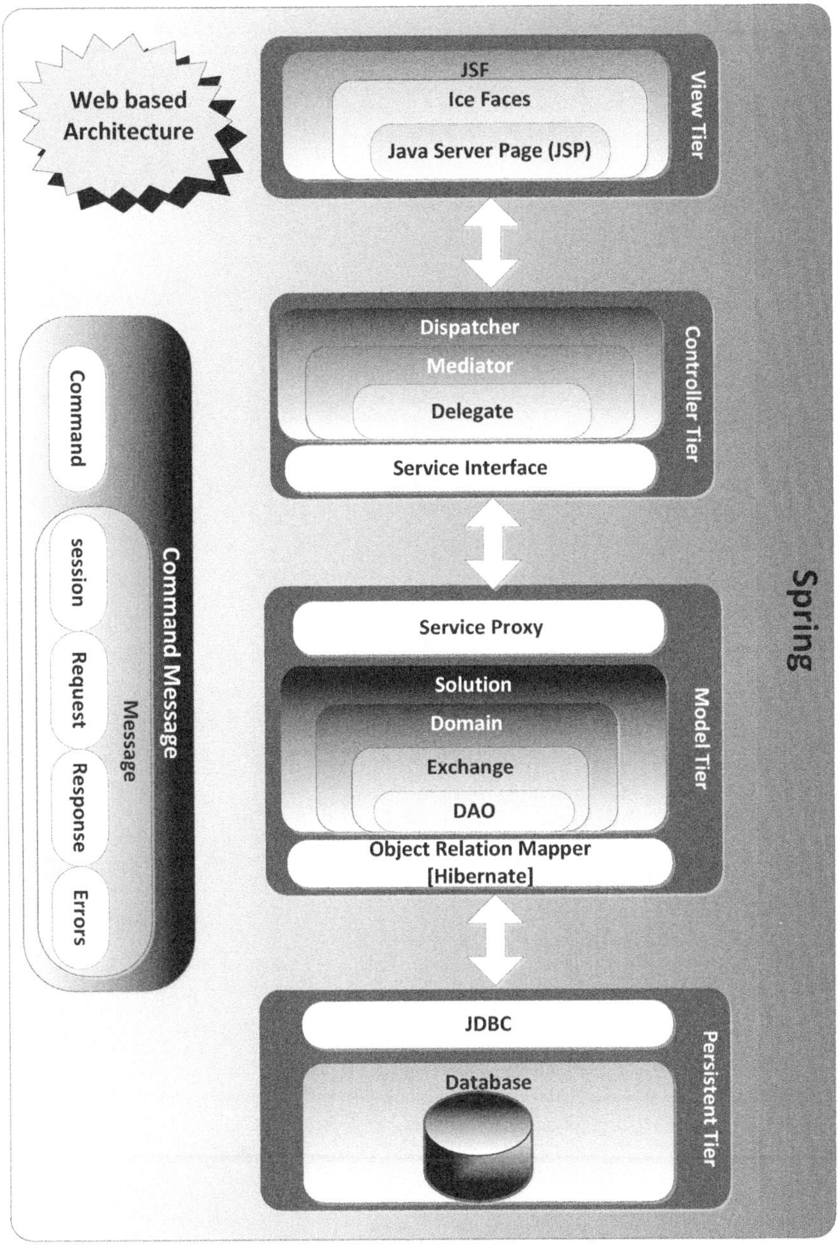

The Agile Architecture framework displayed above consists of a set of principle tiers and layers. The difference between a tier and layer are important concept. A tier is a physical separation based on technology while the layers are conceptual divisions in the software. In order to be a tier, the software must be capable of physical separation from its counterpart. For instance, the View, Controller, Service, the Model and the Persistent Layer can exist independent of each other a provide functionality.

- The View
    - JSP
    - JSF
    - Icefaces
- Controller
    - Mediators
    - Delegates
- Service
    - Proxy
- Model
    - Solution
    - Domain
    - Exchange
        - Data Access Object
- Persistent Layer
    - Hibernate
    - Database
- Command Message
    - Command
    - Message
        - Session
        - Request
        - Response
        - Errors

3.7 Message Driven Architecture and Tiers

The Message Driven Architecture is similar to the Web Based Architecture except for the External Interface. Instead of a web page being the root of the interface, the message Driven Bean is. When a message is received for the Queue, a Message Driven Beans is automatically created and called by the container. The bean can then request the message and translate it into a Message that can be understood by the rest of the system. Once the dispatcher is called, the architecture works exactly like it would in the web based Architecture.

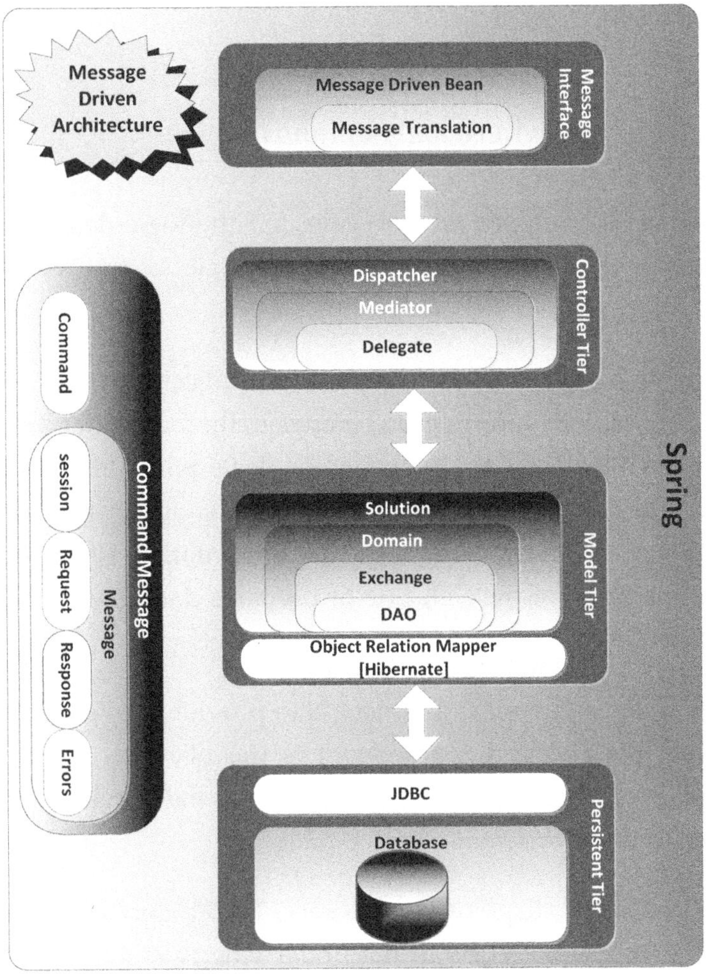

3.8 Inter and Intra Communications

Any communications between Tiers are considered Inter-Communication since they can span physical hardware or technology. Any communications between Layers are Intra-communications. For instance, communication between the view and the controller are accomplished using browser/servlet technology, while communications between the controller and the mediator is an internal or intra-communications. An example of intra-communication is when one object/class calls another and using the class/object method signature. In this case, the communication is handling entirely within the application code (or JVM).

3.9 Understanding where logic belongs

The first decision a developer must decide is if the logic deals with the Model (business logic) or the Controller (Presentation Logic) or the View (Presentation display).

If the information deals with direct communication with the View or Presentation tier, then the information belongs in the Controller Tier, Application Display Manager Layer. If the information deals with Presentation Tier data manipulation and data retrieval, then the logic belongs in the Mediator which retrieves and data and massage data for the Presentation Tier which it retrieves from the Model by way of the Delegate or prepares data sent to the Presentation Tier that is intended for the Model by way of the Delegate.

If the purpose of the software component is to provide a communication path to the Model then the Delegate Component is the place to put the logic. The Delegate provides a Service Request end point for the Service Proxy by way of either local service calls or remote service calls.

When a Service Entry end point is necessary, then a Service Proxy component should be built to control access to the underlying model. Service Proxies can receive request from any number of communication protocols including Web Services, Direct Java Calls, or Message Queues such as a Message Driven bean.

Solution Components provide the top layer of the Model Tier and they are used to provide a complete solution to a business problem. The Solution provides a way to combine Domain logic to the Application Software and can either be a pass through for the Domain; call a collection of Domains or a collection of Solutions or collections of Solutions and Domains. A Solution should never call an Exchange directly, nor should a Domain every call a solution.

Domain Components provide a software component to define well defined business domain logic that can be closely associated with each other. For example, logic that defines a User Profile can be defined in a domain, but a User Profile Domain should never consist of Domain logic that deals with a business organization. A Domain can call other domains and call Exchanges/Data Access Objects.

Low level components that deal with external systems such as databases are defined in the Exchange/Data Access Objects. Exchanges wrap Data Access Objects so that the Data Access Object protocol does not have to conform to the overall component interface hierarchy. Exchanges can wrap external calls such as calls to database, JMS Message posting, data file access.

Data Access Objects (DAO) is the lowest level of composition and provides direct access to external systems such as databases. DAOs may use other software units such as Hibernate to perform their task.

3.10 Generic Patterns

In writing software, there is sometimes code that is so similar that they are varying slightly. In these cases, the framework can be designed using generics. Consider a JMS Component that writes data to a queue. For the most part, the logic flow is the same, create a connection, open a session, and send some data. No matter what the message is or the name of the queue, the basic steps are the same. These can all be wrapped in a simple generic class.

Consider accessing the database in a software system. The basic functions are the same:

Example Generic DAO Interface

```
public interface DAOGeneric<VO, KEY extends Serializable> extends DataAccess
{
  public VO findByKey(KEY aKey,CmdMsg aCmdMsg);
  public Collection<VO> findAll(CmdMsg aCmdMsg);
  public Collection<VO> findByQuery(CmdQuery aCmdQuery,CmdMsg aCmdMsg);
  public Collection<VO> findByQuery(CmdMsg aCmdMsg,String
aName,KeyValue<Object>... aKeyValue);
  public Collection<VO> findByExample(VO aExample,CmdMsg aCmdMsg);
  public VO makePersistent(VO aValueObject,CmdMsg aCmdMsg);
  public void makeTransient(VO aValueObject,CmdMsg aCmdMsg);
}
```

By writing a class that implements this code, we can construct a generic object without ever having to know what was in the Value Object (VO) or what was in the key.

Another type of Generic Patterns are pass through objects where very little is accomplished but they are placed there as a holder so that each layer can be represented.

3.11 Framework and Application Organization

Organizing the software can be a very critical issue. If you try to sub-divide it to granular, you can create confusion of what Framework projects in use. If you don't sub-divide enough, you will have software units available that do not belong in the Application type.

For instance, a Web Service should not have available to it Java Server Faces Project and you would not want to have Java Server Faces available to a Web Service Project.

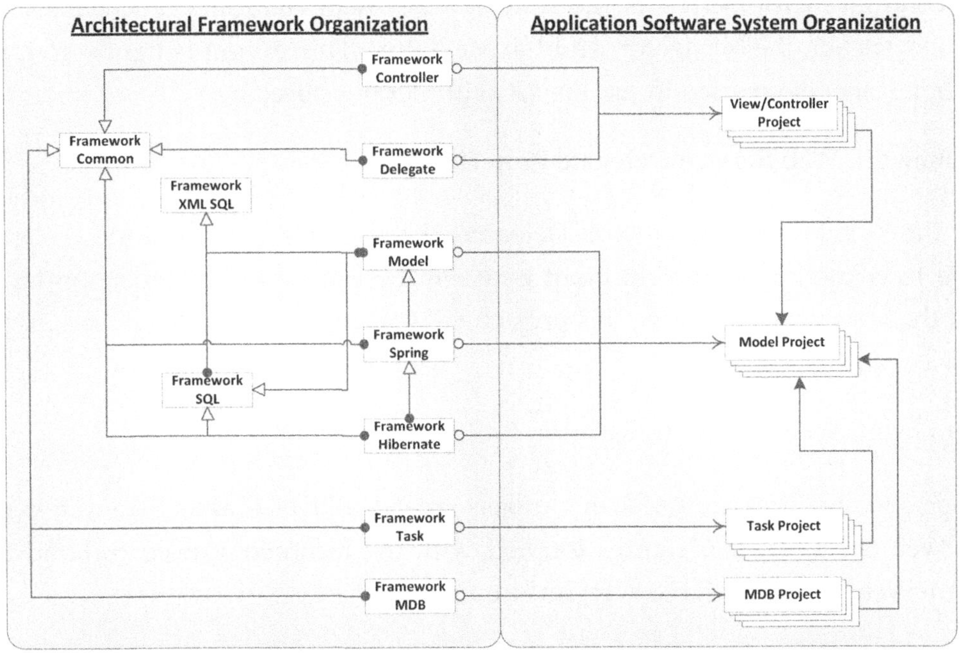

The diagram above shows an example of Frameworks subdivided into regions of concern. For instance, the Framework Hibernate Model region of concern is Hibernate functionality, at the same time, the Framework Spring Model Region of concern is Spring Architecture. By dividing the components of the Architecture this way, the technology and the regions of concern become loosely coupled together and the Architecture is not tightly coupled to any one technology so that changing to a different technology is as simple as using a different Framework Project.

3.11.1 Framework Projects

Framework Common Project:

The intent of this project is to be a holding location for classes that will be used commonly throughout the other projects such as common exceptions, the command message classes, and utilities classes. These classes are cross cutting concerns and do not belong to any particular layer or tier.

JSF Framework Controller Project:

The JSF Framework Controller tier holds those classes that are used to integrate the controller with the rest of the system. They hold controller type classes like the Dispatcher, the Navigator, and the Mediator. This project is tightly coupled with the technology used in the View/Controller interface.

Framework Web Service Delegate Project:

For the Web Service Framework Delegate, the objective is to hold those classes used to create a client access point between the Controller (or other top layer) and the Service Entry Point. This project will contain the technology used for the Service call.

Framework Web Service Integration Project:

When Web Services are used, this project creates a layer that as the entry point for Web Services. It is tightly coupled with the technology used to bond the Client Web Service with the Web Service End Point.

Framework Model Project:

The Framework Model Project is technology agnostic as far as such things as Web Service. It provides the core of the Model including an entry point into the Model (Proxy) and the Layers/Components of the Model Architecture (Solution, Domain, Exchange, and DAO). The Framework Model forms the heart and soul of the abstraction of the Business Logic. When Software Application implements the Model, they use the structure provided in this project to build their logic components.

Framework Spring:

This project, Framework Model Spring integrates the Spring Framework with the rest of the Model. It is tightly coupled with the Spring Framework and is used as integration point between the Spring Framework and the Model. One of the main software units of this project are the Component Spring Factories and Loaders. One of the short comings of the Spring Technology is that when it is used to create software units it must use the higher layer abstract class Java Object to create objects. The intent of this Project is to provide a bridge between the Spring Architecture and the Framework Component Architecture.

Framework Hibernate Project:

Like the Framework Spring Project, the Framework Hibernate Project is a bridge between the Hibernate Architecture and the Model Component Architecture. Among the more important classes in this Project is the DAOGenericHibernate class which is a implementation of the DAO Generic Pattern and provides the implementation for the more abstract concept of the Generalized DAO. This project is tightly coupled to the Hibernate Architecture. In the event a different Architecture for Object Relationship Mapping (ORM) is desired, a different Framework could be constructed using the different technology such as the IBATIS ORM framework.

Framework Task Project:

There are times when a simple main program is useful for executing task oriented work such as reading an input file, parsing it, and storing it in the database. The Framework Task Project is design to handle such tasks. It can be a onetime run, or continues run until told to stop. It can look for trigger files and property files to determine its task flow.

Framework MDB Project:

One of the more success parts of the Enterprise Java Bean Architecture (EJB) is the Message Driven Bean (MDB). Its purpose is to receive JMS messages (Java Message Service) and execute coded logic. The Framework MDB Project is a bridge between the EJB MDB Architecture and the Service Oriented Component Driven Architecture.

Framework Smart SQL Project:

While SQL statements are generally stored in the software based on the ORM Technology such as Hibernate Named Queries, there are times when a more robust technique is required, such as when queries need to be built dynamically based on a set of determined logic. The Framework Smart SQL Project allows the SQL Statements to be built using nondeterministic logic.

Framework Smart XML SQL Project:

There are times when logic for building a query needs to be built before the Model is reached. In order to do this, the XML SQL Framework project creates a set of XML structures that mimic Smart SQL encoded objects. When the Smart XML SQL is processed in the Model, it is converted from XML to SQL statement using the Smart SQL Project.

3.11.2 Application Implementation Software

View Controller Implementation Projects:

The View/Controller Implementation Projects is the implementation of the front end of a software application that uses some GUI technology such as JSF/Icefaces. These Projects uses various framework projects to implement the Software Architecture such as the Controller and Delegate Projects to create the Application Software.

Model Implementation Projects:

The Model Implementation projects are the embodiment of the business logic for the Software Application. The Model Application Software uses various Framework Projects to determine how to implement the Business logic for the Software Application. For instance the Model Application Software might use the base Model Framework to implement the basic features, use the Model Spring Framework to use the Spring Architecture, and use the Model Hibernate Framework to use the Hibernate Architecture. If down the road, the Software Application was to change to use Ibatis, a Model Ibatis Framework project could be created and used instead of the Model Hibernate Framework which would require little changes to the Application Software itself.

Task Implementation Projects:

The Task Implementation Projects bind the Architecture Frameworks necessary to fulfill its jobs as well as implements the logic necessary to complete its intended purpose. A Task who intended target was to read a XML File and send it to a web service for processing might collect the Framework Task Project and the Web Service Integration Project and use the software classes in these projects to implement its classes to complete its execution logic pathways.

MDB Implementation Projects:

The MDB Implementation Project like the name implies is the implementation of the execution units/classes to create a useful MDB Implementation project. This project might utilize the Framework MDB Project, the Framework Model Project, the Framework Spring Project, and the Framework Hibernate Project to implement the MDB Controlling unit (Message Bean) and then use the other projects to implement the business logic. In this case, it is likely the project may not want to utilize the Framework Web Service Delegation since the MDB is already a type of Service and it would simple create a greater latency time reducing the response time of the MDB Service.

Chapter 4 Component Architecture

4.1 General Component Architecture Discussion

All executable units are components. Component is an interface that all components must run. The component interface provides a Façade pattern that all components must implement. It has one method: execute(Command,CmdMsg); Some standard components are:

Solution: Used to solve a business problem.

Domain: Used to run business logic for a specific domain such as a user.

Exchange: Is a wrapper around a DAO and is used to process the Data Access Object (DAO). This allows for technology agnostic software or in other words, the Exchange allows the system to isolate the Data Access technology from the data exchange process.

Data Access: A Data Access Object (DAO) is technology specific logic for access data. For example, the DAO might use Hibernate or Ibatis to access the database. The DAO may be an interface to a JMS object. Regardless of the technology used, the Exchange will not need to understand how the technology is used.

Whenever a component is called and it happens to be a layer component (Solution, Domain, and Exchange), processing begins in the Model execution method which wraps the processing inside a try/catch block. The catch block catches throwable objects. Whenever a throwable object is caught, control is passed to the Exception Handler Manager to either handle the exception or pass exception control to an upper layer by re-throwing the exception.

4.2 Component Architecture Diagram

The Component Architecture is divided into three parts: Common, Controller, and Model. The Common section provides common funcationality to both the Controller and the Model.

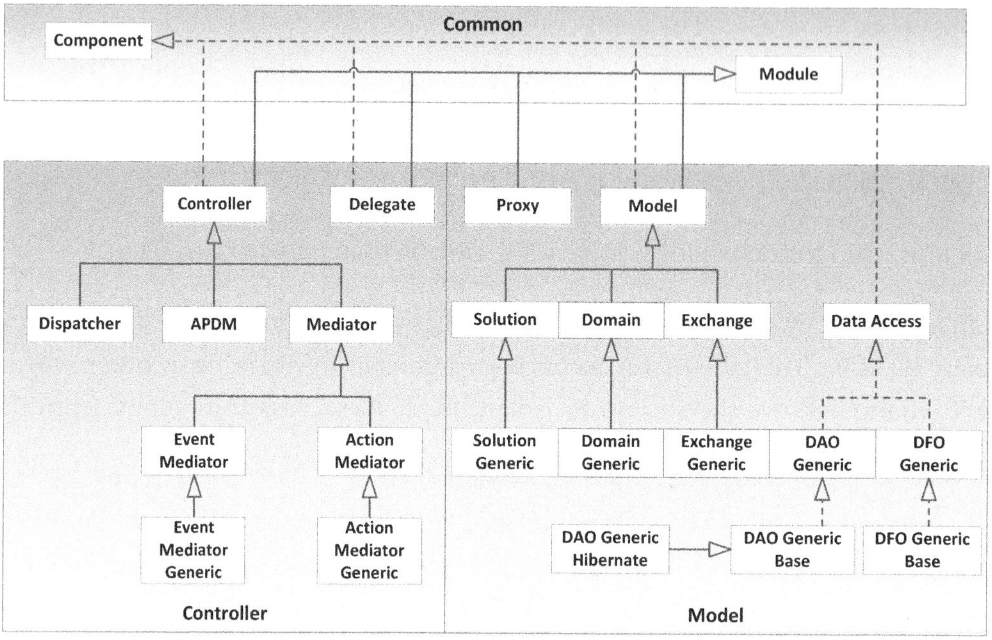

The Controller provides arbitration between the Presentation/View and the Model. The controller behavior is closely related to the Presentation/View and is coupled to the technology used in the Presentation/View while at the same time decoupling the Model from the Presentation/View.

The Model provides the business logic of the system including the access to persistent data storage. The Model is agnostic to the Controller or the Presentation/View other than providing data that the Controller can convert to something useful to the Presentation/View tier.

Chapter 5 The View Layer Patterns

The View is generally made up of HTML and JSP tag and tag libraries. While this book will not dwell too deep on the View layer as there are many good books on the subject.

The best way to build a HTML or JSP View is to use templates. The templates should be able to have insertion points for the heading for the page, a pane for the navigation view and a place for the contents.

The Navigation View will be a set of links that call the Dispatcher layer in the Controller tier to perform some type of action. Typically the Navigator is designed to jump to another page or pages.

The Content View will either be a display only page or a page with a form and HTML/JSP components such as text input fields along with hot links and submit buttons. The Text Fields should be linked to the back end object [View-->Controller[Dispatcher-->APDM-->PTO-->Object]]. The hot links or submit buttons should cause an action to occur in the Controller:Dispatcher.

The Content View may also have AJAX events which will be tied into the Controller:Dispatcher event model.

The View is best seen as a place where data is interfaced with the user. It is either there to display helpfull user information or to receive input from the user. The input tags in a View Page are directly or indirectly linked to the Presentation Data Object through the Application Display Presentation Manager.

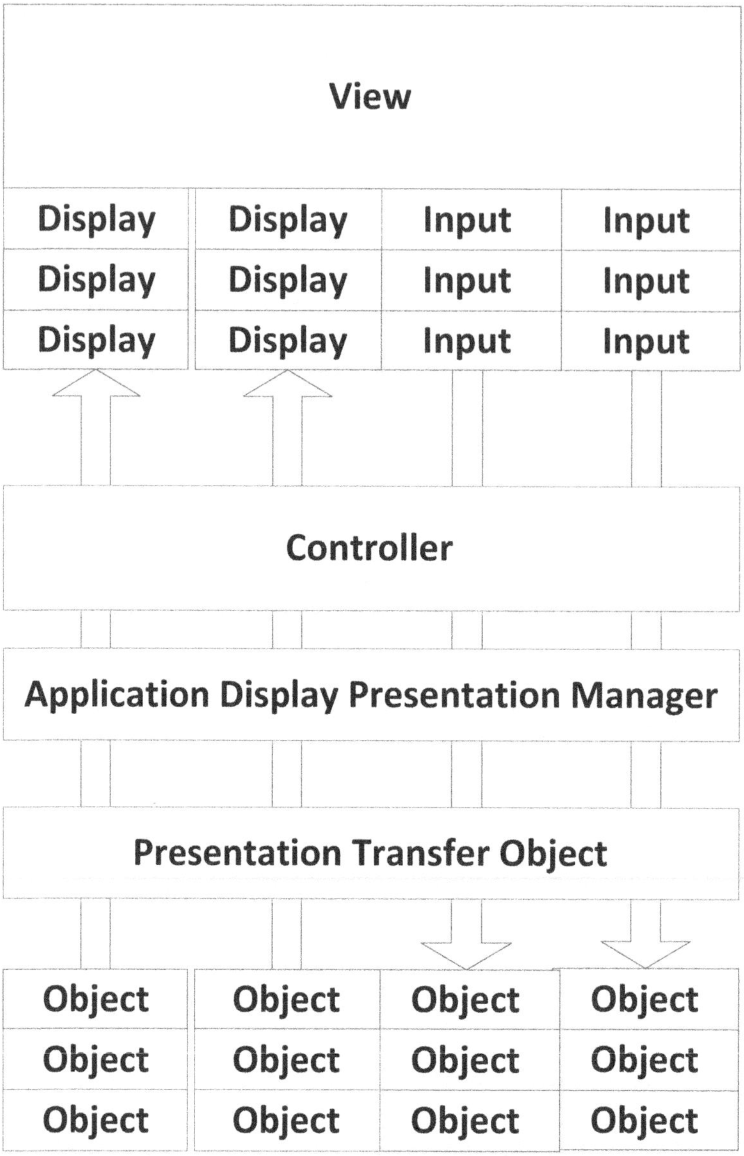
View
Display
Display
Display
Display
Display
Display
Input
Input
Input
Input
Input
Input
Controller
Application Display Presentation Manager
Presentation Transfer Object
Object
Object
Object
Object
Object
Object
Object
Object
Object
Object
Object
Object

Chapter 6 The Controller Tier

6.1 Overview of the Controller Tier

The controller tier is the main entry point into the architecture. It may be integrated from a View (JSP or other GUI) or it may come from a Message Driven Bean or a main java class.

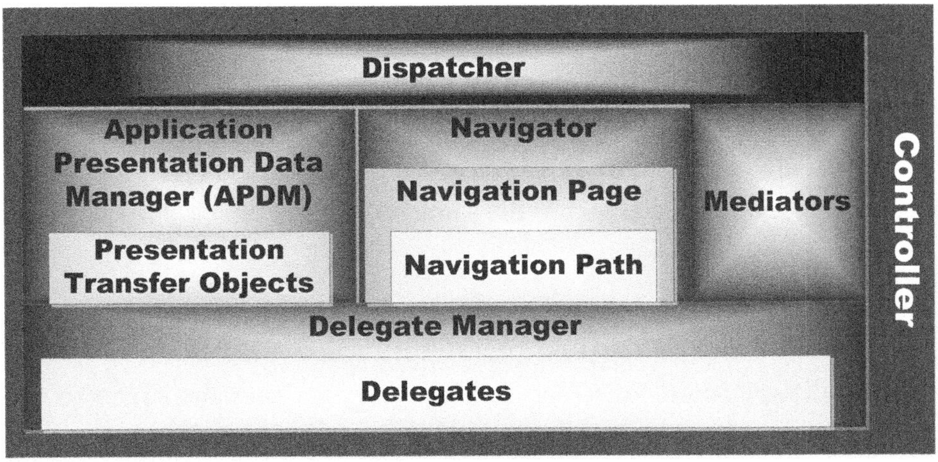

The Controller Tier is made up of several distinct layers:

- The Dispatcher
    - Application Presentation Data Manager
        - Presentation Transfer Objects (PTO)
    - Navigator
        - Navigation Page
            - Navigation Path
    - Mediators
    - Delegate Manager
        - Delegates

Together, these form the Controller Tier.

6.2 Controller Abstraction

Overview:

The Controller Abstract class is a representation of the properties common for the Controller Tier. This is a common interface for the components of the tier which provides a facade so that the objects can share properties without the need to pass them for layer to layer.

Objective:

The objectives of the Controller Abstraction for the tier is to ensure that properties stored in the abstractions are available to other components of the tier such as the Mediator which needs access to the presentation objects as well as the Dispatcher that require the access to the same objects.

Responsibility:

It is the responsibility of the Controller Abstraction to provide a uniformed access to the Application Presentation Data Manager and the Error list. This allows the objects which access the Dispatcher Layer such as the Views to access the same information as other layer classes such as the Mediators.

Pattern Type:

The Controller Abstraction uses the Facade Pattern to provide a uniformed access to the objects in the Controller Tier. Using Inverse of Control, each class in the Tier that inherits the Controller Abstraction uses dependency injection to inject common used Objects into the inheriting class.

Code Sample:

```
public abstract class Controller extends Module implements Component
{
 private AppPresentationDataMgr appPresDataMgr;
 private ErrorList errorList = new ErrorList();

 public void setAppPresentationDataMgr(AppPresentationDataMgr aAppPresDataMgr)
 {
  appPresDataMgr = aAppPresDataMgr;
 }

 public PTO getPto()
 {
  return appPresDataMgr.getCurrentPto();
 }

 public void setPto(PTO pto)
 {
  appPresDataMgr.setCurrentPto(pto);
 }

 public void setId(String aId)
 {
  setValue("id", appPresDataMgr.getCurrentPto(), aId);
 }

 public void addError(Exception aException)
 {
  errorList.addError(aException);
 }

 public void addError(Throwable aThrowable)
 {
  errorList.addError(aThrowable);
 }
}
```

6.3 Dispatcher Layer

Overview:

The top layer of the Controller tier is the Dispatcher layer. Sub-classing of the Dispatcher is usually not necessary as its behavior is controlled by the objects that are injected into it. It is the entry point of the application from the Presentation Tier.

Objective:

The objective of Dispatcher is to act as the initial point of contact with the View. The Dispatcher is the gate keeper of information between the View and the rest of the system. The Dispatcher is also the logic execution traffic controller, controlling what page is next and controlling the flow of execution to the layers that handle the Business Logic. It performs these tasks with the injected objects into its properties such as the Navigation Properties and the Mediators.

Responsibility:

The responsibility of the Dispatcher is to receive information from the Presentation tier above it, store it in the Application Presentation Data Manger [Presentation Transfer Object] or cause some action to occur including either calling the Event Mediator or the Action Mediator.

Pattern Type:

The Dispatcher is a Behavioral Pattern which uses Inversion of Control and Dependency Inject in determining its logical flow.

Structure:

The Dispatcher inherits the abstract class Controller and is a composition of Action Mediator, Event Mediator, and the Navigator.

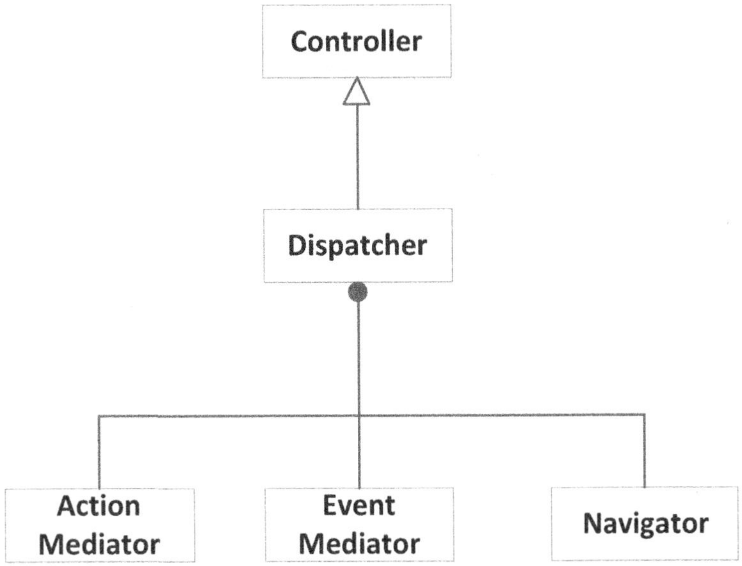

Work Flow:

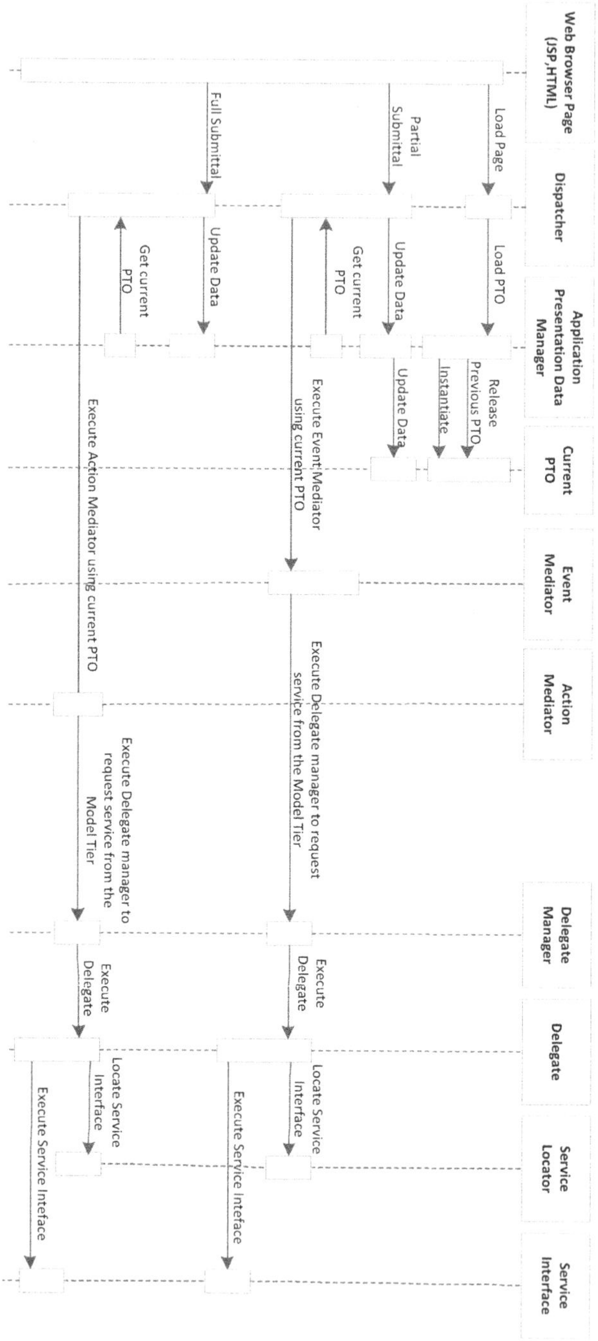
Web Browser Page (JSP,HTML)
Dispatcher
Application Presentation Data Manager
Current PTO
Event Mediator
Action Mediator
Delegate Manager
Delegate
Service Locator
Service Interface
Load Page
Partial Submittal
Full Submittal
Load PTO
Update Data
Get current PTO
Update Data
Get current PTO
Release Previous PTO
Instantiate
Update Data
Execute Event Mediator using current PTO
Execute Action Mediator using current PTO
Execute Delegate manager to request service from the Model Tier
Execute Delegate manager to request service from the Model Tier
Execute Delegate
Execute Delegate
Locate Service Interface
Locate Service Interface
Execute Service Inteface
Execute Service Inteface

Code Sample:

```
public class Dispatcher extends Controller
{
 private static final String ACTION = "Action";
 private static final String ACTION_EVENT = "ActionEvent";
 private static final String ROW_SELECTOR_EVENT = "RowSelectorEvent";
 private static final String VALUE_CHANGE_EVENT = "ValueChangeEvent";
 private String dispatcherName;
 private Navigator navigator;
 private Mediator  actionMediator;
 private EventMediator  actionEventMediator;
 private Command command = new Cmd();

 public void setDispatcherName(String aName)
 {
  dispatcherName = aName;
 }

 public String getDispatcherName()
 {
  return dispatcherName;
 }

 public Navigator getNavigator()
 {
  return navigator;
 }

 public void setNavigator(Navigator aNavigator)
 {
  navigator = aNavigator;
 }

 public Command getCommand()
 {
  return command;
 }

 public void setCommand(Command aCommand)
 {
  command = aCommand;
```

```
}

public void setActionMediator(Mediator aActionMediator)
{
 actionMediator = aActionMediator;
}

public Mediator getActionMediator()
{
 return actionMediator;
}

public void setActionEventMediator(EventMediator aActionEventMediator)
{
 actionEventMediator = aActionEventMediator;
}

public EventMediator getActionEventMediator()
{
 return actionEventMediator;
}


public final String execute()
{
 execute(getCommand(),new CommandMsg());
 String mRtnValue = navigator.getNextPage();
 setValue("view", getPto(), navigator.getView());
 return mRtnValue;
}

public void execute(ActionEvent aActionEvent)
{
 execute(aActionEvent,getCommand(),new CommandMsg());
}
```

```
public void execute(RowSelectorEvent aRowSelectorEvent)

{
 execute(aRowSelectorEvent,getCommand(),new CommandMsg());
}

public void execute(ValueChangeEvent aValueChangeEvent)
{
 execute(aValueChangeEvent,getCommand(),new CommandMsg());
}

@Override
public void execute(Command aCommand, CmdMsg aCmdMsg)
{
 try
 {
  callBack(this, ACTION,aCommand,aCmdMsg);
 }
 catch (Throwable aThrowable)
 {
  addError(aThrowable);
 }
}

public void execute(ActionEvent aActionEvent,Command aCommand, CmdMsg
aCmdMsg)
{
 try
 {
  callBack(this, ACTION_EVENT,aActionEvent,aCommand,aCmdMsg);
 }
 catch (Throwable aThrowable)
 {
  addError(aThrowable);
 }
}
```

```
public void execute(RowSelectorEvent aRowSelectorEvent,Command aCommand,
CmdMsg aCmdMsg)
{
  try
  {
    callBack(this, ROW_SELECTOR_EVENT,aRowSelectorEvent,aCommand,aCmdMsg);
  }
  catch (Throwable aThrowable)
  {
    addError(aThrowable);
  }
}

public void execute(ValueChangeEvent aValueChangeEvent,Command aCommand,
CmdMsg aCmdMsg)
{
  try
  {
    callBack(this,
VALUE_CHANGE_EVENT,aValueChangeEvent,aCommand,aCmdMsg);
  }
  catch (Throwable aThrowable)
  {
    addError(aThrowable);
  }
}

public String genericAction()
{
  getCondParam();
  return execute();
}

public void genericActionEvent(ActionEvent aActionEvent)
{
  getCondParam();
  execute(aActionEvent);
}
public void genericRowSelectorEvent(RowSelectorEvent aRowSelectorEvent)
{
  getCondParam();
  execute(aRowSelectorEvent);
```

```
}

public void genericValueChangeEvent(ValueChangeEvent aValueChangeEvent)
{
  getCondParam();
  execute(aValueChangeEvent);
}

private void getCondParam()
{
  FacesContext context = FacesContext.getCurrentInstance();
  String mCondition = getCondition(context);
  String mId = getId(context);
  if(mId != null) setId(mId);
  setCondition(mCondition);
}

private String getCondition(FacesContext aContext)
{
  Map<String,String> params =
aContext.getExternalContext().getRequestParameterMap();
  return params.get("condition");
}

private String getId(FacesContext aContext)
{
  Map<String,String> params =
aContext.getExternalContext().getRequestParameterMap();
  return params.get("id");
}
```

```
public String genericAction(Command aCommand, CmdMsg aCmdMsg)
{
  Mediator mMediator = getActionMediator();
  if(mMediator != null)
  {
    mMediator.execute(aCommand, aCmdMsg);
  }

  String mNextPage = navigator.getNextPage();
  return mNextPage;
}

public void genericActionEvent(ActionEvent aActionEvent,Command aCommand,
CmdMsg aCmdMsg)
{
  EventMediator mMediator = getActionEventMediator();
  if(mMediator != null)
  {
    mMediator.execute(aActionEvent,aCommand, aCmdMsg);
  }
}

public void genericRowSelectorEvent(RowSelectorEvent aRowSelectorEvent,Command
aCommand, CmdMsg aCmdMsg)
{
  EventMediator mMediator = getActionEventMediator();
  if(mMediator != null)
  {
    mMediator.execute(aRowSelectorEvent,aCommand, aCmdMsg);
  }
}

public void genericValueChangeEvent(ValueChangeEvent
aValueChangeEvent,Command aCommand, CmdMsg aCmdMsg)
{
  EventMediator mMediator = getActionEventMediator();
  if(mMediator != null)
  {
    mMediator.execute(aValueChangeEvent,aCommand, aCmdMsg);
  }
}
```

```
public String getCondition()
{
  return navigator.getCondition();
}

public void setCondition(String condition)
{
  if(condition != null && condition.trim().length() >0)
  {
    navigator.setCondition(condition);
  }
}

@Override
protected Class<?> getTheClass()
{
  return Dispatcher.class;
}

}
```

Dependency Injection:

When the system is first brought up, the Navigator is created and injected with its dependencies, and then injected into the Dispatcher. Then the Mediators are created and injected with their dependencies and then injected into Dispatcher.

The examples below use Spring and Icefaces configurations.

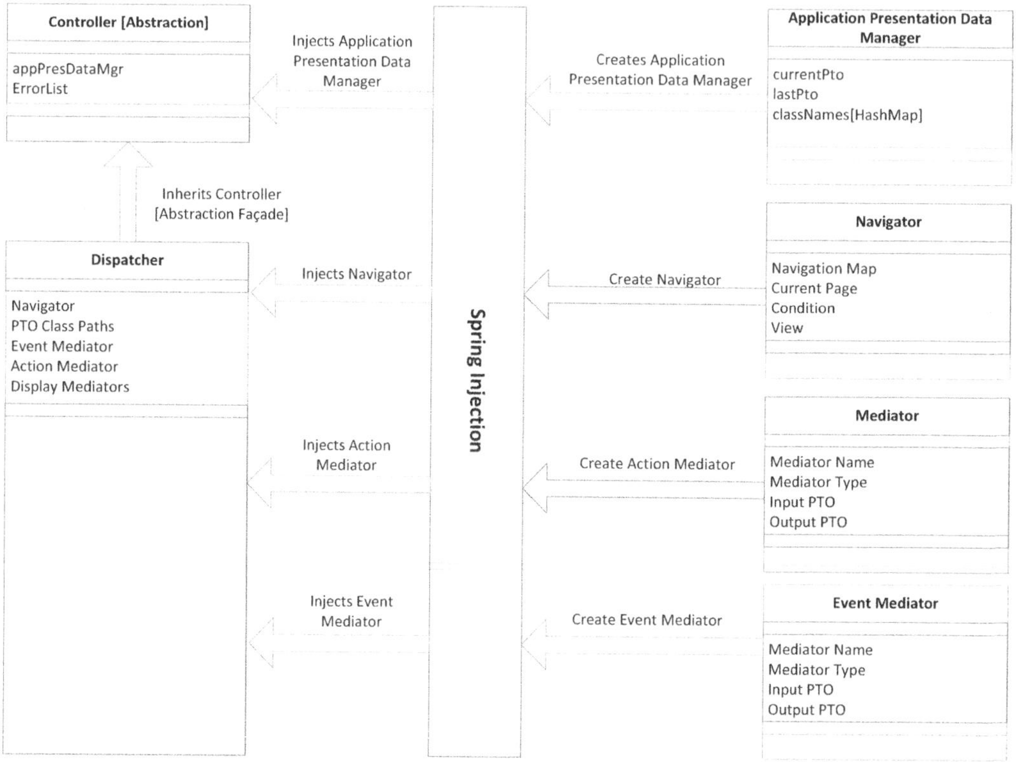

Example icefaces configuration file [faces-config.xml]

```
<managed-bean>
  <managed-bean-name>Welcome</managed-bean-name>
    <managed-bean-class>
       com.dth.fmw.ctl.control.Dispatcher
    </managed-bean-class>
    <managed-bean-scope>request</managed-bean-scope>
    <managed-property>
     <property-name>dispatcherName</property-name>
    <value>Welcome</value>
```

```
  </managed-property>
  <managed-property>
    <property-name>appPresDataMgr</property-name>
    <value>#{welcomeAppPresDataMgr}</value>
  </managed-property>
  <managed-property>
    <property-name>navigator</property-name>
    <value>#{WelcomeNavigator}</value>
  </managed-property>
</managed-bean>
<managed-bean>
  <managed-bean-name>Page2</managed-bean-name>
  <managed-bean-class>
    com.dth.fmw.ctl.control.Dispatcher
  </managed-bean-class>
  <managed-bean-scope>request</managed-bean-scope>
  <managed-property>
    <property-name>dispatcherName</property-name>
    <value>Page2</value>
  </managed-property>
  <managed-property>
    <property-name> appPresDataMgr </property-name>
    <value>#{page2AppPresDataMgr }</value>
  </managed-property>
  <managed-property>
    <property-name>navigator</property-name>
    <value>#{Page2Navigator}</value>
  </managed-property>
  <managed-property>
    <property-name>actionMediator</property-name>
    <value>#{Page2ActionMediator}</value>
  </managed-property>
</managed-bean>
```

Example Spring Configuration:

```
<?xml version="1.0" encoding="UTF-8"?>
<!DOCTYPE beans PUBLIC "-//SPRING//DTD BEAN//EN"
"http://www.springframework.org/dtd/spring-beans.dtd">
<beans>

 <!-- ****************************************************************** -->
 <!-- ************** Page2   *************************************** -->
 <!-- ****************************************************************** -->

 <bean id="page2NavPath" class="com.dth.fmw.ctl.navigator.NavigationPath">
  <constructor-arg value="Page2"/>     <!-- Current Page -->
  <constructor-arg value="goPage3"/>   <!-- Condition    -->
  <constructor-arg value="Page3"/>     <!-- Next Page    -->
  <constructor-arg value="Page3.jspx"/> <!-- Next View    -->
 </bean>

 <bean id="page2NavPage" class="com.dth.fmw.ctl.navigator.NavigationPage">
  <constructor-arg>
   <list>
    <ref bean="page2NavPagePath"/>
   </list>
  </constructor-arg>
 </bean>

 <bean id="page2Navigator" class="com.dth.fmw.ctl.navigator.Navigator">
  <property name="navigationPage" ref="page2NavPage"/>
  <property name="currentPage" value="Page2"/>
  <property name="condition" value="goPage3"/> <!-- default condition -->
 </bean>

 <bean id="page2ActionMediator" class="com.dth.fmw.ctl.mediator.MediatorGeneric">
  <property name="name" value="Page2ActionMediator"/>
  <property name="type" value="action"/>
  <property name="inputPtoName" value="inputPtoName"/>
  <property name="outputPtoName" value="outputPtoName"/>
 </bean>
</beans>
```

6.4 Application Presentation Data Manger Layer

Overview:

The Application Presentation Data Manager [APDM] is the manager of the Presentation Transfer Object [PTO].

Objective:

The APDM objective is to ensure that the correct PTO is used at the current time in the flow of the system and make it available to other parts of the Controller Tier. When there is no current PTO and there is a request for one, the APDM uses the PTOFactory to create a new PTO that lives until it is no longer required.

Responsibility

The Application Presentation Data Manager is responsible for load, updating and release Presentation Data Objects. When a new page is loaded, the Application Presentation Data Manager loads the appropriate Presentation Transfer Object. During the processing of the page, the properties of the Presentation Transfer Objects are updated and available for use by the rest of the system. Once the Presentation Transfer Object is no longer required, the Application Presentation Data Manager is responsible for releasing the PTO so that the Garbage collector can recycle the memory for future use.

Pattern Type:

The APDM is a creation pattern that uses dependency injection to inject that class path of the objects to create and hold during the life cycle of the PTO.

Structure:

The Application Presentation Data Manager is a composite of the Current Active Presentation Transfer Object and a Map of PTODefinitions.

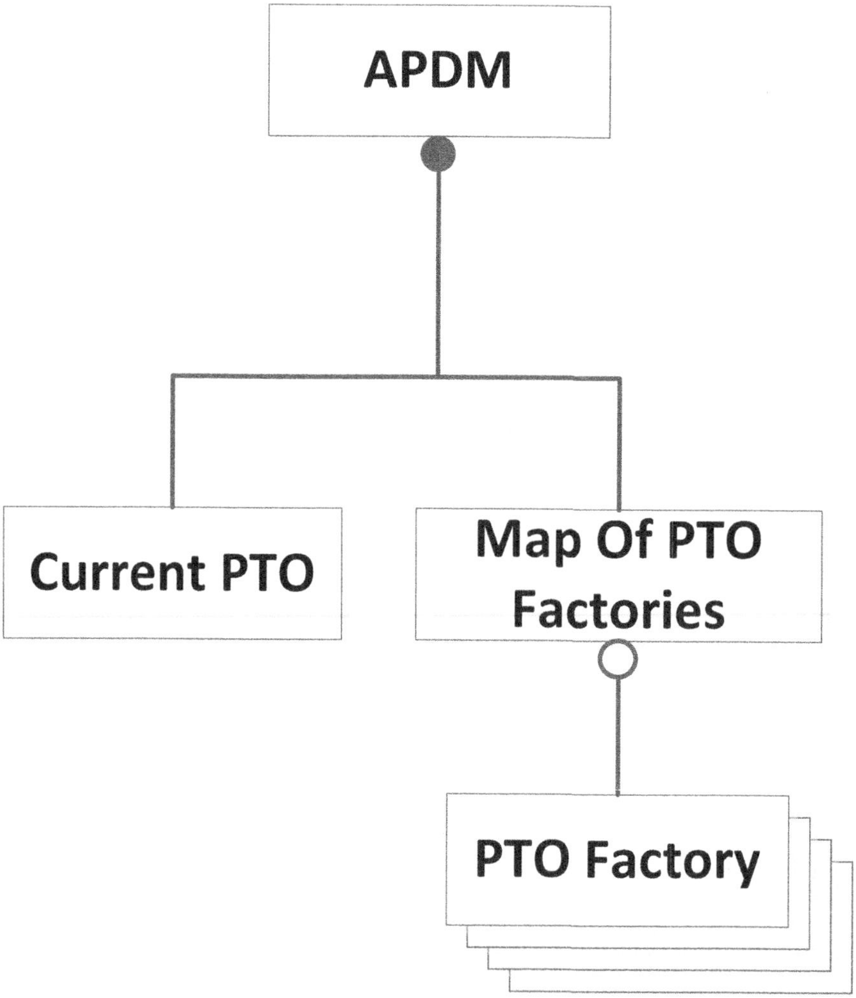

Work Flow:

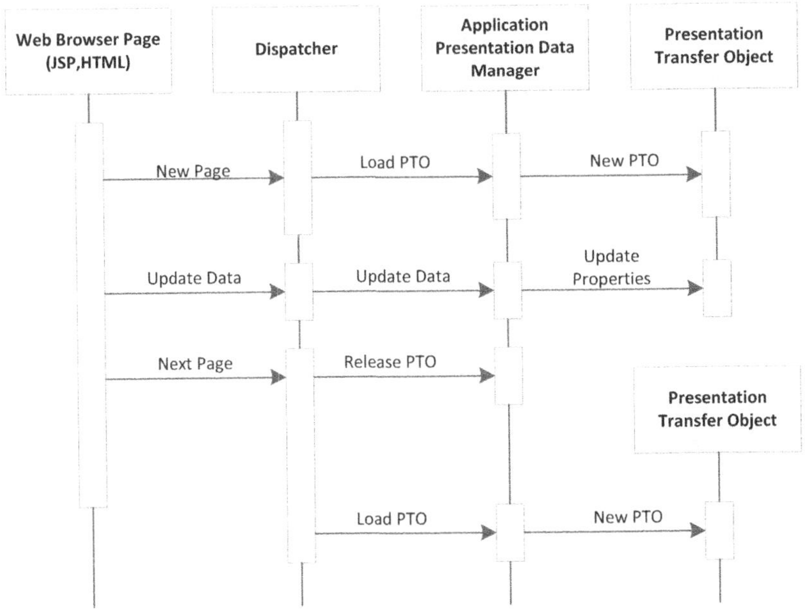
Web Browser Page (JSP,HTML)
Dispatcher
Application Presentation Data Manager
Presentation Transfer Object
New Page
Load PTO
New PTO
Update Data
Update Data
Update Properties
Next Page
Release PTO
Presentation Transfer Object
Load PTO
New PTO

Code Sample:

```
public class AppPresentationDataMgr
{
 private PTO currentPto;
  private Map<String, PTOFactory> classNames = new HashMap<String, PTOFactory>();

 public AppPresentationDataMgr()
 {
  }

 public AppPresentationDataMgr(Map<String,PTOFactory> aClassNames)
 {
  classNames = aClassNames;
 }

 public PTO getCurrentPto()
 {
  return currentPto;
 }

 public void setCurrentPto(PTO aCurrentPto)
 {
  currentPto = aCurrentPto;
 }

 public void loadClassNames(Map<String,PTOFactory> aClassNames)
 {
  classNames = aClassNames;
 }
```

```
public void loadPto(String aNameOfPTO)
{
  currentPto = null;
  PTOFactory mPTOFactory = classNames.get(aNameOfPTO);
  if(mPTOFactory != null)
  {
    currentPto = mPTOFactory.createPTO();
  }
 }
}
```

Dependency Injection:

When the system is first brought up, the PTO Factory objects are created and injected with their Meta Information. These are then injected into the Application Presentation Data Manager.

The examples below use Spring configurations to define the Dependency injection.

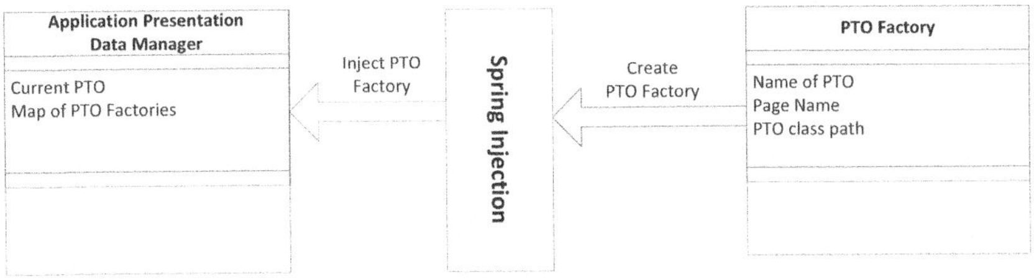

Example of Spring Configuration:

```
<?xml version="1.0" encoding="UTF-8"?>
<!DOCTYPE beans PUBLIC "-//SPRING//DTD BEAN//EN"
"http://www.springframework.org/dtd/spring-beans.dtd">
<beans>
 <bean id="applicationPresentationDataManager"
            class="com.dth.fmw.ctl.apdm.AppPresentationDataMgr">
 <constructor-arg>
   <map>
    <entry key="page2PTODefinition" value-ref="page2PTODefinition" />
     <entry key="page3PTODefinition" value-ref="page3PTODefinition" />
   </map>
 </constructor-arg>
 </bean>
</beans>
```

6.5 Presentation Transfer Object Factory

Overview:

Throughout the duration of the lifecycle of a View, data is transported between the View and the Controller. This data is closely mapped to the information contained in the View most of which is available to the user either visualize or as input information to the Controller Tier. These Presentation Transfer Objects are destroyed when no longer required, but must be constructed when the visual display to the user is changed. The PTOFactory receives key information in order to determine what PTO to create.

Objective:

The Objective of the Presentation Transfer Object Factory [PTOFactory] is to create a new Presentation Transfer Object upon request.

Responsibility

The PTOFacotry is responsible for creating new PTOs upon request based on key information provided to it from the Application Presentation Display Manager.

Pattern Type:

The PTOFactory is a creation pattern used to create Presentation Transfer Objects on demand.

Structure:

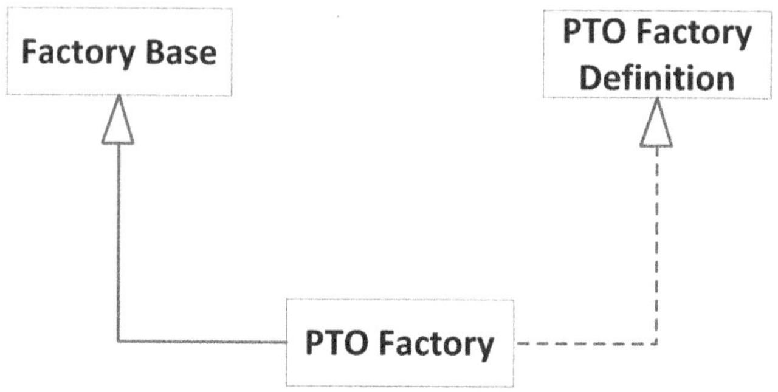

Work Flow:

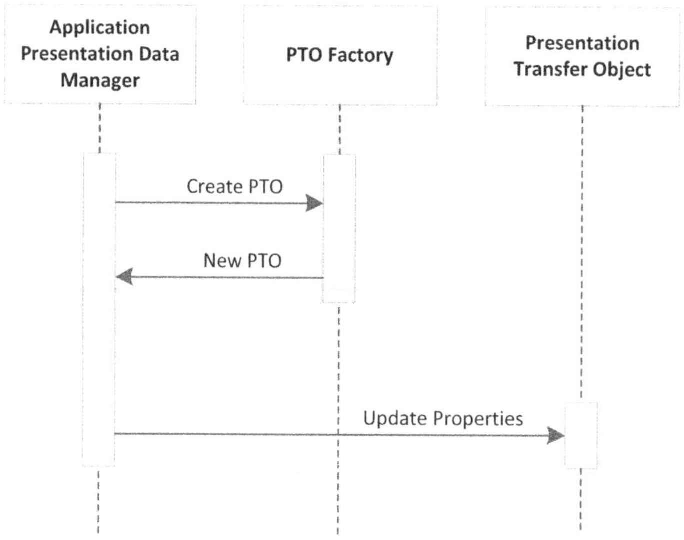

Code Sample:

```
public class PTOFactory extends FactoryBase<PTO> implements PTOFactoryDefinition
{
  private String nameOfPTO;
  private String pageName;
  private String classPath;

  public String getNameOfPTO()
  {
```

```
  return nameOfPTO;
 }

 public void setNameOfPTO(String nameOfPTO)
 {
  this.nameOfPTO = nameOfPTO;
 }

 public String getPageName()
 {
  return pageName;
 }

 public void setPageName(String pageName)
 {
  this.pageName = pageName;
 }

 public String getClassPath()
 {
  return classPath;
 }

 public void setClassPath(String classPath)
 {
  this.classPath = classPath;
 }

 public PTO createPTO()
 {
  String mClassPath = getClassPath();
  PTO mRtnValue = create(mClassPath);
  return mRtnValue;
 }
}
```

Dependency Injection:

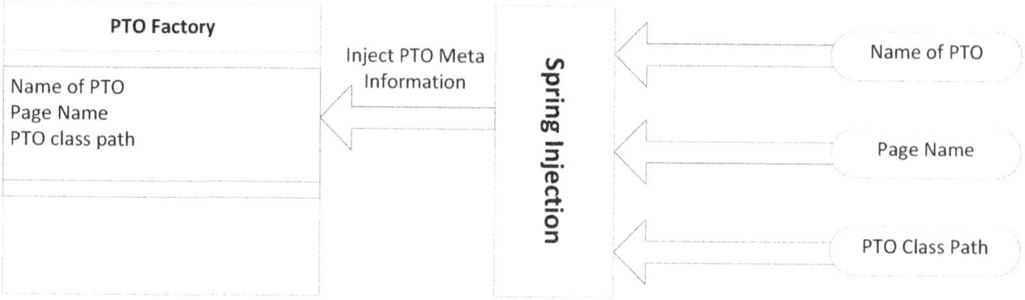

Example of Spring Configuration:

```
<?xml version="1.0" encoding="UTF-8"?>
<!DOCTYPE beans PUBLIC "-//SPRING//DTD BEAN//EN"
"http://www.springframework.org/dtd/spring-beans.dtd">
<beans>
  <bean id="ptoPage2Factory" class="com.dth.pto.factory.PTOPage2Factory">
    <property name="nameOfPTO" value="PTOPage2"/>
    <property name=" nameOfPage " value="Page2"/>
    <property name="ptoClassPath" value="com.dth.example_app.pto.PTOPage2"/>
  </bean>
</beans>
```

6.6 Presentation Transfer Objects

Overview:

The Presentation Transfer Objects (PTO) is nothing more than Data Transfer Objects (DTO) designed specifically to transfer data between the View and the Controller Tier. Each Presentation Transfer Object property should map directly or indirectly to properties in the view (Browser Page). The PTO is a serializable object that is designed to hold properties defined in the View and to provide public access to these properties using getters and setters. The PTOs are designed specifically for the Application and View pages of the system and therefore are arbitrary in nature depending on system requirements.

Objective:

The objective of the Presentation Transfer Objects (PTO) is to provide a simple to use serializable object for transferring data between the View and the Controller Tier.

Responsibility:

The PTO is responsible for holding the data elements represented in the View in the Controller tier. The PTO is also responsible for making these data elements available to the components of the Controller including the Dispatcher and the Mediators.

Pattern Type:

Presentation Transfer Object is a structural pattern providing organization in order to transfer data between the View and the Controller Tier.

Structure:

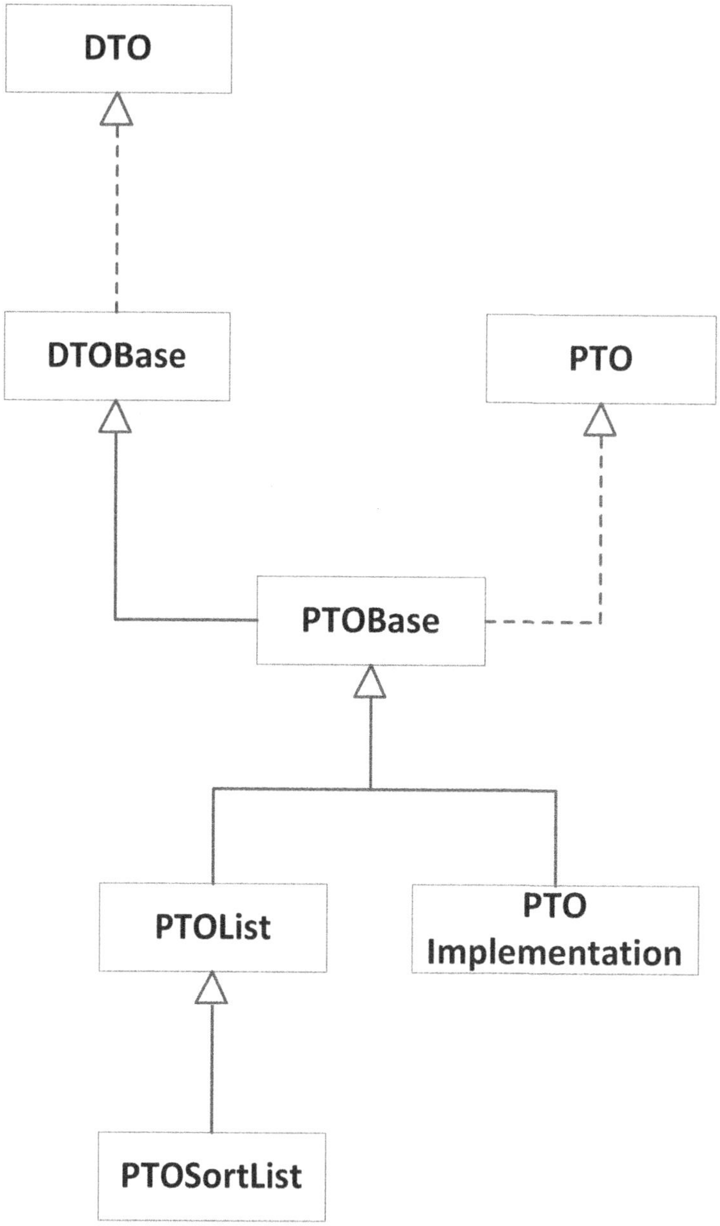
DTO
DTOBase
PTO
PTOBase
PTOList
PTO Implementation
PTOSortList

Work Flow:

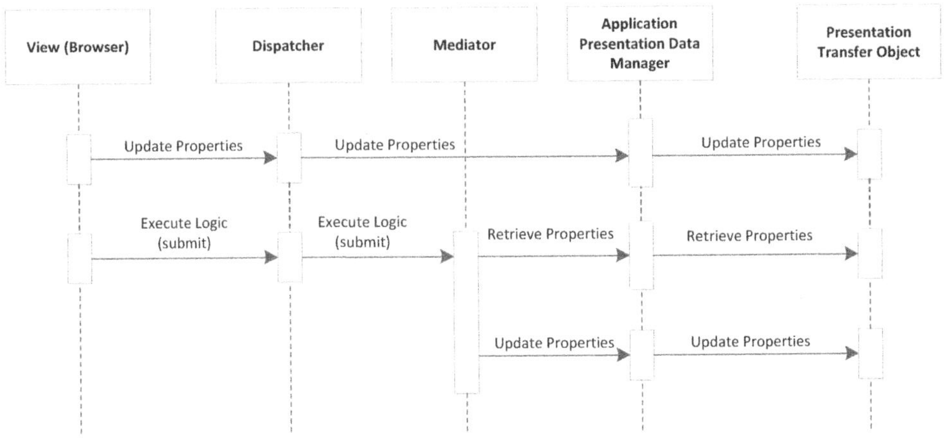

Code Sample:

```
public interface PTO extends DTO
{

}


public abstract class PTOBase extends DTOBase implements PTO
{
  private static final long serialVersionUID = 1L;

}
```

```
public class PTOExample extends PTOBase
{
 private String firstName;
 private String middleName;
 private String lastName;
 private String address1;
 private String address2;
 private String city;
 private String state;
 private String state;

 public String getFirstName()
 {
  return firstName;
 }

 public void setFirstName(String firstName)
 {
  this.firstName = firstName;
 }

 public String getMiddleName()
 {
  return middleName;
 }

 public void setMiddleName(String middleName)
 {
  this.middleName = middleName;
 }

 public String getLastName()
 {
  return lastName;
 }

 public void setLastName(String lastName)
 {
  this.lastName = lastName;
 }

 public String getAddress1()
```

```
{
 return address1;
}

public void setAddress1(String address1)
{
 this.address1 = address1;
}

public String getAddress2()
{
 return address2;
}

public void setAddress2(String address2)
{
 this.address2 = address2;
}

public String getCity()
{
 return city;
}

public void setCity(String city)
{
 this.city = city;
}

public String getState()
{
 return state;
}

public void setState(String state)
{
 this.state = state;
}

public String getState()
{
 return state;
```

```
  }

  public void setState(String state)
  {
    this.state = state;
  }
}
```

Dependency Injection:

None:

6.7 Navigator Layer

Overview:

Each Dispatcher object contains a Navigator. Each Navigator holds a Navigation Map Object, the current Page Name (String Value), the current condition, and the current View name. Each Navigation Map Object contains a list of objects containing a Navigation Path.

Objective:

The Objective of the Navigator is to control the flow of user experience. The Navigator uses the available information from the view to determine if a new page/view should be displayed and if so which page/view.

Responsibility:

The Navigator is responsible for receiving information from the page/view including the current page and a condition value. Based on these criteria, the Navigator uses its contents to determine the next page/view to display.

Pattern Type:

The Navigator is a behavioral pattern using chain of responsibility to perform its tasks.

Structure:

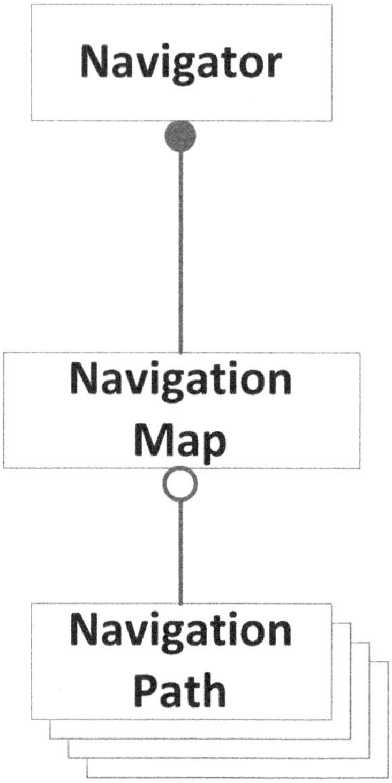

Work Flow:

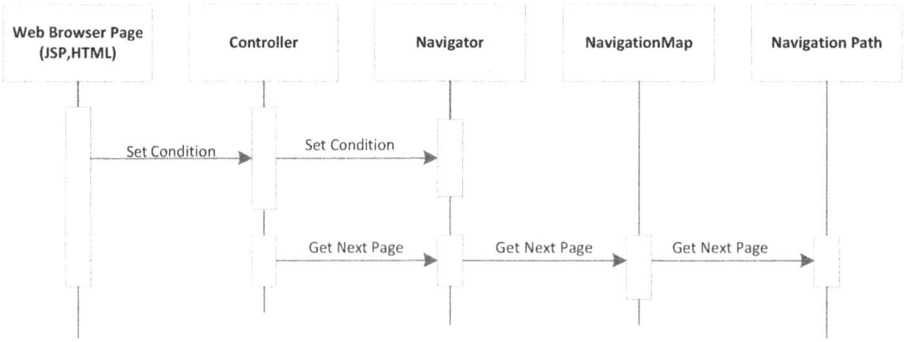

Code Sample:

```
public class Navigator
{
 private NavigationMap navigationMap;
 private String currentPage;
 private String condition;
 private String view;

 public NavigationMap getNavigationMap()
 {
  return navigationMap;
 }

 public void setNavigationMap(NavigationMap navigationMap)
 {
  this.navigationMap = navigationMap;
 }

 public String getCurrentPage()
 {
  return currentPage;
 }

 public void setCurrentPage(String currentPage)
 {
  this.currentPage = currentPage;
 }

 public String getCondition()
 {
  return condition;
 }

 public void setCondition(String condition)
 {
  this.condition = condition;
 }

 public String getNextPage()
 {
  String mRtnValue = navigationMap.getNextPage(currentPage, condition);
```

```
    view = navigationMap.getView();
    return mRtnValue;
  }

  public String getView()
  {
    return view;
  }

}
```

Dependency Injection:

When the application starts up, Spring will create a set of Objects based on the configuration setup provided by the developers. When talking about the Navigator and its parts, Spring will start by constructing a set of Objects of the type Navigation Path. Spring will then construct the Navigation Map Objects and for each object, it will insert a set of Navigation Paths. Spring will then continue to insert the Navigator into the Dispatcher.

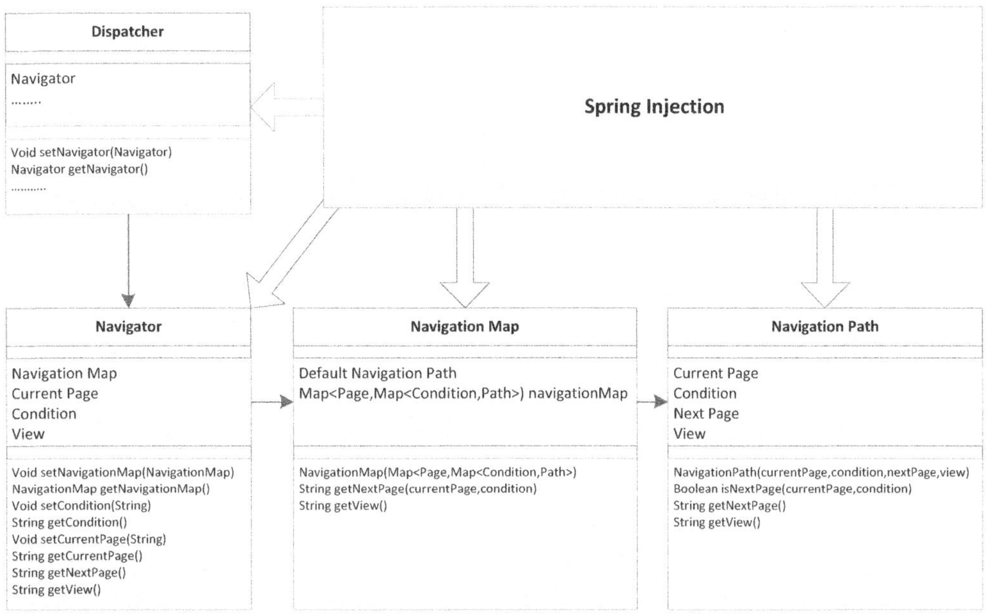

6.8 Navigation Map

Overview:

The Navigation Map is used to find the proper Navigation Path based on the current Page and a Condition value. Using this information, the Navigation Map will find the appropriate Navigation Path.

Objective:

The Objective of the Navigation Map is to provide the next Page to be displayed to the user based on the current page and the condition.

Responsibility:

The Navigation Map along with the Navigator is responsible for determining what page to return to the Dispatcher in order to display the new content to the user using the browser or other GUI processing system.

Pattern Type:

The Navigator Map is a Structural Pattern that holds a set of objects stored by Name and Condition.

Structure:

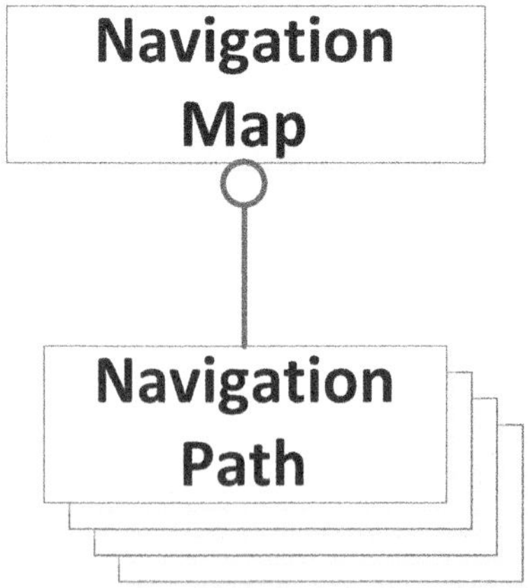

Work Flow:

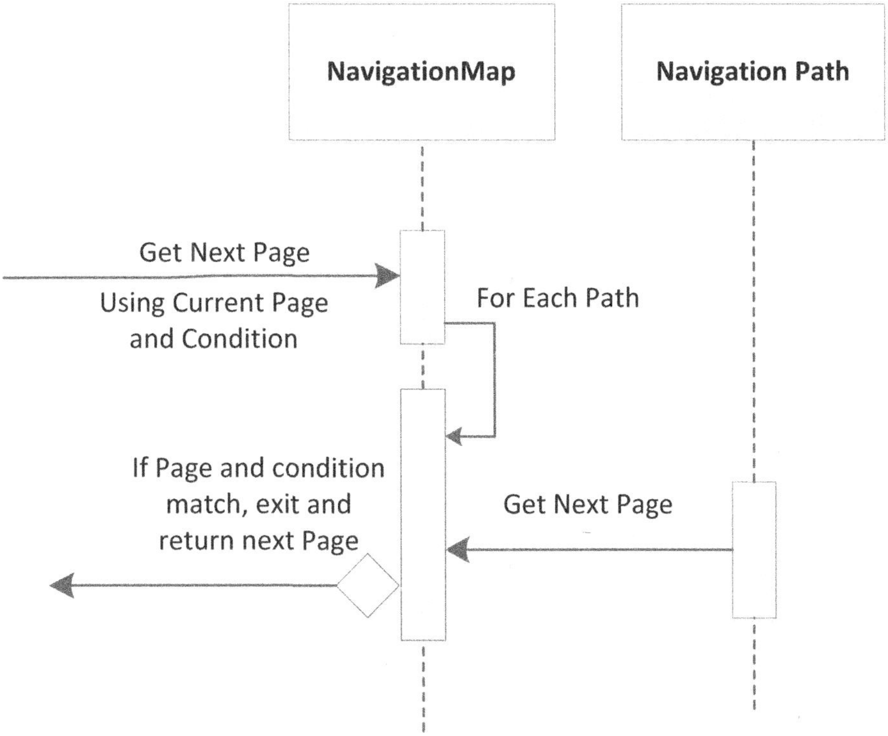
NavigationMap
Navigation Path
Get Next Page
Using Current Page
and Condition
For Each Path
If Page and condition
match, exit and
return next Page
Get Next Page

Code Sample:

```
public class NavigationMap
{
 private final static String NO_PAGE = "NO_PAGE";
 private NavigationPath navPath = null;
 private Map<String,Map<String,NavigationPath>> navigationMap;

 public NavigationMap()
 {
  navigationMap = new HashMap<String, Map<String,NavigationPath>>();
 }

 public NavigationMap(List<NavigationPath> aNavigationPath)
 {
  this();
  for(NavigationPath mNavigationPath:aNavigationPath)
  {
   addNavigationPath(mNavigationPath);
  }
 }

 public void setNavigationPath(String aCurrentPage,String aCondition,String
aNextPage)
 {
  addNavigationPath(new NavigationPath(aCurrentPage,aCondition,aNextPage));
 }

 public void addNavigationPath(NavigationPath aNavigationPath)
 {
  if(aNavigationPath != null)
  {
   String mCurrentPage = aNavigationPath.getCurrentPage();
   String mCondition = aNavigationPath.getCondition();
   Map<String,NavigationPath> mMap = navigationMap.get(mCurrentPage);
   if(mMap == null)
   {
    mMap = new HashMap<String,NavigationPath>();
    navigationMap.put(mCurrentPage, mMap);
   }
   mMap.put(mCondition, aNavigationPath);
  }
```

```
  }

  private NavigationPath getNavigationPath(String aCurrentPage,String aCondition)
  {
   NavigationPath mRtnValue = null;
   Map<String,NavigationPath> mMap = navigationMap.get(aCurrentPage);
   if(mMap != null)
   {
    mRtnValue = mMap.get(aCondition);
   }
   navPath = mRtnValue;
   return mRtnValue;
  }

  public String getNextPage(String aCurrentPage,String aCondition)
  {
   String mRtnValue = NO_PAGE;
   NavigationPath mNavPath = getNavigationPath(aCurrentPage,aCondition);
   if(mNavPath != null)
   {
    mRtnValue = mNavPath.getNextPage();
   }
   return mRtnValue;
  }

  public String getView()
  {
   String mRtnValue = "";
   if(navPath != null)
   {
    mRtnValue = navPath.getView();
   }
   return mRtnValue;
  }

  public static boolean isNoPage(String aPage)
  {
   return NO_PAGE.equals(aPage);
  }
}
```

Dependency Injection:

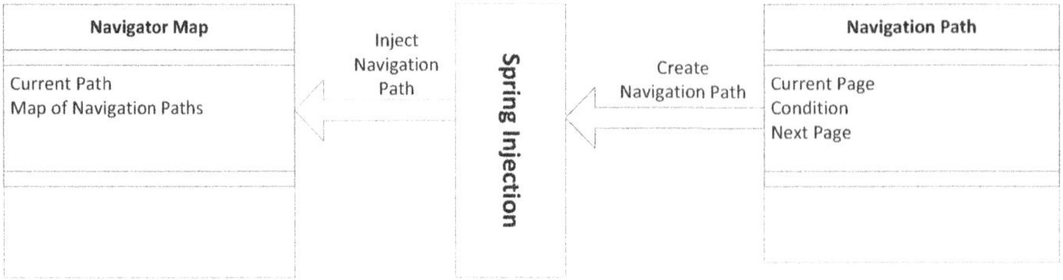

Example of Spring Configuration

```
<?xml version="1.0" encoding="UTF-8"?>
<!DOCTYPE beans PUBLIC "-//SPRING//DTD BEAN//EN"
"http://www.springframework.org/dtd/spring-beans.dtd">
<beans>

  <bean id="page2NavPath" class="com.dth.fmw.ctl.navigator.NavigationPath">
    <constructor-arg value="Page2"/>      <!-- Current Page -->
    <constructor-arg value="goPage3"/>   <!-- Condition   -->
    <constructor-arg value="Page3"/>      <!-- Next Page   -->
    <constructor-arg value="Page3.jspx"/> <!-- Next View    -->
  </bean>
</beans>
```

6.9 Navigation Path

Overview:

The Navigation Path is a set of information used to determine what the next page display is.

Objective:

The Objective of the Navigation Path is to provide the information necessary to determine what the next page is.

Responsibility:

The Navigation Path is responsible for supplying the contents to the Navigator used in determining what the next Path (Page/View) will be based on the current page and a condition supplied to the navigator.

Pattern Type:

The Navigation Path is a Structural Pattern used to hold information elements in making logical decisions on what should be the next page.

Structure:

Work Flow:

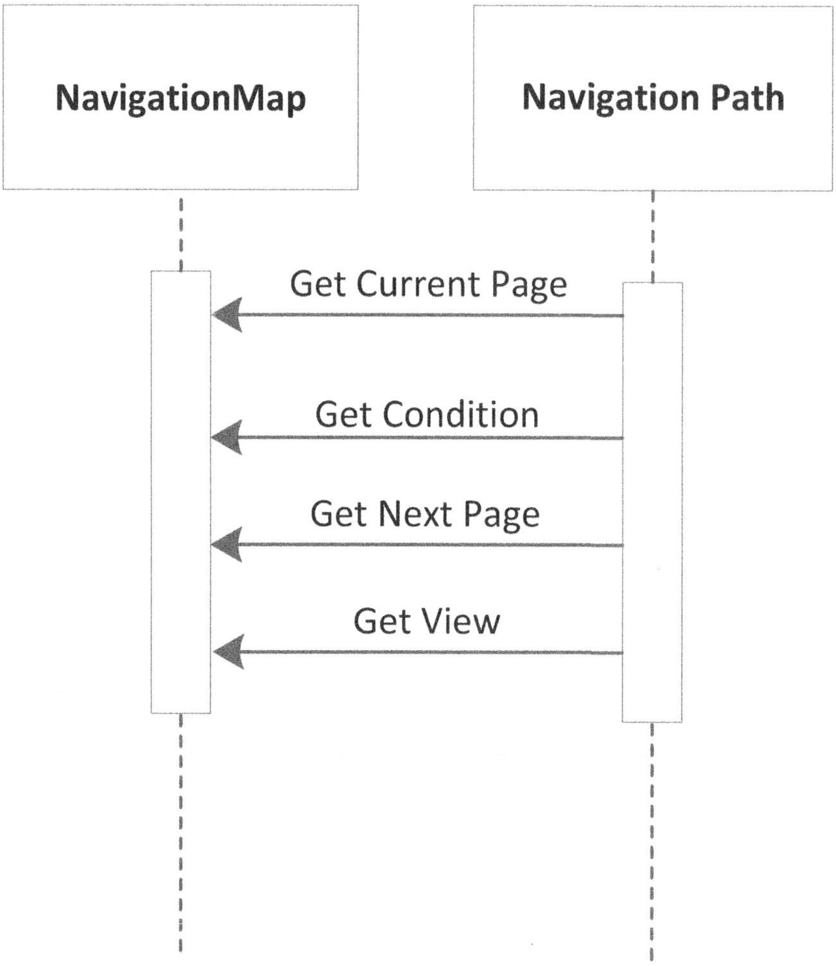
NavigationMap
Navigation Path
Get Current Page
Get Condition
Get Next Page
Get View

Code Sample:

```
public interface NavigationPathDef
{
 public String getCurrentPage();
 public String getCondition();
 public String getNextPage();
 public String getView();
 public String toString();
}


public class NavigationPath implements NavigationPathDef
{
 private String currentPage;
 private String condition;
 private String nextPage;
 private String view;

 public NavigationPath(String aCurrentPage,String aCondition,String aNextPage)
 {
  currentPage = aCurrentPage;
  condition = aCondition;
  nextPage = aNextPage;
  view = "";
 }

 public NavigationPath(String aCurrentPage,String aCondition,String aNextPage,String
aView)
 {
  this(aCurrentPage,aCondition,aNextPage);
  view = aView;
 }

 public String getCurrentPage()
 {
  return currentPage;
 }

 public String getCondition()
 {
  return condition;
```

```
  }

  public String getNextPage()
  {
   return nextPage;
  }

  public String getView()
  {
   return view;
  }

  public String toString()
  {
   return "Current Page["+currentPage+"] Condition ["+condition+"] Next Page
["+nextPage+"]";
  }
}
```

Dependency Injection:

Example of Spring Configuration

```
<?xml version="1.0" encoding="UTF-8"?>
<!DOCTYPE beans PUBLIC "-//SPRING//DTD BEAN//EN"
"http://www.springframework.org/dtd/spring-beans.dtd">
<beans>

  <bean id="page2NavPath" class="com.dth.fmw.ctl.navigator.NavigationPath">
    <constructor-arg value="Page2"/>      <!-- Current Page -->
    <constructor-arg value="goPage3"/>    <!-- Condition    -->
    <constructor-arg value="Page3"/>      <!-- Next Page    -->
    <constructor-arg value="Page3.jspx"/> <!-- Next View    -->
  </bean>
 </beans>
```

6.10 Mediator Layer

Overview:

The Mediator layer is provided to handle the transition from the Controller Layer of the architecture to the Model using the Delegate Layer and then receive return data from the Model and prepare it for use by the Controller Layer. The Mediator converts the data format from that of the View into a format that the backend logic uses to complete its tasks.

Objective:

The Mediator Pattern acts as a buffer between the View and the Model. The Mediator decouples the controller layer from the Model by keeping the backend Model from referring to the Presentation Transfer Objects and keeping the View/Dispatcher from referring to the Data Transfer Objects in the Model. One of the Objectives of the Mediator is to provide logic to convert display data into data that can be processed by the Model (business logic). A second object is the reverse the process by converting business logic data into display data that can be eventually displayed by the View.

Responsibility:

The Mediator is responsible for translation of the Presentation Data (PTO) into the Model Data (DTO), and calling the Model using the Delegate Layer. Once the Model is complete, and the Delegate Layer returns control to the Mediator. The Mediator is then responsible to translate the Model Data (DTO) back into a format that the View/Dispatcher can understand (PTO).

Pattern Type:

The Mediator is a behavioral Pattern used to decouple objects from referring to each other allow them to work independent of each other.

Structure:

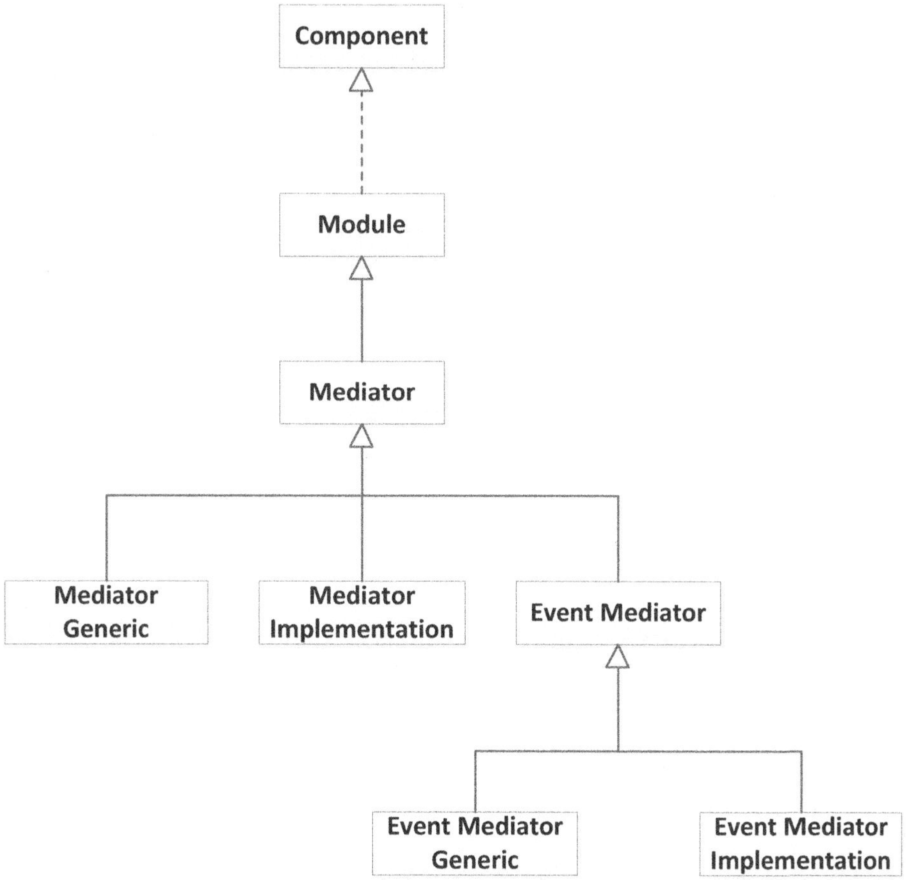

Work Flow:

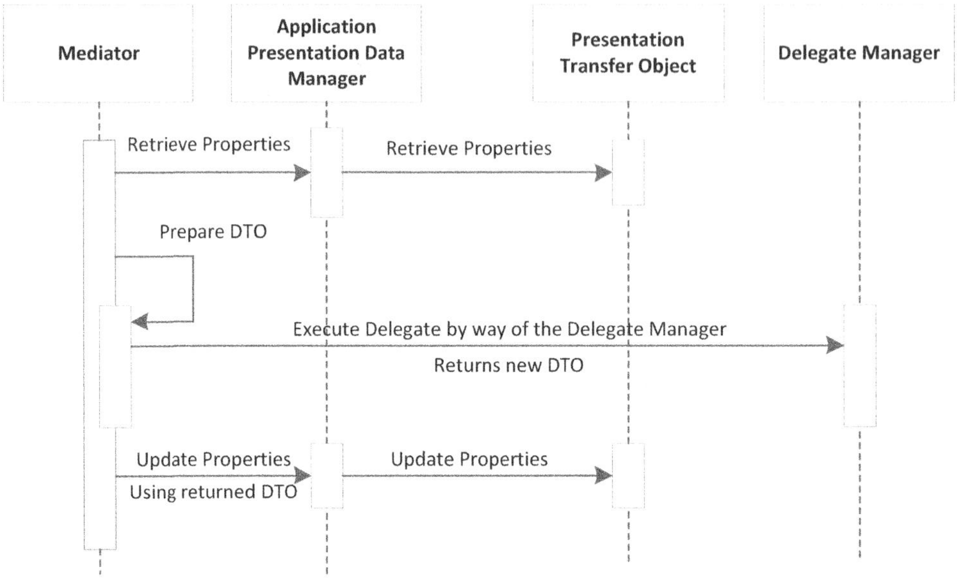
Mediator
Application Presentation Data Manager
Presentation Transfer Object
Delegate Manager
Retrieve Properties
Retrieve Properties
Prepare DTO
Execute Delegate by way of the Delegate Manager
Returns new DTO
Update Properties
Using returned DTO
Update Properties

Code Sample:

```
public enum MediatorType
{
 ACTION("ACTION"),
 EVENT("EVENT") ;
 private String type;

 private MediatorType(String aType)
 {
  type = aType;
 }

 public String getType()
 {
  return type;
 }

 public static MediatorType getType(String aName)
 {
  MediatorType mRtnValue = null;
  for(MediatorType mediatorType:MediatorType.values())
  {
   if(mediatorType.getType().equalsIgnoreCase(aName))
   {
    mRtnValue = mediatorType;
    break;
   }
  }
  return mRtnValue;
 }
}

public abstract class Mediator extends Controller implements Component
{
 private String name;
 private MediatorType mediatorType;
 private AppPresentationDataMgr appPresDataMgr;
 private String delegateName;
 private String dtoClassPath;

 public void setName(String aName)
```

```
{
  name = aName;
}

public String getName()
{
  return name;
}

public boolean isName(String aName)
{
  return (name == null || name.equals(aName));
}

public void setType(String aType)
{
  mediatorType = MediatorType.getType(aType);
}

public void setMediatorType(MediatorType aType)
{
  mediatorType = aType;
}

public String getType()
{
  return mediatorType.getType();
}

public MediatorType getMediatorType()
{
  return mediatorType;
}

@Override
protected Class<?> getTheClass()
{
  return Mediator.class;
}

public AppPresentationDataMgr getAppPresDataMgr()
{
```

```
  return appPresDataMgr;
 }

 public void setAppPresDataMgr(AppPresentationDataMgr appPresDataMgr)
 {
  this.appPresDataMgr = appPresDataMgr;
 }

 public String getDelegateName()
 {
  return delegateName; }

 public void setDelegateName(String delegateName)
 {
  this.delegateName = delegateName; }

 public String getDtoClassPath()
 {
  return dtoClassPath; }

  public void setDtoClassPath(String dtoClassPath)
 {
  this.dtoClassPath = dtoClassPath; }
}
```

Dependency Injection:

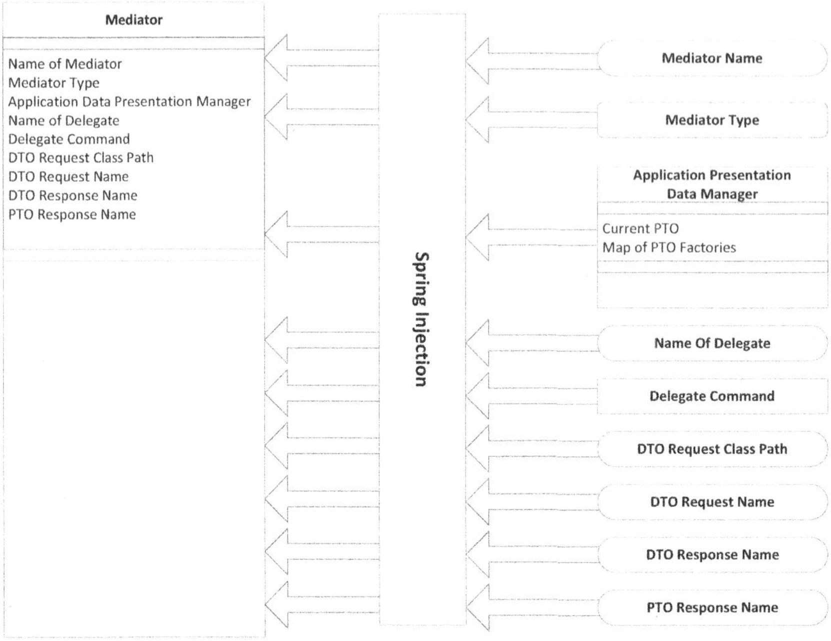

Example of Spring Configuration

```
<?xml version="1.0" encoding="UTF-8"?>
<!DOCTYPE beans PUBLIC "-//SPRING//DTD BEAN//EN"
"http://www.springframework.org/dtd/spring-beans.dtd">
<beans>
  <bean id="exampleActionMediator"
class="com.dth.fmw.ctl.mediator.MediatorGeneric">
  <property name="name" value="ExampleActionMediator"/>
  <property name="type" ref="actionMediatorType"/>
  <property name="appPresDataMgr" ref="exampleAppPresDataMgr"/>
  <property name="delegateName" value="exampleDelegateName"/>
  <property name="dtoRequestClassPath" value="com.dth.example.dto.exampleDto"/>
  <property name="delegateCmd" ref="exampleDelegateCmd"/>
  <property name="dtoRequestName" value="exampleDtoReqName"/>
  <property name="dtoResponseName" value="exampleDtoRespName"/>
  <property name="ptoResponseName" value="examplePtoRespName"/>
 </bean>
</beans>
```

6.11 Delegate Layer

Overview:

The Delegate Layer is divided into two parts, the Delegate Manager and the Delegates. The Delegate Manager provides a lookup for the Delegates by name. When the Delegate Manager is called, it will retrieve the delegate and pass control to it by passing it a Command Message.

There two types of Delegates, Remote and Local. Local Delegates use java methods calls access the Model Tier using the proxies, while Remote Delegates use communication protocol such as Web Services to access the Model Tier.

Objective:

The objective of the delegate layer is to separate the transport technology from the application implementation. This allows the application to be agnostic to the transport communication technology. This technology may be a local java call; it may be a SOAP call or any other technology that passes messages between application tiers.

- Improve Maintainability by making it easy to switch the underlying technology
- Reduces Coupling by encapsulating the communications between the model tier and the controller tier.
- Translates model tier errors and exceptions into user friendly error messages by shielding technical details of the underlying model implementation from the user community.
- Provides for the ability for auto recovery which improves availability of services.

Responsibility:

It is the responsibility of the delegate layer to facilitate transportation of information between the controller tier and the model tier. This allows the two tiers to treat the communication between the two layers as a black box. This allows the tiers to be on the same box or multiple boxes. It also allows for the possibility of multiple server containing duplicate controller tiers and duplicate model tiers which would provide for distribution of work load over multiple servers.

Pattern Type:

The Delegator layer uses a combination of the Adapter and Proxy pattern. The Delegate provides gateway to the backend Model tier by providing an adapter to the communication protocol, which in turn will call a model service interface to eventually call the proxy.

Structure:

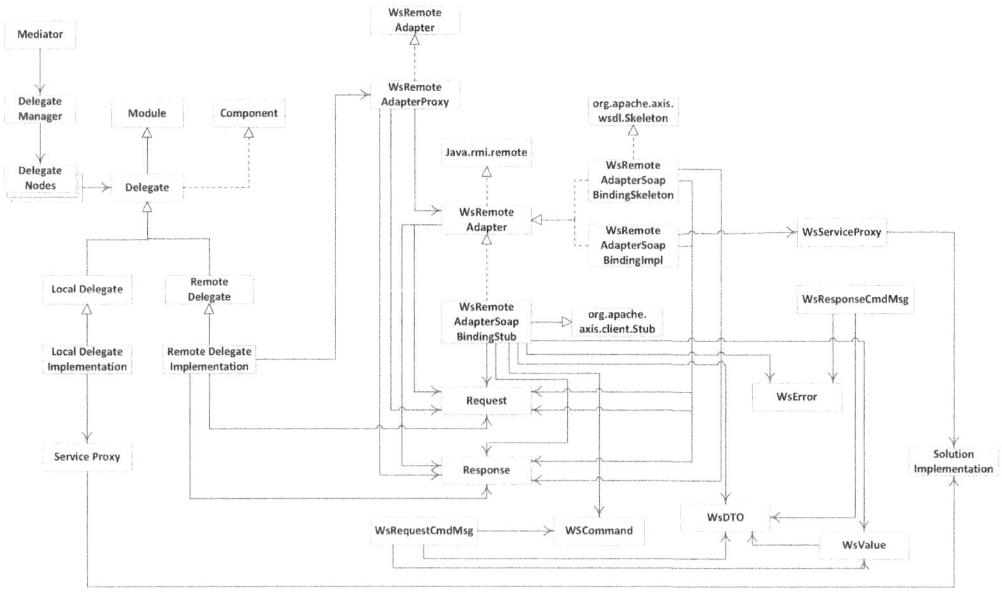

Work Flow:

Local Delegate

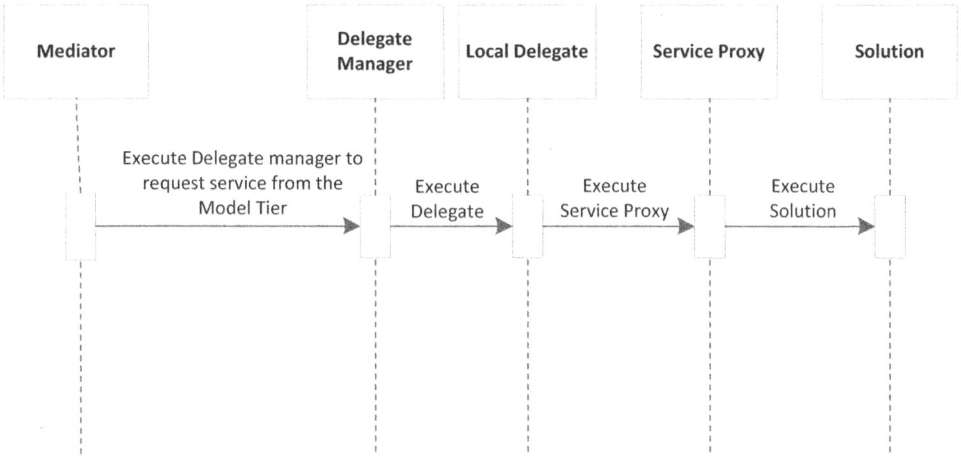

Remote Delegate

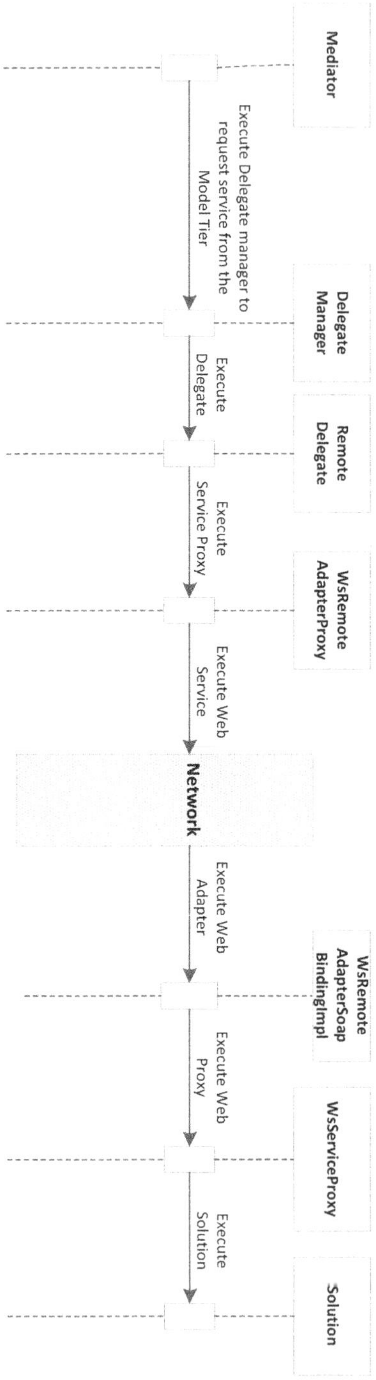

Code Sample:

```
public class DelegateManager
{
 private static Map<String,Delegate> delegates = new HashMap<String,Delegate>();

 @SuppressWarnings("unchecked")
 public DelegateManager(Map aDelegates)
 {
  delegates.putAll(aDelegates);
 }

 @SuppressWarnings("unchecked")
 public void setDelegates(Map aDelegates)
 {
  delegates.putAll(aDelegates);
 }

 public static void execute(String aName,Command aCommand,CmdMsg aCmdMsg)
 {
  Delegate mDelegate = delegates.get(aName);
  if(mDelegate != null)
  {
   mDelegate.execute(aCommand,aCmdMsg);
  }
 }
}

public abstract class Delegate  extends Module implements Component
{

 private static ExceptionHandlerManager exceptionHandlerManager;

 public void execute(Command aCommand,CmdMsg aCmdMsg)
 {
  try
  {
   preProcess(aCommand,aCmdMsg);
   process(aCommand,aCmdMsg);
   postProcess(aCommand,aCmdMsg);
  }
  catch(Throwable aThrowable)
```

```
  {
    try
    {
     if(getExceptionHandlerManager() == null)
     {
       throw new DelegateException(aThrowable);
     }
     else
     {
       getExceptionHandlerManager().handle(aCmdMsg,aThrowable);
     }

    }
    catch(Throwable aException)
    {
     throw new DelegateException(aThrowable);
    }
  }
}

protected void preProcess(Command aCommand,CmdMsg aCmdMsg)
{
  // Left Intentionally empty
}

protected abstract void process(Command aCommand,CmdMsg aCmdMsg);

protected void postProcess(Command aCommand,CmdMsg aCmdMsg)
{
  // Left Intentionally empty
}

protected void doWork(Command aCommand,CmdMsg aCmdMsg)
{
  // Left Intentionally empty
}

protected ExceptionHandlerManager getExceptionHandlerManager()
{
  return exceptionHandlerManager;
}
```

```
 @Override
 protected Class<?> getTheClass()
 {
  return Delegate.class;
 }

}
public class DelegateRemoteExample extends Delegate
{

 @Override
 protected void process(Command aCommand, CmdMsg aCmdMsg)
 {
  WsRemoteAdapterProxy mTest = new WsRemoteAdapterProxy();
  try
  {
   Request parameters = new Request();
   com.dth.wse.service.impl.Response mResponse = mTest.execute(parameters);
  }
  catch (RemoteException eException)
  {
   System.out.println(eException);
  }
 }

}
public class DelegateLocalExample extends Delegate
{

       @Override
       protected void process(Command aCommand, CmdMsg aCmdMsg)
       {
        ExampleProxy.execute("CmdExampleSolution", aCmdMsg);
       }


        @Override
        protected Class<?> getTheClass()
        {
         return DelegateLocalExample.class;
        }
}
```

WSDL Definition

```
<?xml version="1.0" encoding="UTF-8"?>
<wsdl:definitions targetNamespace="http://impl.service.wse.dth.com"
xmlns:apachesoap="http://xml.apache.org/xml-soap"
xmlns:impl="http://impl.service.wse.dth.com"
xmlns:intf="http://impl.service.wse.dth.com"
xmlns:wsdl="http://schemas.xmlsoap.org/wsdl/"
xmlns:wsdlsoap="http://schemas.xmlsoap.org/wsdl/soap/"
xmlns:xsd="http://www.w3.org/2001/XMLSchema">
<!--WSDL created by Apache Axis version: 1.4
Built on Apr 22, 2006 (06:55:48 PDT)-->
 <wsdl:types>
  <schema elementFormDefault="qualified"
targetNamespace="http://impl.service.wse.dth.com"
xmlns="http://www.w3.org/2001/XMLSchema">
   <element name="request">
  <complexType>
    <sequence>
     <element name="requestCmdMsg" type="impl:wsRequestCmdMsg" minOccurs="0"/>
    </sequence>
  </complexType>
   </element>
   <element name="response">
  <complexType>
    <sequence>
     <element name="responseCmdMsg" type="impl:wsResponseCmdMsg"
minOccurs="0"/>
    </sequence>
  </complexType>
   </element>

  <complexType name="wsRequestCmdMsg">
    <sequence>
     <element name="command" type="impl:wsCommands"/>
     <element name="session" type="impl:wsValues"/>
     <element name="request" type="impl:wsDTOs"/>
    </sequence>
  </complexType>
  <complexType name="wsCommands">
    <sequence>
```

```
      <element name="comand" type="impl:wsCommand" minOccurs="0"
maxOccurs="99"/>
    </sequence>
  </complexType>
  <complexType name="wsCommand">
    <sequence>
      <element name="service" type="xsd:string" minOccurs="1" maxOccurs="1"/>
      <element name="task" type="xsd:string" minOccurs="1"/>
    </sequence>
  </complexType>
   <complexType name="wsDTOs">
    <sequence>
      <element name="dto" type="impl:wsDTO" minOccurs="0" maxOccurs="99"/>
    </sequence>
  </complexType>
  <complexType name="wsDTO">
    <sequence>
      <element name="name" type="xsd:string" minOccurs="1"/>
      <element name="type" type="xsd:string" minOccurs="1"/>
      <element name="data" type="impl:wsValue" minOccurs="0" maxOccurs="99"/>
      <element name="dtoSet" type="impl:wsDTO" minOccurs="0" maxOccurs="99"/>
    </sequence>
  </complexType>
  <complexType name="wsResponseCmdMsg">
    <sequence>
      <element name="response" type="impl:wsDTOs"/>
      <element name="errors" type="impl:wsErrors"/>
    </sequence>
  </complexType>
  <complexType name="wsErrors">
    <sequence>
      <element name="error" type="impl:wsError" minOccurs="0" maxOccurs="99"/>
    </sequence>
  </complexType>
  <complexType name="wsError">
    <sequence>
      <element name="number" type="xsd:string" minOccurs="1"/>
      <element name="title" type="xsd:string" minOccurs="1"/>
      <element name="time" type="xsd:string" minOccurs="1"/>
      <element name="type" type="xsd:string" minOccurs="1"/>
      <element name="catagory" type="xsd:string" minOccurs="1"/>
      <element name="source" type="xsd:string" minOccurs="1"/>
```

```
    <element name="reference" type="xsd:string" minOccurs="1"/>
    <element name="displayMessage" type="xsd:string" minOccurs="1"/>
    <element name="logMessage" type="xsd:string" minOccurs="1"/>
    <element name="disregard" type="xsd:string" minOccurs="1"/>
    <element name="initialCause" type="impl:wsError" minOccurs="0"/>
  </sequence>
 </complexType>
 <complexType name="wsValues">
  <sequence>
    <element name="valueSet" type="impl:wsValue" minOccurs="0" maxOccurs="99"/>
  </sequence>
 </complexType>

 <complexType name="wsValue">
  <sequence>
    <element name="name" type="xsd:string" minOccurs="1"/>
    <element name="type" type="xsd:string" minOccurs="1"/>
    <element name="value" type="xsd:string" minOccurs="0"/>
  </sequence>
 </complexType>
 </schema>
 </wsdl:types>

<wsdl:message name="getMsgRequest">
    <wsdl:part element="impl:request" name="parameters"/>
</wsdl:message>
<wsdl:message name="getMsgResponse">
   <wsdl:part element="impl:response" name="parameters"/>
</wsdl:message>
<wsdl:portType name="WsRemoteAdapter">
 <wsdl:operation name="execute">
 <wsdl:input message="impl:getMsgRequest" name="getMsgRequest"/>

<wsdl:output message="impl:getMsgResponse" name="getMsgResponse"/>
</wsdl:operation>
  </wsdl:portType>
  <wsdl:binding name="WsRemoteAdapterSoapBinding"
type="impl:WsRemoteAdapter">
    <wsdlsoap:binding style="document"
transport="http://schemas.xmlsoap.org/soap/http"/>
    <wsdl:operation name="execute">
       <wsdlsoap:operation soapAction=""/>
```

```
    <wsdl:input name="getMsgRequest">
     <wsdlsoap:body use="literal"/>
</wsdl:input>
<wsdl:output name="getMsgResponse">
   <wsdlsoap:body use="literal"/>
</wsdl:output>
</wsdl:operation>
</wsdl:binding>
<wsdl:service name="WsRemoteAdapterService">
 <wsdl:port binding="impl:WsRemoteAdapterSoapBinding"
name="WsReportAdapterPort">
<wsdlsoap:address
location="http://localhost:8080/ThunderWs/services/WsReportAdapter"/>
</wsdl:port>
</wsdl:service>
</wsdl:definitions>
```

Web Service Proxy

```
public class WsServiceProxy extends ServiceProxy
{
 public static Response execute(Request aRequest) throws java.rmi.RemoteException
 {
  Response mRtnValue = new Response();
  CmdMsg mCmdMsg = new CommandMsg();
  WsRequestCmdMsg mReqCmdMsg = aRequest.getRequestCmdMsg();
  WsDTO mWsDTOs[] =mReqCmdMsg.getRequest();
  if(mWsDTOs != null && mWsDTOs.length>0)
  {
   for(WsDTO mWsDTO:mWsDTOs)
   {
    String mType = mWsDTO.getType();
    String mName = mWsDTO.getName();
    DTO mDTO = createDTO(mType);
    mCmdMsg.setRequest(mName, mDTO);
    WsValue mValues[] = mWsDTO.getData();
    if(mValues != null && mValues.length > 0)
    {
     for(WsValue mValue:mValues)
     {
      String mObjectValue = mValue.getValue();
      String mValueName = mValue.getName();
```

```
        setValue(mValueName,mDTO,mObjectValue);
       }
      }
     }
    }
    WsCommand[] mCommands = mReqCmdMsg.getCommand();
    if(mCommands != null && mCommands.length > 0)
    {
     for(WsCommand mCommand:mCommands)
     {
      String mTask = mCommand.getTask();
      execute(mTask,mCmdMsg);
     }
    }
    return mRtnValue;
   }

   public static void execute(String mCmdSolutionId,CmdMsg aCmdMsg)
   {
    runCommand(ComponentType.SOLUTION.getName(),mCmdSolutionId,aCmdMsg);
   }

   @Override
   protected Class<?> getTheClass()
   {
    return WsServiceProxy.class;
   }
  }

public interface WsRemoteAdapter extends java.rmi.Remote {
  public com.dth.wse.service.impl.Response execute(com.dth.wse.service.impl.Request
parameters) throws java.rmi.RemoteException;
}
```

Web Service Adapter Proxy

```
package com.dth.wse.service.impl;

public class WsRemoteAdapterProxy implements
com.dth.wse.service.impl.WsRemoteAdapter {
 private String _endpoint = null;
 private com.dth.wse.service.impl.WsRemoteAdapter wsRemoteAdapter = null;

 public WsRemoteAdapterProxy() {
  _initWsRemoteAdapterProxy();
 }

 public WsRemoteAdapterProxy(String endpoint) {
  _endpoint = endpoint;
  _initWsRemoteAdapterProxy();
 }

 private void _initWsRemoteAdapterProxy() {
  try {
   wsRemoteAdapter = (new
com.dth.wse.service.impl.WsRemoteAdapterServiceLocator()).getWsReportAdapterPort(
);
    if (wsRemoteAdapter != null) {
     if (_endpoint != null)

((javax.xml.rpc.Stub)wsRemoteAdapter)._setProperty("javax.xml.rpc.service.endpoint.ad
dress", _endpoint);
     else
      _endpoint =
(String)((javax.xml.rpc.Stub)wsRemoteAdapter)._getProperty("javax.xml.rpc.service.end
point.address");
    }

  }
  catch (javax.xml.rpc.ServiceException serviceException) {}
 }

 public String getEndpoint() {
  return _endpoint;
 }
```

```
 public void setEndpoint(String endpoint) {
   _endpoint = endpoint;
   if (wsRemoteAdapter != null)

((javax.xml.rpc.Stub)wsRemoteAdapter)._setProperty("javax.xml.rpc.service.endpoint.ad
dress", _endpoint);

 }

 public com.dth.wse.service.impl.WsRemoteAdapter getWsRemoteAdapter() {
   if (wsRemoteAdapter == null)
     _initWsRemoteAdapterProxy();
   return wsRemoteAdapter;
 }

 public com.dth.wse.service.impl.Response execute(com.dth.wse.service.impl.Request
parameters) throws java.rmi.RemoteException{
   if (wsRemoteAdapter == null)
     _initWsRemoteAdapterProxy();
   return wsRemoteAdapter.execute(parameters);
 }


}

/**
 * WsRemoteAdapterService.java
 *
 * This file was auto-generated from WSDL
 * by the Apache Axis 1.4 Apr 22, 2006 (06:55:48 PDT) WSDL2Java emitter.
 */

package com.dth.wse.service.impl;

public interface WsRemoteAdapterService extends javax.xml.rpc.Service {
   public java.lang.String getWsReportAdapterPortAddress();

   public com.dth.wse.service.impl.WsRemoteAdapter getWsReportAdapterPort()
throws javax.xml.rpc.ServiceException;
```

```
   public com.dth.wse.service.impl.WsRemoteAdapter
getWsReportAdapterPort(java.net.URL portAddress) throws
javax.xml.rpc.ServiceException;
}

/**
 * WsRemoteAdapterServiceLocator.java
 *
 * This file was auto-generated from WSDL
 * by the Apache Axis 1.4 Apr 22, 2006 (06:55:48 PDT) WSDL2Java emitter.
 */

package com.dth.wse.service.impl;

public class WsRemoteAdapterServiceLocator extends org.apache.axis.client.Service
implements com.dth.wse.service.impl.WsRemoteAdapterService {

   public WsRemoteAdapterServiceLocator() {
   }


   public WsRemoteAdapterServiceLocator(org.apache.axis.EngineConfiguration config)
{
      super(config);
   }

   public WsRemoteAdapterServiceLocator(java.lang.String wsdlLoc,
javax.xml.namespace.QName sName) throws javax.xml.rpc.ServiceException {
      super(wsdlLoc, sName);
   }

   // Use to get a proxy class for WsReportAdapterPort
   private java.lang.String WsReportAdapterPort_address =
"http://localhost:8080/ThunderWs/services/WsReportAdapter";

   public java.lang.String getWsReportAdapterPortAddress() {
      return WsReportAdapterPort_address;
   }

   // The WSDD service name defaults to the port name.
   private java.lang.String WsReportAdapterPortWSDDServiceName =
"WsReportAdapterPort";
```

```
  public java.lang.String getWsReportAdapterPortWSDDServiceName() {
    return WsReportAdapterPortWSDDServiceName;
  }

  public void setWsReportAdapterPortWSDDServiceName(java.lang.String name) {
    WsReportAdapterPortWSDDServiceName = name;
  }

  public com.dth.wse.service.impl.WsRemoteAdapter getWsReportAdapterPort()
throws javax.xml.rpc.ServiceException {
     java.net.URL endpoint;
    try {
      endpoint = new java.net.URL(WsReportAdapterPort_address);
    }
    catch (java.net.MalformedURLException e) {
      throw new javax.xml.rpc.ServiceException(e);
    }
    return getWsReportAdapterPort(endpoint);
  }

  public com.dth.wse.service.impl.WsRemoteAdapter
getWsReportAdapterPort(java.net.URL portAddress) throws
javax.xml.rpc.ServiceException {
    try {
      com.dth.wse.service.impl.WsRemoteAdapterSoapBindingStub _stub = new
com.dth.wse.service.impl.WsRemoteAdapterSoapBindingStub(portAddress, this);
      _stub.setPortName(getWsReportAdapterPortWSDDServiceName());
      return _stub;
    }
    catch (org.apache.axis.AxisFault e) {
      return null;
    }
  }

  public void setWsReportAdapterPortEndpointAddress(java.lang.String address) {
    WsReportAdapterPort_address = address;
  }

  /**
   * For the given interface, get the stub implementation.
   * If this service has no port for the given interface,
```

```
  * then ServiceException is thrown.
  */
  public java.rmi.Remote getPort(Class serviceEndpointInterface) throws
javax.xml.rpc.ServiceException {
    try {
      if
(com.dth.wse.service.impl.WsRemoteAdapter.class.isAssignableFrom(serviceEndpointIn
terface)) {
        com.dth.wse.service.impl.WsRemoteAdapterSoapBindingStub _stub = new
com.dth.wse.service.impl.WsRemoteAdapterSoapBindingStub(new
java.net.URL(WsReportAdapterPort_address), this);
        _stub.setPortName(getWsReportAdapterPortWSDDServiceName());
        return _stub;
      }
    }
    catch (java.lang.Throwable t) {
      throw new javax.xml.rpc.ServiceException(t);
    }
    throw new javax.xml.rpc.ServiceException("There is no stub implementation for the
interface:  " + (serviceEndpointInterface == null ? "null" :
serviceEndpointInterface.getName()));
  }

  /**
  * For the given interface, get the stub implementation.
  * If this service has no port for the given interface,
  * then ServiceException is thrown.
  */
  public java.rmi.Remote getPort(javax.xml.namespace.QName portName, Class
serviceEndpointInterface) throws javax.xml.rpc.ServiceException {
    if (portName == null) {
      return getPort(serviceEndpointInterface);
    }
    java.lang.String inputPortName = portName.getLocalPart();
    if ("WsReportAdapterPort".equals(inputPortName)) {
      return getWsReportAdapterPort();
    }
    else {
      java.rmi.Remote _stub = getPort(serviceEndpointInterface);
      ((org.apache.axis.client.Stub) _stub).setPortName(portName);
      return _stub;
    }
```

```
  }

  public javax.xml.namespace.QName getServiceName() {
     return new javax.xml.namespace.QName("http://impl.service.wse.dth.com",
"WsRemoteAdapterService");
  }

  private java.util.HashSet ports = null;

  public java.util.Iterator getPorts() {
     if (ports == null) {
        ports = new java.util.HashSet();
        ports.add(new javax.xml.namespace.QName("http://impl.service.wse.dth.com",
"WsReportAdapterPort"));
     }
     return ports.iterator();
  }

  /**
  * Set the endpoint address for the specified port name.
  */
  public void setEndpointAddress(java.lang.String portName, java.lang.String address)
throws javax.xml.rpc.ServiceException {

if ("WsReportAdapterPort".equals(portName)) {
        setWsReportAdapterPortEndpointAddress(address);
     }
     else
{ // Unknown Port Name
        throw new javax.xml.rpc.ServiceException(" Cannot set Endpoint Address for
Unknown Port" + portName);
     }
  }

  /**
  * Set the endpoint address for the specified port name.
  */
  public void setEndpointAddress(javax.xml.namespace.QName portName,
java.lang.String address) throws javax.xml.rpc.ServiceException {
     setEndpointAddress(portName.getLocalPart(), address);
  }
```

```
}

/**
 * WsRemoteAdapterSoapBindingImpl.java
 *
 * This file was auto-generated from WSDL
 * by the Apache Axis 1.4 Apr 22, 2006 (06:55:48 PDT) WSDL2Java emitter.
 */

package com.dth.wse.service.impl;

import com.dth.svc.impl.user.WsServiceProxy;

public class WsRemoteAdapterSoapBindingImpl implements
com.dth.wse.service.impl.WsRemoteAdapter{
  public com.dth.wse.service.impl.Response execute(com.dth.wse.service.impl.Request
parameters) throws java.rmi.RemoteException {
      return WsServiceProxy.execute(parameters);
  }

}

public class WsRemoteAdapterSoapBindingSkeleton implements
com.dth.wse.service.impl.WsRemoteAdapter, org.apache.axis.wsdl.Skeleton {
  private com.dth.wse.service.impl.WsRemoteAdapter impl;
  private static java.util.Map _myOperations = new java.util.Hashtable();
  private static java.util.Collection _myOperationsList = new java.util.ArrayList();

  /**
  * Returns List of OperationDesc objects with this name
  */
  public static java.util.List getOperationDescByName(java.lang.String methodName) {
     return (java.util.List)_myOperations.get(methodName);
  }

  /**
  * Returns Collection of OperationDescs
  */
  public static java.util.Collection getOperationDescs() {
     return _myOperationsList;
  }
```

```
  static {
    org.apache.axis.description.OperationDesc _oper;
    org.apache.axis.description.FaultDesc _fault;
    org.apache.axis.description.ParameterDesc [] _params;
    _params = new org.apache.axis.description.ParameterDesc [] {
      new org.apache.axis.description.ParameterDesc(new
javax.xml.namespace.QName("http://impl.service.wse.dth.com", "request"),
org.apache.axis.description.ParameterDesc.IN, new
javax.xml.namespace.QName("http://impl.service.wse.dth.com", ">request"),
com.dth.wse.service.impl.Request.class, false, false),
    };
    _oper = new org.apache.axis.description.OperationDesc("execute", _params, new
javax.xml.namespace.QName("http://impl.service.wse.dth.com", "response"));
    _oper.setReturnType(new
javax.xml.namespace.QName("http://impl.service.wse.dth.com", ">response"));
    _oper.setElementQName(new javax.xml.namespace.QName("", "execute"));
    _oper.setSoapAction("");
    _myOperationsList.add(_oper);
    if (_myOperations.get("execute") == null) {
      _myOperations.put("execute", new java.util.ArrayList());
    }
    ((java.util.List)_myOperations.get("execute")).add(_oper);
  }

  public WsRemoteAdapterSoapBindingSkeleton() {
    this.impl = new com.dth.wse.service.impl.WsRemoteAdapterSoapBindingImpl();
  }

  public
WsRemoteAdapterSoapBindingSkeleton(com.dth.wse.service.impl.WsRemoteAdapter
impl) {
    this.impl = impl;
  }
  public com.dth.wse.service.impl.Response execute(com.dth.wse.service.impl.Request
parameters) throws java.rmi.RemoteException
  {
    com.dth.wse.service.impl.Response ret = impl.execute(parameters);
    return ret;
  }

}
```

```
public class WsRemoteAdapterSoapBindingStub extends org.apache.axis.client.Stub
implements com.dth.wse.service.impl.WsRemoteAdapter {
   private java.util.Vector cachedSerClasses = new java.util.Vector();
   private java.util.Vector cachedSerQNames = new java.util.Vector();
   private java.util.Vector cachedSerFactories = new java.util.Vector();
   private java.util.Vector cachedDeserFactories = new java.util.Vector();

   static org.apache.axis.description.OperationDesc [] _operations;

   static {
      _operations = new org.apache.axis.description.OperationDesc[1];
      _initOperationDesc1();
   }

   private static void _initOperationDesc1(){
      org.apache.axis.description.OperationDesc oper;
      org.apache.axis.description.ParameterDesc param;
      oper = new org.apache.axis.description.OperationDesc();
      oper.setName("execute");
      param = new org.apache.axis.description.ParameterDesc(new
javax.xml.namespace.QName("http://impl.service.wse.dth.com", "request"),
org.apache.axis.description.ParameterDesc.IN, new
javax.xml.namespace.QName("http://impl.service.wse.dth.com", ">request"),
com.dth.wse.service.impl.Request.class, false, false);
      oper.addParameter(param);
      oper.setReturnType(new
javax.xml.namespace.QName("http://impl.service.wse.dth.com", ">response"));
      oper.setReturnClass(com.dth.wse.service.impl.Response.class);
      oper.setReturnQName(new
javax.xml.namespace.QName("http://impl.service.wse.dth.com", "response"));
      oper.setStyle(org.apache.axis.constants.Style.DOCUMENT);
      oper.setUse(org.apache.axis.constants.Use.LITERAL);
      _operations[0] = oper;

   }

   public WsRemoteAdapterSoapBindingStub() throws org.apache.axis.AxisFault {
       this(null);
   }
```

```
  public WsRemoteAdapterSoapBindingStub(java.net.URL endpointURL,
javax.xml.rpc.Service service) throws org.apache.axis.AxisFault {
      this(service);
      super.cachedEndpoint = endpointURL;
  }

  public WsRemoteAdapterSoapBindingStub(javax.xml.rpc.Service service) throws
org.apache.axis.AxisFault {
     if (service == null) {
        super.service = new org.apache.axis.client.Service();
     } else {
        super.service = service;
     }
     ((org.apache.axis.client.Service)super.service).setTypeMappingVersion("1.2");
        java.lang.Class cls;
        javax.xml.namespace.QName qName;
        javax.xml.namespace.QName qName2;
        java.lang.Class beansf = org.apache.axis.encoding.ser.BeanSerializerFactory.class;
        java.lang.Class beandf =
org.apache.axis.encoding.ser.BeanDeserializerFactory.class;
        java.lang.Class enumsf =
org.apache.axis.encoding.ser.EnumSerializerFactory.class;
        java.lang.Class enumdf =
org.apache.axis.encoding.ser.EnumDeserializerFactory.class;
        java.lang.Class arraysf = org.apache.axis.encoding.ser.ArraySerializerFactory.class;
        java.lang.Class arraydf =
org.apache.axis.encoding.ser.ArrayDeserializerFactory.class;
        java.lang.Class simplesf =
org.apache.axis.encoding.ser.SimpleSerializerFactory.class;
        java.lang.Class simpledf =
org.apache.axis.encoding.ser.SimpleDeserializerFactory.class;
        java.lang.Class simplelistsf =
org.apache.axis.encoding.ser.SimpleListSerializerFactory.class;
        java.lang.Class simplelistdf =
org.apache.axis.encoding.ser.SimpleListDeserializerFactory.class;
        qName = new javax.xml.namespace.QName("http://impl.service.wse.dth.com",
">request");
        cachedSerQNames.add(qName);
        cls = com.dth.wse.service.impl.Request.class;
        cachedSerClasses.add(cls);
        cachedSerFactories.add(beansf);
        cachedDeserFactories.add(beandf);
```

```
        qName = new javax.xml.namespace.QName("http://impl.service.wse.dth.com",
">response");
        cachedSerQNames.add(qName);
        cls = com.dth.wse.service.impl.Response.class;
        cachedSerClasses.add(cls);
        cachedSerFactories.add(beansf);
        cachedDeserFactories.add(beandf);

        qName = new javax.xml.namespace.QName("http://impl.service.wse.dth.com",
"wsCommand");
        cachedSerQNames.add(qName);
        cls = com.dth.wse.service.impl.WsCommand.class;
        cachedSerClasses.add(cls);
        cachedSerFactories.add(beansf);
        cachedDeserFactories.add(beandf);

        qName = new javax.xml.namespace.QName("http://impl.service.wse.dth.com",
"wsCommands");
        cachedSerQNames.add(qName);
        cls = com.dth.wse.service.impl.WsCommand[].class;
        cachedSerClasses.add(cls);
        qName = new javax.xml.namespace.QName("http://impl.service.wse.dth.com",
"wsCommand");
        qName2 = new javax.xml.namespace.QName("http://impl.service.wse.dth.com",
"comand");
        cachedSerFactories.add(new
org.apache.axis.encoding.ser.ArraySerializerFactory(qName, qName2));
        cachedDeserFactories.add(new
org.apache.axis.encoding.ser.ArrayDeserializerFactory());

        qName = new javax.xml.namespace.QName("http://impl.service.wse.dth.com",
"wsDTO");
        cachedSerQNames.add(qName);
        cls = com.dth.wse.service.impl.WsDTO.class;
        cachedSerClasses.add(cls);
        cachedSerFactories.add(beansf);
        cachedDeserFactories.add(beandf);

        qName = new javax.xml.namespace.QName("http://impl.service.wse.dth.com",
"wsDTOs");
        cachedSerQNames.add(qName);
```

```
        cls = com.dth.wse.service.impl.WsDTO[].class;
        cachedSerClasses.add(cls);
        qName = new javax.xml.namespace.QName("http://impl.service.wse.dth.com",
"wsDTO");
        qName2 = new javax.xml.namespace.QName("http://impl.service.wse.dth.com",
"dto");
        cachedSerFactories.add(new
org.apache.axis.encoding.ser.ArraySerializerFactory(qName, qName2));
        cachedDeserFactories.add(new
org.apache.axis.encoding.ser.ArrayDeserializerFactory());

        qName = new javax.xml.namespace.QName("http://impl.service.wse.dth.com",
"wsError");
        cachedSerQNames.add(qName);
        cls = com.dth.wse.service.impl.WsError.class;
        cachedSerClasses.add(cls);
        cachedSerFactories.add(beansf);
        cachedDeserFactories.add(beandf);

        qName = new javax.xml.namespace.QName("http://impl.service.wse.dth.com",
"wsErrors");
        cachedSerQNames.add(qName);
        cls = com.dth.wse.service.impl.WsError[].class;
        cachedSerClasses.add(cls);
        qName = new javax.xml.namespace.QName("http://impl.service.wse.dth.com",
"wsError");
        qName2 = new javax.xml.namespace.QName("http://impl.service.wse.dth.com",
"error");
        cachedSerFactories.add(new
org.apache.axis.encoding.ser.ArraySerializerFactory(qName, qName2));
        cachedDeserFactories.add(new
org.apache.axis.encoding.ser.ArrayDeserializerFactory());

        qName = new javax.xml.namespace.QName("http://impl.service.wse.dth.com",
"wsRequestCmdMsg");
        cachedSerQNames.add(qName);
        cls = com.dth.wse.service.impl.WsRequestCmdMsg.class;
        cachedSerClasses.add(cls);
        cachedSerFactories.add(beansf);
        cachedDeserFactories.add(beandf);
```

```
        qName = new javax.xml.namespace.QName("http://impl.service.wse.dth.com",
"wsResponseCmdMsg");
        cachedSerQNames.add(qName);
        cls = com.dth.wse.service.impl.WsResponseCmdMsg.class;
        cachedSerClasses.add(cls);
        cachedSerFactories.add(beansf);
        cachedDeserFactories.add(beandf);

        qName = new javax.xml.namespace.QName("http://impl.service.wse.dth.com",
"wsValue");
        cachedSerQNames.add(qName);
        cls = com.dth.wse.service.impl.WsValue.class;
        cachedSerClasses.add(cls);
        cachedSerFactories.add(beansf);
        cachedDeserFactories.add(beandf);

        qName = new javax.xml.namespace.QName("http://impl.service.wse.dth.com",
"wsValues");
        cachedSerQNames.add(qName);
        cls = com.dth.wse.service.impl.WsValue[].class;
        cachedSerClasses.add(cls);
        qName = new javax.xml.namespace.QName("http://impl.service.wse.dth.com",
"wsValue");
        qName2 = new javax.xml.namespace.QName("http://impl.service.wse.dth.com",
"valueSet");
        cachedSerFactories.add(new
org.apache.axis.encoding.ser.ArraySerializerFactory(qName, qName2));
        cachedDeserFactories.add(new
org.apache.axis.encoding.ser.ArrayDeserializerFactory());

  }

  protected org.apache.axis.client.Call createCall() throws java.rmi.RemoteException {
    try {
        org.apache.axis.client.Call _call = super._createCall();
        if (super.maintainSessionSet) {
          _call.setMaintainSession(super.maintainSession);
        }
        if (super.cachedUsername != null) {
          _call.setUsername(super.cachedUsername);
        }
        if (super.cachedPassword != null) {
```

```
      _call.setPassword(super.cachedPassword);
    }
    if (super.cachedEndpoint != null) {
      _call.setTargetEndpointAddress(super.cachedEndpoint);
    }
    if (super.cachedTimeout != null) {
      _call.setTimeout(super.cachedTimeout);
    }
    if (super.cachedPortName != null) {
      _call.setPortName(super.cachedPortName);
    }
    java.util.Enumeration keys = super.cachedProperties.keys();
    while (keys.hasMoreElements()) {
      java.lang.String key = (java.lang.String) keys.nextElement();
      _call.setProperty(key, super.cachedProperties.get(key));
    }
    // All the type mapping information is registered
    // when the first call is made.
    // The type mapping information is actually registered in
    // the TypeMappingRegistry of the service, which
    // is the reason why registration is only needed for the first call.
    synchronized (this) {
      if (firstCall()) {
        // must set encoding style before registering serializers
        _call.setEncodingStyle(null);
        for (int i = 0; i < cachedSerFactories.size(); ++i) {
          java.lang.Class cls = (java.lang.Class) cachedSerClasses.get(i);
          javax.xml.namespace.QName qName =
              (javax.xml.namespace.QName) cachedSerQNames.get(i);
          java.lang.Object x = cachedSerFactories.get(i);
          if (x instanceof Class) {
            java.lang.Class sf = (java.lang.Class)
              cachedSerFactories.get(i);
            java.lang.Class df = (java.lang.Class)
              cachedDeserFactories.get(i);
            _call.registerTypeMapping(cls, qName, sf, df, false);
          }
          else if (x instanceof javax.xml.rpc.encoding.SerializerFactory) {
            org.apache.axis.encoding.SerializerFactory sf =
(org.apache.axis.encoding.SerializerFactory)
              cachedSerFactories.get(i);
```

```
                org.apache.axis.encoding.DeserializerFactory df =
(org.apache.axis.encoding.DeserializerFactory)
                    cachedDeserFactories.get(i);
                _call.registerTypeMapping(cls, qName, sf, df, false);
              }
            }
          }
        }
        return _call;
      }
      catch (java.lang.Throwable _t) {
        throw new org.apache.axis.AxisFault("Failure trying to get the Call object", _t);
      }
    }

    public com.dth.wse.service.impl.Response execute(com.dth.wse.service.impl.Request
parameters) throws java.rmi.RemoteException {
      if (super.cachedEndpoint == null) {
        throw new org.apache.axis.NoEndPointException();
      }
      org.apache.axis.client.Call _call = createCall();
      _call.setOperation(_operations[0]);
      _call.setUseSOAPAction(true);
      _call.setSOAPActionURI("");
      _call.setEncodingStyle(null);
      _call.setProperty(org.apache.axis.client.Call.SEND_TYPE_ATTR, Boolean.FALSE);
      _call.setProperty(org.apache.axis.AxisEngine.PROP_DOMULTIREFS,
Boolean.FALSE);

_call.setSOAPVersion(org.apache.axis.soap.SOAPConstants.SOAP11_CONSTANTS);
      _call.setOperationName(new javax.xml.namespace.QName("", "execute"));

      setRequestHeaders(_call);
      setAttachments(_call);
 try {      java.lang.Object _resp = _call.invoke(new java.lang.Object[] {parameters});

      if (_resp instanceof java.rmi.RemoteException) {
        throw (java.rmi.RemoteException)_resp;
      }
      else {
        extractAttachments(_call);
        try {
```

```
            return (com.dth.wse.service.impl.Response) _resp;
        } catch (java.lang.Exception _exception) {
            return (com.dth.wse.service.impl.Response)
org.apache.axis.utils.JavaUtils.convert(_resp, com.dth.wse.service.impl.Response.class);
        }
      }
  } catch (org.apache.axis.AxisFault axisFaultException) {
  throw axisFaultException;
}
   }

}

public class WsRequestCmdMsg  implements java.io.Serializable {
   private com.dth.wse.service.impl.WsCommand[] command;

   private com.dth.wse.service.impl.WsValue[] session;

   private com.dth.wse.service.impl.WsDTO[] request;

   public WsRequestCmdMsg() {
   }

   public WsRequestCmdMsg(
        com.dth.wse.service.impl.WsCommand[] command,
        com.dth.wse.service.impl.WsValue[] session,
        com.dth.wse.service.impl.WsDTO[] request) {
        this.command = command;
        this.session = session;
        this.request = request;
   }


   /**
    * Gets the command value for this WsRequestCmdMsg.
    *
    * @return command
    */
   public com.dth.wse.service.impl.WsCommand[] getCommand() {
      return command;
   }
```

```
/**
 * Sets the command value for this WsRequestCmdMsg.
 *
 * @param command
 */
public void setCommand(com.dth.wse.service.impl.WsCommand[] command) {
   this.command = command;
}


/**
 * Gets the session value for this WsRequestCmdMsg.
 *
 * @return session
 */
public com.dth.wse.service.impl.WsValue[] getSession() {
   return session;
}


/**
 * Sets the session value for this WsRequestCmdMsg.
 *
 * @param session
 */
public void setSession(com.dth.wse.service.impl.WsValue[] session) {
   this.session = session;
}


/**
 * Gets the request value for this WsRequestCmdMsg.
 *
 * @return request
 */
public com.dth.wse.service.impl.WsDTO[] getRequest() {
   return request;
}


/**
```

```
 * Sets the request value for this WsRequestCmdMsg.
 *
 * @param request
 */
public void setRequest(com.dth.wse.service.impl.WsDTO[] request) {
   this.request = request;
}

private java.lang.Object __equalsCalc = null;
public synchronized boolean equals(java.lang.Object obj) {
   if (!(obj instanceof WsRequestCmdMsg)) return false;
   WsRequestCmdMsg other = (WsRequestCmdMsg) obj;
   if (obj == null) return false;
   if (this == obj) return true;
   if (__equalsCalc != null) {
      return (__equalsCalc == obj);
   }
   __equalsCalc = obj;
   boolean _equals;
   _equals = true &&
      ((this.command==null && other.getCommand()==null) ||
       (this.command!=null &&
        java.util.Arrays.equals(this.command, other.getCommand()))) &&
      ((this.session==null && other.getSession()==null) ||
       (this.session!=null &&
        java.util.Arrays.equals(this.session, other.getSession()))) &&
      ((this.request==null && other.getRequest()==null) ||
       (this.request!=null &&
        java.util.Arrays.equals(this.request, other.getRequest())));
   __equalsCalc = null;
   return _equals;
}

private boolean __hashCodeCalc = false;
public synchronized int hashCode() {
   if (__hashCodeCalc) {
      return 0;
   }
   __hashCodeCalc = true;
   int _hashCode = 1;
   if (getCommand() != null) {
      for (int i=0;
```

```
          i<java.lang.reflect.Array.getLength(getCommand());
          i++) {
         java.lang.Object obj = java.lang.reflect.Array.get(getCommand(), i);
         if (obj != null &&
            !obj.getClass().isArray()) {
            _hashCode += obj.hashCode();
         }
      }
   }
   if (getSession() != null) {
      for (int i=0;
          i<java.lang.reflect.Array.getLength(getSession());
          i++) {
         java.lang.Object obj = java.lang.reflect.Array.get(getSession(), i);
         if (obj != null &&
            !obj.getClass().isArray()) {
            _hashCode += obj.hashCode();
         }
      }
   }
   if (getRequest() != null) {
      for (int i=0;
          i<java.lang.reflect.Array.getLength(getRequest());
          i++) {
         java.lang.Object obj = java.lang.reflect.Array.get(getRequest(), i);
         if (obj != null &&
            !obj.getClass().isArray()) {
            _hashCode += obj.hashCode();
         }
      }
   }
   __hashCodeCalc = false;
   return _hashCode;
}

// Type metadata
private static org.apache.axis.description.TypeDesc typeDesc =
   new org.apache.axis.description.TypeDesc(WsRequestCmdMsg.class, true);

static {
   typeDesc.setXmlType(new
javax.xml.namespace.QName("http://impl.service.wse.dth.com", "wsRequestCmdMsg"));
```

```
        org.apache.axis.description.ElementDesc elemField = new
org.apache.axis.description.ElementDesc();
        elemField.setFieldName("command");
        elemField.setXmlName(new
javax.xml.namespace.QName("http://impl.service.wse.dth.com", "command"));
        elemField.setXmlType(new
javax.xml.namespace.QName("http://impl.service.wse.dth.com", "wsCommand"));
        elemField.setNillable(false);
        elemField.setItemQName(new
javax.xml.namespace.QName("http://impl.service.wse.dth.com", "comand"));
        typeDesc.addFieldDesc(elemField);
        elemField = new org.apache.axis.description.ElementDesc();
        elemField.setFieldName("session");
        elemField.setXmlName(new
javax.xml.namespace.QName("http://impl.service.wse.dth.com", "session"));
        elemField.setXmlType(new
javax.xml.namespace.QName("http://impl.service.wse.dth.com", "wsValue"));
        elemField.setNillable(false);
        elemField.setItemQName(new
javax.xml.namespace.QName("http://impl.service.wse.dth.com", "valueSet"));
        typeDesc.addFieldDesc(elemField);
        elemField = new org.apache.axis.description.ElementDesc();
        elemField.setFieldName("request");
        elemField.setXmlName(new
javax.xml.namespace.QName("http://impl.service.wse.dth.com", "request"));
        elemField.setXmlType(new
javax.xml.namespace.QName("http://impl.service.wse.dth.com", "wsDTO"));
        elemField.setNillable(false);
        elemField.setItemQName(new
javax.xml.namespace.QName("http://impl.service.wse.dth.com", "dto"));
        typeDesc.addFieldDesc(elemField);
    }

    /**
     * Return type metadata object
     */
    public static org.apache.axis.description.TypeDesc getTypeDesc() {
        return typeDesc;
    }

    /**
     * Get Custom Serializer
```

```
  */
  public static org.apache.axis.encoding.Serializer getSerializer(
      java.lang.String mechType,
      java.lang.Class _javaType,
      javax.xml.namespace.QName _xmlType) {
    return
     new  org.apache.axis.encoding.ser.BeanSerializer(
      _javaType, _xmlType, typeDesc);
  }

  /**
   * Get Custom Deserializer
   */
  public static org.apache.axis.encoding.Deserializer getDeserializer(
      java.lang.String mechType,
      java.lang.Class _javaType,
      javax.xml.namespace.QName _xmlType) {
    return
     new  org.apache.axis.encoding.ser.BeanDeserializer(
      _javaType, _xmlType, typeDesc);
  }

}


public class WsResponseCmdMsg  implements java.io.Serializable {
  private com.dth.wse.service.impl.WsDTO[] response;

  private com.dth.wse.service.impl.WsError[] errors;

  public WsResponseCmdMsg() {
  }

  public WsResponseCmdMsg(
      com.dth.wse.service.impl.WsDTO[] response,
      com.dth.wse.service.impl.WsError[] errors) {
      this.response = response;
      this.errors = errors;
  }


  /**
```

```
 * Gets the response value for this WsResponseCmdMsg.
 *
 * @return response
 */
public com.dth.wse.service.impl.WsDTO[] getResponse() {
   return response;
}


/**
 * Sets the response value for this WsResponseCmdMsg.
 *
 * @param response
 */
public void setResponse(com.dth.wse.service.impl.WsDTO[] response) {
   this.response = response;
}


/**
 * Gets the errors value for this WsResponseCmdMsg.
 *
 * @return errors
 */
public com.dth.wse.service.impl.WsError[] getErrors() {
   return errors;
}


/**
 * Sets the errors value for this WsResponseCmdMsg.
 *
 * @param errors
 */
public void setErrors(com.dth.wse.service.impl.WsError[] errors) {
   this.errors = errors;
}

private java.lang.Object __equalsCalc = null;
public synchronized boolean equals(java.lang.Object obj) {
   if (!(obj instanceof WsResponseCmdMsg)) return false;
   WsResponseCmdMsg other = (WsResponseCmdMsg) obj;
```

```
    if (obj == null) return false;
    if (this == obj) return true;
    if (__equalsCalc != null) {
        return (__equalsCalc == obj);
    }
    __equalsCalc = obj;
    boolean _equals;
    _equals = true &&
        ((this.response==null && other.getResponse()==null) ||
         (this.response!=null &&
          java.util.Arrays.equals(this.response, other.getResponse()))) &&
        ((this.errors==null && other.getErrors()==null) ||
         (this.errors!=null &&
          java.util.Arrays.equals(this.errors, other.getErrors())));
    __equalsCalc = null;
    return _equals;
}

private boolean __hashCodeCalc = false;
public synchronized int hashCode() {
    if (__hashCodeCalc) {
        return 0;
    }
    __hashCodeCalc = true;
    int _hashCode = 1;
    if (getResponse() != null) {
        for (int i=0;
             i<java.lang.reflect.Array.getLength(getResponse());
             i++) {
            java.lang.Object obj = java.lang.reflect.Array.get(getResponse(), i);
            if (obj != null &&
                !obj.getClass().isArray()) {
                _hashCode += obj.hashCode();
            }
        }
    }
    if (getErrors() != null) {
        for (int i=0;
             i<java.lang.reflect.Array.getLength(getErrors());
             i++) {
            java.lang.Object obj = java.lang.reflect.Array.get(getErrors(), i);
            if (obj != null &&
```

```
                !obj.getClass().isArray()) {
                _hashCode += obj.hashCode();
            }
        }
    }
    __hashCodeCalc = false;
    return _hashCode;
}

// Type metadata
private static org.apache.axis.description.TypeDesc typeDesc =
    new org.apache.axis.description.TypeDesc(WsResponseCmdMsg.class, true);

static {
    typeDesc.setXmlType(new
javax.xml.namespace.QName("http://impl.service.wse.dth.com",
"wsResponseCmdMsg"));
    org.apache.axis.description.ElementDesc elemField = new
org.apache.axis.description.ElementDesc();
    elemField.setFieldName("response");
    elemField.setXmlName(new
javax.xml.namespace.QName("http://impl.service.wse.dth.com", "response"));
    elemField.setXmlType(new
javax.xml.namespace.QName("http://impl.service.wse.dth.com", "wsDTO"));
    elemField.setNillable(false);
    elemField.setItemQName(new
javax.xml.namespace.QName("http://impl.service.wse.dth.com", "dto"));
    typeDesc.addFieldDesc(elemField);
    elemField = new org.apache.axis.description.ElementDesc();
    elemField.setFieldName("errors");
    elemField.setXmlName(new
javax.xml.namespace.QName("http://impl.service.wse.dth.com", "errors"));
    elemField.setXmlType(new
javax.xml.namespace.QName("http://impl.service.wse.dth.com", "wsError"));
    elemField.setNillable(false);
    elemField.setItemQName(new
javax.xml.namespace.QName("http://impl.service.wse.dth.com", "error"));
    typeDesc.addFieldDesc(elemField);
}

/**
 * Return type metadata object
```

```
     */
    public static org.apache.axis.description.TypeDesc getTypeDesc() {
        return typeDesc;
    }

    /**
     * Get Custom Serializer
     */
    public static org.apache.axis.encoding.Serializer getSerializer(
           java.lang.String mechType,
           java.lang.Class _javaType,
           javax.xml.namespace.QName _xmlType) {
        return
          new  org.apache.axis.encoding.ser.BeanSerializer(
            _javaType, _xmlType, typeDesc);
    }

    /**
     * Get Custom Deserializer
     */
    public static org.apache.axis.encoding.Deserializer getDeserializer(
           java.lang.String mechType,
           java.lang.Class _javaType,
           javax.xml.namespace.QName _xmlType) {
        return
          new  org.apache.axis.encoding.ser.BeanDeserializer(
            _javaType, _xmlType, typeDesc);
    }

}


public class Request  implements java.io.Serializable {
    private com.dth.wse.service.impl.WsRequestCmdMsg requestCmdMsg;

    public Request() {
    }

    public Request(
           com.dth.wse.service.impl.WsRequestCmdMsg requestCmdMsg) {
           this.requestCmdMsg = requestCmdMsg;
    }
```

```
/**
 * Gets the requestCmdMsg value for this Request.
 *
 * @return requestCmdMsg
 */
public com.dth.wse.service.impl.WsRequestCmdMsg getRequestCmdMsg() {
    return requestCmdMsg;
}


/**
 * Sets the requestCmdMsg value for this Request.
 *
 * @param requestCmdMsg
 */
public void setRequestCmdMsg(com.dth.wse.service.impl.WsRequestCmdMsg
requestCmdMsg) {
    this.requestCmdMsg = requestCmdMsg;
}

private java.lang.Object __equalsCalc = null;
public synchronized boolean equals(java.lang.Object obj) {
    if (!(obj instanceof Request)) return false;
    Request other = (Request) obj;
    if (obj == null) return false;
    if (this == obj) return true;
    if (__equalsCalc != null) {
        return (__equalsCalc == obj);
    }
    __equalsCalc = obj;
    boolean _equals;
    _equals = true &&
        ((this.requestCmdMsg==null && other.getRequestCmdMsg()==null) ||
         (this.requestCmdMsg!=null &&
          this.requestCmdMsg.equals(other.getRequestCmdMsg())));
    __equalsCalc = null;
    return _equals;
}

private boolean __hashCodeCalc = false;
```

```
  public synchronized int hashCode() {
    if (__hashCodeCalc) {
      return 0;
    }
    __hashCodeCalc = true;
    int _hashCode = 1;
    if (getRequestCmdMsg() != null) {
      _hashCode += getRequestCmdMsg().hashCode();
    }
    __hashCodeCalc = false;
    return _hashCode;
  }

  // Type metadata
  private static org.apache.axis.description.TypeDesc typeDesc =
    new org.apache.axis.description.TypeDesc(Request.class, true);

  static {
    typeDesc.setXmlType(new
javax.xml.namespace.QName("http://impl.service.wse.dth.com", ">request"));
    org.apache.axis.description.ElementDesc elemField = new
org.apache.axis.description.ElementDesc();
    elemField.setFieldName("requestCmdMsg");
    elemField.setXmlName(new
javax.xml.namespace.QName("http://impl.service.wse.dth.com", "requestCmdMsg"));
    elemField.setXmlType(new
javax.xml.namespace.QName("http://impl.service.wse.dth.com", "wsRequestCmdMsg"));
    elemField.setMinOccurs(0);
    elemField.setNillable(false);
    typeDesc.addFieldDesc(elemField);
  }

  /**
   * Return type metadata object
   */
  public static org.apache.axis.description.TypeDesc getTypeDesc() {
    return typeDesc;
  }

  /**
   * Get Custom Serializer
   */
```

```
  public static org.apache.axis.encoding.Serializer getSerializer(
       java.lang.String mechType,
       java.lang.Class _javaType,
       javax.xml.namespace.QName _xmlType) {
     return
      new  org.apache.axis.encoding.ser.BeanSerializer(
       _javaType, _xmlType, typeDesc);
  }

  /**
   * Get Custom Deserializer
   */
  public static org.apache.axis.encoding.Deserializer getDeserializer(
       java.lang.String mechType,
       java.lang.Class _javaType,
       javax.xml.namespace.QName _xmlType) {
     return
      new  org.apache.axis.encoding.ser.BeanDeserializer(
       _javaType, _xmlType, typeDesc);
  }

}


public class Response  implements java.io.Serializable {
  private com.dth.wse.service.impl.WsResponseCmdMsg responseCmdMsg;

  public Response() {
  }

  public Response(
       com.dth.wse.service.impl.WsResponseCmdMsg responseCmdMsg) {
       this.responseCmdMsg = responseCmdMsg;
  }


  /**
   * Gets the responseCmdMsg value for this Response.
   *
   * @return responseCmdMsg
   */
  public com.dth.wse.service.impl.WsResponseCmdMsg getResponseCmdMsg() {
```

```
        return responseCmdMsg;
    }


    /**
     * Sets the responseCmdMsg value for this Response.
     *
     * @param responseCmdMsg
     */
    public void setResponseCmdMsg(com.dth.wse.service.impl.WsResponseCmdMsg
responseCmdMsg) {
        this.responseCmdMsg = responseCmdMsg;
    }

    private java.lang.Object __equalsCalc = null;
    public synchronized boolean equals(java.lang.Object obj) {
        if (!(obj instanceof Response)) return false;
        Response other = (Response) obj;
        if (obj == null) return false;
        if (this == obj) return true;
        if (__equalsCalc != null) {
            return (__equalsCalc == obj);
        }
        __equalsCalc = obj;
        boolean _equals;
        _equals = true &&
            ((this.responseCmdMsg==null && other.getResponseCmdMsg()==null) ||
             (this.responseCmdMsg!=null &&
              this.responseCmdMsg.equals(other.getResponseCmdMsg())));
        __equalsCalc = null;
        return _equals;
    }

    private boolean __hashCodeCalc = false;
    public synchronized int hashCode() {
        if (__hashCodeCalc) {
            return 0;
        }
        __hashCodeCalc = true;
        int _hashCode = 1;
        if (getResponseCmdMsg() != null) {
            _hashCode += getResponseCmdMsg().hashCode();
```

```
    }
    __hashCodeCalc = false;
    return _hashCode;
  }

  // Type metadata
  private static org.apache.axis.description.TypeDesc typeDesc =
    new org.apache.axis.description.TypeDesc(Response.class, true);

  static {
    typeDesc.setXmlType(new
javax.xml.namespace.QName("http://impl.service.wse.dth.com", ">response"));
    org.apache.axis.description.ElementDesc elemField = new
org.apache.axis.description.ElementDesc();
    elemField.setFieldName("responseCmdMsg");
    elemField.setXmlName(new
javax.xml.namespace.QName("http://impl.service.wse.dth.com", "responseCmdMsg"));
    elemField.setXmlType(new
javax.xml.namespace.QName("http://impl.service.wse.dth.com",
"wsResponseCmdMsg"));
    elemField.setMinOccurs(0);
    elemField.setNillable(false);
    typeDesc.addFieldDesc(elemField);
  }

  /**
   * Return type metadata object
   */
  public static org.apache.axis.description.TypeDesc getTypeDesc() {
    return typeDesc;
  }

  /**
   * Get Custom Serializer
   */
  public static org.apache.axis.encoding.Serializer getSerializer(
      java.lang.String mechType,
      java.lang.Class _javaType,
      javax.xml.namespace.QName _xmlType) {
    return
     new  org.apache.axis.encoding.ser.BeanSerializer(
      _javaType, _xmlType, typeDesc);
```

```
    }

    /**
     * Get Custom Deserializer
     */
    public static org.apache.axis.encoding.Deserializer getDeserializer(
           java.lang.String mechType,
           java.lang.Class _javaType,
           javax.xml.namespace.QName _xmlType) {
        return
          new  org.apache.axis.encoding.ser.BeanDeserializer(
            _javaType, _xmlType, typeDesc);
    }

}


public class WsCommand  implements java.io.Serializable {
    private java.lang.String service;

    private java.lang.String task;

    public WsCommand() {
    }

    public WsCommand(
           java.lang.String service,
           java.lang.String task) {
           this.service = service;
           this.task = task;
    }


    /**
     * Gets the service value for this WsCommand.
     *
     * @return service
     */
    public java.lang.String getService() {
        return service;
    }
```

```
/**
 * Sets the service value for this WsCommand.
 *
 * @param service
 */
public void setService(java.lang.String service) {
   this.service = service;
}


/**
 * Gets the task value for this WsCommand.
 *
 * @return task
 */
public java.lang.String getTask() {
   return task;
}


/**
 * Sets the task value for this WsCommand.
 *
 * @param task
 */
public void setTask(java.lang.String task) {
   this.task = task;
}

private java.lang.Object __equalsCalc = null;
public synchronized boolean equals(java.lang.Object obj) {
   if (!(obj instanceof WsCommand)) return false;
   WsCommand other = (WsCommand) obj;
   if (obj == null) return false;
   if (this == obj) return true;
   if (__equalsCalc != null) {
      return (__equalsCalc == obj);
   }
   __equalsCalc = obj;
   boolean _equals;
   _equals = true &&
```

```
        ((this.service==null && other.getService()==null) ||
         (this.service!=null &&
          this.service.equals(other.getService()))) &&
        ((this.task==null && other.getTask()==null) ||
         (this.task!=null &&
          this.task.equals(other.getTask())));
      __equalsCalc = null;
      return _equals;
   }

   private boolean __hashCodeCalc = false;
   public synchronized int hashCode() {
      if (__hashCodeCalc) {
         return 0;
      }
      __hashCodeCalc = true;
      int _hashCode = 1;
      if (getService() != null) {
         _hashCode += getService().hashCode();
      }
      if (getTask() != null) {
         _hashCode += getTask().hashCode();
      }
      __hashCodeCalc = false;
      return _hashCode;
   }

   // Type metadata
   private static org.apache.axis.description.TypeDesc typeDesc =
      new org.apache.axis.description.TypeDesc(WsCommand.class, true);

   static {
      typeDesc.setXmlType(new
javax.xml.namespace.QName("http://impl.service.wse.dth.com", "wsCommand"));
      org.apache.axis.description.ElementDesc elemField = new
org.apache.axis.description.ElementDesc();
      elemField.setFieldName("service");
      elemField.setXmlName(new
javax.xml.namespace.QName("http://impl.service.wse.dth.com", "service"));
      elemField.setXmlType(new
javax.xml.namespace.QName("http://www.w3.org/2001/XMLSchema", "string"));
      elemField.setNillable(false);
```

```
        typeDesc.addFieldDesc(elemField);
        elemField = new org.apache.axis.description.ElementDesc();
        elemField.setFieldName("task");
        elemField.setXmlName(new
javax.xml.namespace.QName("http://impl.service.wse.dth.com", "task"));
        elemField.setXmlType(new
javax.xml.namespace.QName("http://www.w3.org/2001/XMLSchema", "string"));
        elemField.setNillable(false);
        typeDesc.addFieldDesc(elemField);
    }

    /**
     * Return type metadata object
     */
    public static org.apache.axis.description.TypeDesc getTypeDesc() {
        return typeDesc;
    }

    /**
     * Get Custom Serializer
     */
    public static org.apache.axis.encoding.Serializer getSerializer(
           java.lang.String mechType,
           java.lang.Class _javaType,
           javax.xml.namespace.QName _xmlType) {
        return
          new  org.apache.axis.encoding.ser.BeanSerializer(
            _javaType, _xmlType, typeDesc);
    }

    /**
     * Get Custom Deserializer
     */
    public static org.apache.axis.encoding.Deserializer getDeserializer(
           java.lang.String mechType,
           java.lang.Class _javaType,
           javax.xml.namespace.QName _xmlType) {
        return
          new  org.apache.axis.encoding.ser.BeanDeserializer(
            _javaType, _xmlType, typeDesc);
    }
```

```
}

public class WsDTO  implements java.io.Serializable {
   private java.lang.String name;

   private java.lang.String type;

   private com.dth.wse.service.impl.WsValue[] data;

   private com.dth.wse.service.impl.WsDTO[] dtoSet;

   public WsDTO() {
   }

   public WsDTO(
        java.lang.String name,
        java.lang.String type,
        com.dth.wse.service.impl.WsValue[] data,
        com.dth.wse.service.impl.WsDTO[] dtoSet) {
        this.name = name;
        this.type = type;
        this.data = data;
        this.dtoSet = dtoSet;
   }


   /**
    * Gets the name value for this WsDTO.
    *
    * @return name
    */
   public java.lang.String getName() {
      return name;
   }


   /**
    * Sets the name value for this WsDTO.
    *
    * @param name
    */
```

```
public void setName(java.lang.String name) {
    this.name = name;
}


/**
 * Gets the type value for this WsDTO.
 *
 * @return type
 */
public java.lang.String getType() {
    return type;
}


/**
 * Sets the type value for this WsDTO.
 *
 * @param type
 */
public void setType(java.lang.String type) {
    this.type = type;
}


/**
 * Gets the data value for this WsDTO.
 *
 * @return data
 */
public com.dth.wse.service.impl.WsValue[] getData() {
    return data;
}


/**
 * Sets the data value for this WsDTO.
 *
 * @param data
 */
public void setData(com.dth.wse.service.impl.WsValue[] data) {
    this.data = data;
```

```
}

public com.dth.wse.service.impl.WsValue getData(int i) {
   return this.data[i];
}

public void setData(int i, com.dth.wse.service.impl.WsValue _value) {
   this.data[i] = _value;
}


/**
 * Gets the dtoSet value for this WsDTO.
 *
 * @return dtoSet
 */
public com.dth.wse.service.impl.WsDTO[] getDtoSet() {
   return dtoSet;
}


/**
 * Sets the dtoSet value for this WsDTO.
 *
 * @param dtoSet
 */
public void setDtoSet(com.dth.wse.service.impl.WsDTO[] dtoSet) {
   this.dtoSet = dtoSet;
}

public com.dth.wse.service.impl.WsDTO getDtoSet(int i) {
   return this.dtoSet[i];
}

public void setDtoSet(int i, com.dth.wse.service.impl.WsDTO _value) {
   this.dtoSet[i] = _value;
}

private java.lang.Object __equalsCalc = null;
public synchronized boolean equals(java.lang.Object obj) {
   if (!(obj instanceof WsDTO)) return false;
   WsDTO other = (WsDTO) obj;
```

```
    if (obj == null) return false;
    if (this == obj) return true;
    if (__equalsCalc != null) {
        return (__equalsCalc == obj);
    }
    __equalsCalc = obj;
    boolean _equals;
    _equals = true &&
        ((this.name==null && other.getName()==null) ||
         (this.name!=null &&
          this.name.equals(other.getName()))) &&
        ((this.type==null && other.getType()==null) ||
         (this.type!=null &&
          this.type.equals(other.getType()))) &&
        ((this.data==null && other.getData()==null) ||
         (this.data!=null &&
          java.util.Arrays.equals(this.data, other.getData()))) &&
        ((this.dtoSet==null && other.getDtoSet()==null) ||
         (this.dtoSet!=null &&
          java.util.Arrays.equals(this.dtoSet, other.getDtoSet())));
    __equalsCalc = null;
    return _equals;
}

private boolean __hashCodeCalc = false;
public synchronized int hashCode() {
    if (__hashCodeCalc) {
        return 0;
    }
    __hashCodeCalc = true;
    int _hashCode = 1;
    if (getName() != null) {
        _hashCode += getName().hashCode();
    }
    if (getType() != null) {
        _hashCode += getType().hashCode();
    }
    if (getData() != null) {
        for (int i=0;
             i<java.lang.reflect.Array.getLength(getData());
             i++) {
            java.lang.Object obj = java.lang.reflect.Array.get(getData(), i);
```

```
            if (obj != null &&
                !obj.getClass().isArray()) {
                _hashCode += obj.hashCode();
            }
        }
    }
    if (getDtoSet() != null) {
        for (int i=0;
             i<java.lang.reflect.Array.getLength(getDtoSet());
             i++) {
            java.lang.Object obj = java.lang.reflect.Array.get(getDtoSet(), i);
            if (obj != null &&
                !obj.getClass().isArray()) {
                _hashCode += obj.hashCode();
            }
        }
    }
    __hashCodeCalc = false;
    return _hashCode;
}

// Type metadata
private static org.apache.axis.description.TypeDesc typeDesc =
    new org.apache.axis.description.TypeDesc(WsDTO.class, true);

static {
    typeDesc.setXmlType(new
javax.xml.namespace.QName("http://impl.service.wse.dth.com", "wsDTO"));
    org.apache.axis.description.ElementDesc elemField = new
org.apache.axis.description.ElementDesc();
    elemField.setFieldName("name");
    elemField.setXmlName(new
javax.xml.namespace.QName("http://impl.service.wse.dth.com", "name"));
    elemField.setXmlType(new
javax.xml.namespace.QName("http://www.w3.org/2001/XMLSchema", "string"));
    elemField.setNillable(false);
    typeDesc.addFieldDesc(elemField);
    elemField = new org.apache.axis.description.ElementDesc();
    elemField.setFieldName("type");
    elemField.setXmlName(new
javax.xml.namespace.QName("http://impl.service.wse.dth.com", "type"));
```

```
    elemField.setXmlType(new
javax.xml.namespace.QName("http://www.w3.org/2001/XMLSchema", "string"));
    elemField.setNillable(false);
    typeDesc.addFieldDesc(elemField);
    elemField = new org.apache.axis.description.ElementDesc();
    elemField.setFieldName("data");
    elemField.setXmlName(new
javax.xml.namespace.QName("http://impl.service.wse.dth.com", "data"));
    elemField.setXmlType(new
javax.xml.namespace.QName("http://impl.service.wse.dth.com", "wsValue"));
    elemField.setMinOccurs(0);
    elemField.setNillable(false);
    typeDesc.addFieldDesc(elemField);
    elemField = new org.apache.axis.description.ElementDesc();
    elemField.setFieldName("dtoSet");
    elemField.setXmlName(new
javax.xml.namespace.QName("http://impl.service.wse.dth.com", "dtoSet"));
    elemField.setXmlType(new
javax.xml.namespace.QName("http://impl.service.wse.dth.com", "wsDTO"));
    elemField.setMinOccurs(0);
    elemField.setNillable(false);
    typeDesc.addFieldDesc(elemField);
  }

  /**
   * Return type metadata object
   */
  public static org.apache.axis.description.TypeDesc getTypeDesc() {
    return typeDesc;
  }

  /**
   * Get Custom Serializer
   */
  public static org.apache.axis.encoding.Serializer getSerializer(
      java.lang.String mechType,
      java.lang.Class _javaType,
      javax.xml.namespace.QName _xmlType) {
    return
     new  org.apache.axis.encoding.ser.BeanSerializer(
      _javaType, _xmlType, typeDesc);
  }
```

```
    /**
     * Get Custom Deserializer
     */
    public static org.apache.axis.encoding.Deserializer getDeserializer(
           java.lang.String mechType,
           java.lang.Class _javaType,
           javax.xml.namespace.QName _xmlType) {
        return
          new  org.apache.axis.encoding.ser.BeanDeserializer(
            _javaType, _xmlType, typeDesc);
    }

}

public class WsValue  implements java.io.Serializable {
    private java.lang.String name;

    private java.lang.String type;

    private java.lang.String value;

    public WsValue() {
    }

    public WsValue(
           java.lang.String name,
           java.lang.String type,
           java.lang.String value) {
           this.name = name;
           this.type = type;
           this.value = value;
    }


    /**
     * Gets the name value for this WsValue.
     *
     * @return name
     */
    public java.lang.String getName() {
        return name;
```

```
}


/**
 * Sets the name value for this WsValue.
 *
 * @param name
 */
public void setName(java.lang.String name) {
   this.name = name;
}


/**
 * Gets the type value for this WsValue.
 *
 * @return type
 */
public java.lang.String getType() {
   return type;
}


/**
 * Sets the type value for this WsValue.
 *
 * @param type
 */
public void setType(java.lang.String type) {
   this.type = type;
}


/**
 * Gets the value value for this WsValue.
 *
 * @return value
 */
public java.lang.String getValue() {
   return value;
}
```

```
/**
 * Sets the value value for this WsValue.
 *
 * @param value
 */
public void setValue(java.lang.String value) {
   this.value = value;
}

private java.lang.Object __equalsCalc = null;
public synchronized boolean equals(java.lang.Object obj) {
   if (!(obj instanceof WsValue)) return false;
   WsValue other = (WsValue) obj;
   if (obj == null) return false;
   if (this == obj) return true;
   if (__equalsCalc != null) {
      return (__equalsCalc == obj);
   }
   __equalsCalc = obj;
   boolean _equals;
   _equals = true &&
      ((this.name==null && other.getName()==null) ||
       (this.name!=null &&
        this.name.equals(other.getName()))) &&
      ((this.type==null && other.getType()==null) ||
       (this.type!=null &&
        this.type.equals(other.getType()))) &&
      ((this.value==null && other.getValue()==null) ||
       (this.value!=null &&
        this.value.equals(other.getValue())));
   __equalsCalc = null;
   return _equals;
}

private boolean __hashCodeCalc = false;
public synchronized int hashCode() {
   if (__hashCodeCalc) {
      return 0;
   }
   __hashCodeCalc = true;
   int _hashCode = 1;
```

```
        if (getName() != null) {
            _hashCode += getName().hashCode();
        }
        if (getType() != null) {
            _hashCode += getType().hashCode();
        }
        if (getValue() != null) {
            _hashCode += getValue().hashCode();
        }
        __hashCodeCalc = false;
        return _hashCode;
    }

    // Type metadata
    private static org.apache.axis.description.TypeDesc typeDesc =
        new org.apache.axis.description.TypeDesc(WsValue.class, true);

    static {
        typeDesc.setXmlType(new
javax.xml.namespace.QName("http://impl.service.wse.dth.com", "wsValue"));
        org.apache.axis.description.ElementDesc elemField = new
org.apache.axis.description.ElementDesc();
        elemField.setFieldName("name");
        elemField.setXmlName(new
javax.xml.namespace.QName("http://impl.service.wse.dth.com", "name"));
        elemField.setXmlType(new
javax.xml.namespace.QName("http://www.w3.org/2001/XMLSchema", "string"));
        elemField.setNillable(false);
        typeDesc.addFieldDesc(elemField);
        elemField = new org.apache.axis.description.ElementDesc();
        elemField.setFieldName("type");
        elemField.setXmlName(new
javax.xml.namespace.QName("http://impl.service.wse.dth.com", "type"));
        elemField.setXmlType(new
javax.xml.namespace.QName("http://www.w3.org/2001/XMLSchema", "string"));
        elemField.setNillable(false);
        typeDesc.addFieldDesc(elemField);
        elemField = new org.apache.axis.description.ElementDesc();
        elemField.setFieldName("value");
        elemField.setXmlName(new
javax.xml.namespace.QName("http://impl.service.wse.dth.com", "value"));
```

```
        elemField.setXmlType(new
javax.xml.namespace.QName("http://www.w3.org/2001/XMLSchema", "string"));
        elemField.setMinOccurs(0);
        elemField.setNillable(false);
        typeDesc.addFieldDesc(elemField);
    }

    /**
     * Return type metadata object
     */
    public static org.apache.axis.description.TypeDesc getTypeDesc() {
        return typeDesc;
    }

    /**
     * Get Custom Serializer
     */
    public static org.apache.axis.encoding.Serializer getSerializer(
           java.lang.String mechType,
           java.lang.Class _javaType,
           javax.xml.namespace.QName _xmlType) {
        return
          new  org.apache.axis.encoding.ser.BeanSerializer(
            _javaType, _xmlType, typeDesc);
    }

    /**
     * Get Custom Deserializer
     */
    public static org.apache.axis.encoding.Deserializer getDeserializer(
           java.lang.String mechType,
           java.lang.Class _javaType,
           javax.xml.namespace.QName _xmlType) {
        return
          new  org.apache.axis.encoding.ser.BeanDeserializer(
            _javaType, _xmlType, typeDesc);
    }

}


public class WsError  implements java.io.Serializable {
```

```
private java.lang.String number;

private java.lang.String title;

private java.lang.String time;

private java.lang.String type;

private java.lang.String catagory;

private java.lang.String source;

private java.lang.String reference;

private java.lang.String displayMessage;

private java.lang.String logMessage;

private java.lang.String disregard;

private com.dth.wse.service.impl.WsError initialCause;

public WsError() {
}

public WsError(
    java.lang.String number,
    java.lang.String title,
    java.lang.String time,
    java.lang.String type,
    java.lang.String catagory,
    java.lang.String source,
    java.lang.String reference,
    java.lang.String displayMessage,
    java.lang.String logMessage,
    java.lang.String disregard,
    com.dth.wse.service.impl.WsError initialCause) {
    this.number = number;
    this.title = title;
    this.time = time;
    this.type = type;
    this.catagory = catagory;
```

```
        this.source = source;
        this.reference = reference;
        this.displayMessage = displayMessage;
        this.logMessage = logMessage;
        this.disregard = disregard;
        this.initialCause = initialCause;
    }


    /**
     * Gets the number value for this WsError.
     *
     * @return number
     */
    public java.lang.String getNumber() {
      return number;
    }


    /**
     * Sets the number value for this WsError.
     *
     * @param number
     */
    public void setNumber(java.lang.String number) {
      this.number = number;
    }


    /**
     * Gets the title value for this WsError.
     *
     * @return title
     */
    public java.lang.String getTitle() {
      return title;
    }


    /**
     * Sets the title value for this WsError.
     *
```

```
 * @param title
 */
public void setTitle(java.lang.String title) {
   this.title = title;
}


/**
 * Gets the time value for this WsError.
 *
 * @return time
 */
public java.lang.String getTime() {
   return time;
}


/**
 * Sets the time value for this WsError.
 *
 * @param time
 */
public void setTime(java.lang.String time) {
   this.time = time;
}


/**
 * Gets the type value for this WsError.
 *
 * @return type
 */
public java.lang.String getType() {
   return type;
}


/**
 * Sets the type value for this WsError.
 *
 * @param type
 */
```

```
public void setType(java.lang.String type) {
   this.type = type;
}


/**
 * Gets the catagory value for this WsError.
 *
 * @return catagory
 */
public java.lang.String getCatagory() {
   return catagory;
}


/**
 * Sets the catagory value for this WsError.
 *
 * @param catagory
 */
public void setCatagory(java.lang.String catagory) {
   this.catagory = catagory;
}


/**
 * Gets the source value for this WsError.
 *
 * @return source
 */
public java.lang.String getSource() {
   return source;
}


/**
 * Sets the source value for this WsError.
 *
 * @param source
 */
public void setSource(java.lang.String source) {
   this.source = source;
```

```
}


/**
 * Gets the reference value for this WsError.
 *
 * @return reference
 */
public java.lang.String getReference() {
  return reference;
}


/**
 * Sets the reference value for this WsError.
 *
 * @param reference
 */
public void setReference(java.lang.String reference) {
  this.reference = reference;
}


/**
 * Gets the displayMessage value for this WsError.
 *
 * @return displayMessage
 */
public java.lang.String getDisplayMessage() {
  return displayMessage;
}


/**
 * Sets the displayMessage value for this WsError.
 *
 * @param displayMessage
 */
public void setDisplayMessage(java.lang.String displayMessage) {
  this.displayMessage = displayMessage;
}
```

```
/**
 * Gets the logMessage value for this WsError.
 *
 * @return logMessage
 */
public java.lang.String getLogMessage() {
   return logMessage;
}


/**
 * Sets the logMessage value for this WsError.
 *
 * @param logMessage
 */
public void setLogMessage(java.lang.String logMessage) {
   this.logMessage = logMessage;
}


/**
 * Gets the disregard value for this WsError.
 *
 * @return disregard
 */
public java.lang.String getDisregard() {
   return disregard;
}


/**
 * Sets the disregard value for this WsError.
 *
 * @param disregard
 */
public void setDisregard(java.lang.String disregard) {
   this.disregard = disregard;
}


/**
```

```
     * Gets the initialCause value for this WsError.
     *
     * @return initialCause
     */
    public com.dth.wse.service.impl.WsError getInitialCause() {
        return initialCause;
    }


    /**
     * Sets the initialCause value for this WsError.
     *
     * @param initialCause
     */
    public void setInitialCause(com.dth.wse.service.impl.WsError initialCause) {
        this.initialCause = initialCause;
    }

    private java.lang.Object __equalsCalc = null;
    public synchronized boolean equals(java.lang.Object obj) {
        if (!(obj instanceof WsError)) return false;
        WsError other = (WsError) obj;
        if (obj == null) return false;
        if (this == obj) return true;
        if (__equalsCalc != null) {
            return (__equalsCalc == obj);
        }
        __equalsCalc = obj;
        boolean _equals;
        _equals = true &&
            ((this.number==null && other.getNumber()==null) ||
             (this.number!=null &&
              this.number.equals(other.getNumber()))) &&
            ((this.title==null && other.getTitle()==null) ||
             (this.title!=null &&
              this.title.equals(other.getTitle()))) &&
            ((this.time==null && other.getTime()==null) ||
             (this.time!=null &&
              this.time.equals(other.getTime()))) &&
            ((this.type==null && other.getType()==null) ||
             (this.type!=null &&
              this.type.equals(other.getType()))) &&
```

```
        ((this.catagory==null && other.getCatagory()==null) ||
         (this.catagory!=null &&
          this.catagory.equals(other.getCatagory()))) &&
        ((this.source==null && other.getSource()==null) ||
         (this.source!=null &&
          this.source.equals(other.getSource()))) &&
        ((this.reference==null && other.getReference()==null) ||
         (this.reference!=null &&
          this.reference.equals(other.getReference()))) &&
        ((this.displayMessage==null && other.getDisplayMessage()==null) ||
         (this.displayMessage!=null &&
          this.displayMessage.equals(other.getDisplayMessage()))) &&
        ((this.logMessage==null && other.getLogMessage()==null) ||
         (this.logMessage!=null &&
          this.logMessage.equals(other.getLogMessage()))) &&
        ((this.disregard==null && other.getDisregard()==null) ||
         (this.disregard!=null &&
          this.disregard.equals(other.getDisregard()))) &&
        ((this.initialCause==null && other.getInitialCause()==null) ||
         (this.initialCause!=null &&
          this.initialCause.equals(other.getInitialCause())));
    __equalsCalc = null;
    return _equals;
}

private boolean __hashCodeCalc = false;
public synchronized int hashCode() {
    if (__hashCodeCalc) {
        return 0;
    }
    __hashCodeCalc = true;
    int _hashCode = 1;
    if (getNumber() != null) {
        _hashCode += getNumber().hashCode();
    }
    if (getTitle() != null) {
        _hashCode += getTitle().hashCode();
    }
    if (getTime() != null) {
        _hashCode += getTime().hashCode();
    }
    if (getType() != null) {
```

```
            _hashCode += getType().hashCode();
        }
        if (getCatagory() != null) {
            _hashCode += getCatagory().hashCode();
        }
        if (getSource() != null) {
            _hashCode += getSource().hashCode();
        }
        if (getReference() != null) {
            _hashCode += getReference().hashCode();
        }
        if (getDisplayMessage() != null) {
            _hashCode += getDisplayMessage().hashCode();
        }
        if (getLogMessage() != null) {
            _hashCode += getLogMessage().hashCode();
        }
        if (getDisregard() != null) {
            _hashCode += getDisregard().hashCode();
        }
        if (getInitialCause() != null) {
            _hashCode += getInitialCause().hashCode();
        }
        __hashCodeCalc = false;
        return _hashCode;
    }

    // Type metadata
    private static org.apache.axis.description.TypeDesc typeDesc =
        new org.apache.axis.description.TypeDesc(WsError.class, true);

    static {
        typeDesc.setXmlType(new
javax.xml.namespace.QName("http://impl.service.wse.dth.com", "wsError"));
        org.apache.axis.description.ElementDesc elemField = new
org.apache.axis.description.ElementDesc();
        elemField.setFieldName("number");
        elemField.setXmlName(new
javax.xml.namespace.QName("http://impl.service.wse.dth.com", "number"));
        elemField.setXmlType(new
javax.xml.namespace.QName("http://www.w3.org/2001/XMLSchema", "string"));
        elemField.setNillable(false);
```

```
    typeDesc.addFieldDesc(elemField);
    elemField = new org.apache.axis.description.ElementDesc();
    elemField.setFieldName("title");
    elemField.setXmlName(new
javax.xml.namespace.QName("http://impl.service.wse.dth.com", "title"));
    elemField.setXmlType(new
javax.xml.namespace.QName("http://www.w3.org/2001/XMLSchema", "string"));
    elemField.setNillable(false);
    typeDesc.addFieldDesc(elemField);
    elemField = new org.apache.axis.description.ElementDesc();
    elemField.setFieldName("time");
    elemField.setXmlName(new
javax.xml.namespace.QName("http://impl.service.wse.dth.com", "time"));
    elemField.setXmlType(new
javax.xml.namespace.QName("http://www.w3.org/2001/XMLSchema", "string"));
    elemField.setNillable(false);
    typeDesc.addFieldDesc(elemField);
    elemField = new org.apache.axis.description.ElementDesc();
    elemField.setFieldName("type");
    elemField.setXmlName(new
javax.xml.namespace.QName("http://impl.service.wse.dth.com", "type"));
    elemField.setXmlType(new
javax.xml.namespace.QName("http://www.w3.org/2001/XMLSchema", "string"));
    elemField.setNillable(false);
    typeDesc.addFieldDesc(elemField);
    elemField = new org.apache.axis.description.ElementDesc();
    elemField.setFieldName("catagory");
    elemField.setXmlName(new
javax.xml.namespace.QName("http://impl.service.wse.dth.com", "catagory"));
    elemField.setXmlType(new
javax.xml.namespace.QName("http://www.w3.org/2001/XMLSchema", "string"));
    elemField.setNillable(false);
    typeDesc.addFieldDesc(elemField);
    elemField = new org.apache.axis.description.ElementDesc();
    elemField.setFieldName("source");
    elemField.setXmlName(new
javax.xml.namespace.QName("http://impl.service.wse.dth.com", "source"));
    elemField.setXmlType(new
javax.xml.namespace.QName("http://www.w3.org/2001/XMLSchema", "string"));
    elemField.setNillable(false);
    typeDesc.addFieldDesc(elemField);
    elemField = new org.apache.axis.description.ElementDesc();
```

```
        elemField.setFieldName("reference");
        elemField.setXmlName(new
javax.xml.namespace.QName("http://impl.service.wse.dth.com", "reference"));
        elemField.setXmlType(new
javax.xml.namespace.QName("http://www.w3.org/2001/XMLSchema", "string"));
        elemField.setNillable(false);
        typeDesc.addFieldDesc(elemField);
        elemField = new org.apache.axis.description.ElementDesc();
        elemField.setFieldName("displayMessage");
        elemField.setXmlName(new
javax.xml.namespace.QName("http://impl.service.wse.dth.com", "displayMessage"));
        elemField.setXmlType(new
javax.xml.namespace.QName("http://www.w3.org/2001/XMLSchema", "string"));
        elemField.setNillable(false);
        typeDesc.addFieldDesc(elemField);
        elemField = new org.apache.axis.description.ElementDesc();
        elemField.setFieldName("logMessage");
        elemField.setXmlName(new
javax.xml.namespace.QName("http://impl.service.wse.dth.com", "logMessage"));
        elemField.setXmlType(new
javax.xml.namespace.QName("http://www.w3.org/2001/XMLSchema", "string"));
        elemField.setNillable(false);
        typeDesc.addFieldDesc(elemField);
        elemField = new org.apache.axis.description.ElementDesc();
        elemField.setFieldName("disregard");
        elemField.setXmlName(new
javax.xml.namespace.QName("http://impl.service.wse.dth.com", "disregard"));
        elemField.setXmlType(new
javax.xml.namespace.QName("http://www.w3.org/2001/XMLSchema", "string"));
        elemField.setNillable(false);
        typeDesc.addFieldDesc(elemField);
        elemField = new org.apache.axis.description.ElementDesc();
        elemField.setFieldName("initialCause");
        elemField.setXmlName(new
javax.xml.namespace.QName("http://impl.service.wse.dth.com", "initialCause"));
        elemField.setXmlType(new
javax.xml.namespace.QName("http://impl.service.wse.dth.com", "wsError"));
        elemField.setMinOccurs(0);
        elemField.setNillable(false);
        typeDesc.addFieldDesc(elemField);
    }
```

```
/**
 * Return type metadata object
 */
public static org.apache.axis.description.TypeDesc getTypeDesc() {
   return typeDesc;
}

/**
 * Get Custom Serializer
 */
public static org.apache.axis.encoding.Serializer getSerializer(
      java.lang.String mechType,
      java.lang.Class _javaType,
      javax.xml.namespace.QName _xmlType) {
   return
     new  org.apache.axis.encoding.ser.BeanSerializer(
       _javaType, _xmlType, typeDesc);
}

/**
 * Get Custom Deserializer
 */
public static org.apache.axis.encoding.Deserializer getDeserializer(
      java.lang.String mechType,
      java.lang.Class _javaType,
      javax.xml.namespace.QName _xmlType) {
   return
     new  org.apache.axis.encoding.ser.BeanDeserializer(
       _javaType, _xmlType, typeDesc);
} }
```

Dependency Injection:

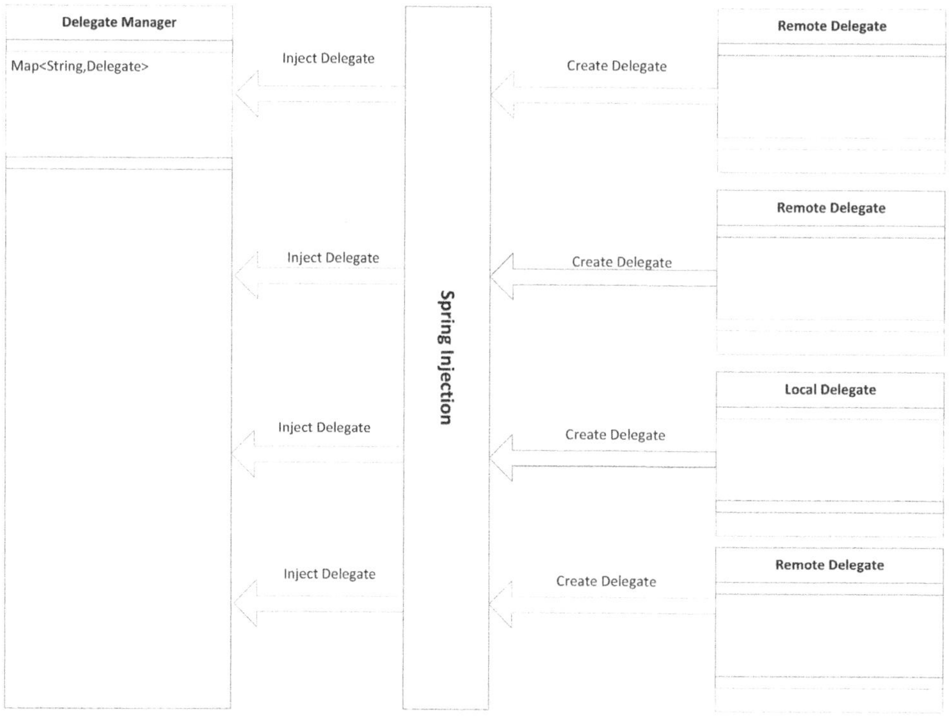

Example of Spring Configuration

```
<?xml version="1.0" encoding="UTF-8"?>
<!DOCTYPE beans PUBLIC "-//SPRING//DTD BEAN//EN"
"http://www.springframework.org/dtd/spring-beans.dtd">
<beans>

  <bean id="remoteExample1Delegate"
class="com.dth.example.delegate.RemoteExample1Delegate"/>
  <bean id="remoteExample2Delegate"
class="com.dth.example.delegate.RemoteExample2Delegate"/>
  <bean id="remoteExample3Delegate
class="com.dth.example.delegate.RemoteExample3Delegate"/>
  <bean id="localExample1Delegate"
class="com.dth.example.delegate.LocalExample1Delegate"/>

  <bean id="delegateManager" class="com.dth.fmw.delegate.DelegateManager">
    <constructor-arg>
```

```
    <map>
     <entry key="remoteExample1Delegate" value-ref="RemoteExample1Delegate"/>
     <entry key="remoteExample2Delegate" value-ref="RemoteExample1Delegate"/>
     <entry key="remoteExample3Delegate" value-ref="RemoteExample1Delegate"/>
     <entry key="localeExample1Delegate" value-ref="RemoteExample1Delegate"/>
    </map>
   </constructor-arg>
  </bean>
</beans>
```

Chapter 7 The Model Tier

7.1 Service Proxy

Overview:

The Service proxy acts as the bridge between the communication technology and the underlying software. In the case of a web service, the web service implementation would make a single call to the Service proxy to start the processing cycle. The Service Proxy has a single static method to start execution.

Objective:

The Objective of the Service Proxy is to provide a gateway into the Model Teir (business logic) of the system.

Responsibility:

The Service Proxy is responsible for running the command that will load and execute the initial Solution. Using the Module Abstract Class, the Service Proxy loads the Solution and execute the proper method.

Pattern Type:

The Service Proxy follows the design pattern proxy which is a place holder or a gateway to another object, or in this case, the Solution.

Structure:

Work Flow:

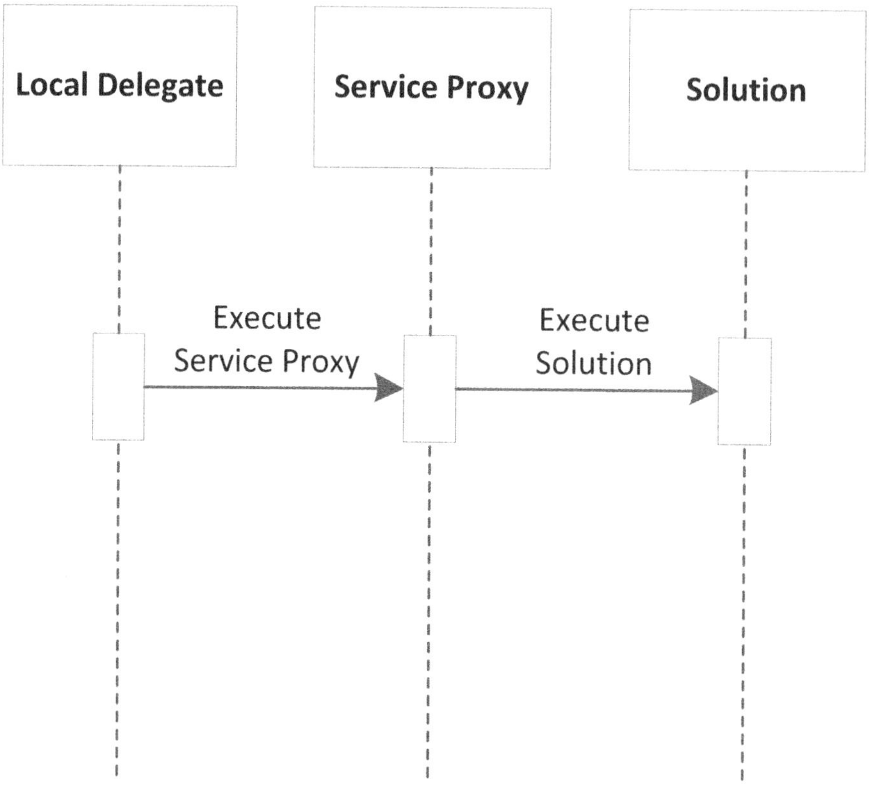
Local Delegate
Service Proxy
Solution
Execute Service Proxy
Execute Solution

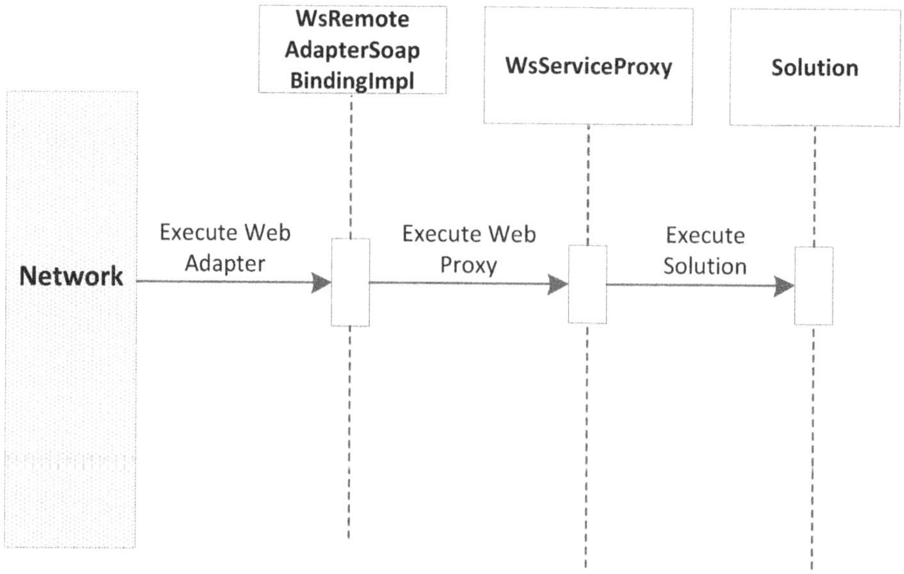
WsRemote AdapterSoap BindingImpl
WsServiceProxy
Solution
Network
Execute Web Adapter
Execute Web Proxy
Execute Solution

Code Sample:

```
public class ServiceProxy extends Module
{
 public static void execute(String mCmdSolutionId,CmdMsg aCmdMsg)
 {
  runCommand(ComponentType.SOLUTION.getName(),mCmdSolutionId,aCmdMsg);
  CmdManager.writeProfileTime();
 }

 @Override
 protected Class<?> getTheClass()
 {
  return ServiceProxy.class;
 }
}

public class WsServiceProxy extends ServiceProxy
{
 public static Response execute(Request aRequest) throws java.rmi.RemoteException
 {
  Response mRtnValue = new Response();
  CmdMsg mCmdMsg = new CommandMsg();
  WsRequestCmdMsg mReqCmdMsg = aRequest.getRequestCmdMsg();
  WsDTO mWsDTOs[] =mReqCmdMsg.getRequest();
  if(mWsDTOs != null && mWsDTOs.length>0)
  {
   for(WsDTO mWsDTO:mWsDTOs)
   {
    String mType = mWsDTO.getType();
    String mName = mWsDTO.getName();
    DTO mDTO = createDTO(mType);
    mCmdMsg.setRequest(mName, mDTO);
    WsValue mValues[] = mWsDTO.getData();
    if(mValues != null && mValues.length > 0)
    {
     for(WsValue mValue:mValues)
     {
      String mObjectValue = mValue.getValue();
      String mValueName = mValue.getName();
```

```
        setValue(mValueName,mDTO,mObjectValue);
       }
      }
     }
    }
    WsCommand[] mCommands = mReqCmdMsg.getCommand();
    if(mCommands != null && mCommands.length > 0)
    {
     for(WsCommand mCommand:mCommands)
     {
      String mTask = mCommand.getTask();
      execute(mTask,mCmdMsg);
     }
    }
    return mRtnValue;
   }

   public static void execute(String mCmdSolutionId,CmdMsg aCmdMsg)
   {
    runCommand(ComponentType.SOLUTION.getName(),mCmdSolutionId,aCmdMsg);
   }

   @Override
   protected Class<?> getTheClass()
   {
    return WsServiceProxy.class;
   }
  }
```

Dependency Injection:

None.

7.2 Module base class <abstract>

Overview:

This is an abstract class used by the framework to create and execute Components in the system. The Module uses the Factory Manager to create objects generated by the Spring framework. The class will also look up stored commands. Additionally, the Module Base has methods that will execute the component operations and the commands.

Objective:

The Objective of the Module base class is to have an abstract class with common behaviors that can be used but multiple components. This may include reflective type behavior such as creating a Data Transfer Object or using the framework to call the next component.

Responsibility:

The Responsibility of the Module base class is to provide services to other components and other Architecture artifacts.

Structure:

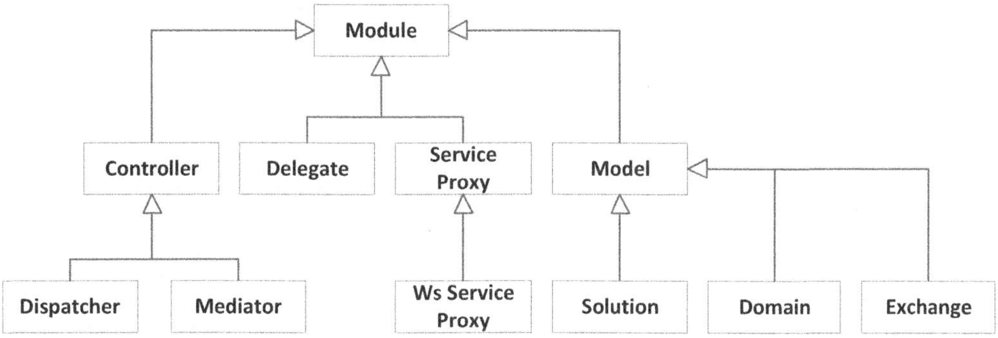

Code Sample:

```
public abstract class Module
{
   protected abstract Class<?> getTheClass();
  private static Map<Class<?>,Logger> logMap = new HashMap<Class<?>, Logger>();

  private static Logger log(Class<?> aClass)
  {
   Logger mRtnValue = logMap.get(aClass);
   if(mRtnValue == null)
   {
    Logger mLog = Logger.getLogger(aClass);
    logMap.put(aClass,mLog);
    mRtnValue = mLog;
   }
   return mRtnValue;
  }

  private Logger log()
  {
   return log(getTheClass());
  }

  protected void trace(String aMessage)
  {
   log().trace(aMessage);
  }

  public static void trace(Class<?> aClass,String aMessage)
  {
   log(aClass).trace(aMessage);
  }

  protected void debug(String aMessage)
  {
   log().debug(aMessage);
  }

  public static void debug(Class<?> aClass,String aMessage)
  {
   log(aClass).debug(aMessage);
```

```
}

protected void info(String aMessage)
{
 log().info(aMessage);
}

public static void info(Class<?> aClass,String aMessage)
{
 log(aClass).info(aMessage);
}

protected void warn(String aMessage)
{
 log().warn(aMessage);
}

public static void warn(Class<?> aClass,String aMessage)
{
 log(aClass).warn(aMessage);
}

protected void error(String aMessage)
{
 log().error(aMessage);
}

public static void error(Class<?> aClass,String aMessage)
{
 log(aClass).error(aMessage);
}

protected void fatal(String aMessage)
{
 log().fatal(aMessage);
}

public static void fatal(Class<?> aClass,String aMessage)
{
 log(aClass).fatal(aMessage);
}
```

```
 protected static void runCommand(String componentType,String
comandName,CmdMsg aCmdMsg)
 {
  List<CmdLibraryEntry> mCmdList =
getLibraryEntries(componentType,comandName);
  for(CmdLibraryEntry mCmdLibraryEntry:mCmdList)
  {
   Command mCommand = mCmdLibraryEntry.getCommand();
   aCmdMsg.addCommand(mCommand);
  }
  runCommand(aCmdMsg);
 }

 protected static void runCommand(Command aCmd,Component
aComponent,CmdMsg aCmdMsg)
 {
  CmdManager.runCommand(aCmd,aComponent,aCmdMsg);
 }

 protected static void runCommand(CmdMsg aCmdMsg)
 {
  CmdManager.runCommands(aCmdMsg);
 }

 public static List<CmdLibraryEntry> getLibraryEntries(String aType,String aId)
 {
  List<CmdLibraryEntry> mRtnValue = null;
  CmdLibrary mLibrary = getCommandLibrary(aType);
  if(mLibrary != null)
  {
   mRtnValue = mLibrary.getLibraryEntries(aId);
  }
  return mRtnValue;
 }

 public static CmdLibrary getCommandLibrary(String aKey)
 {
  return getCommandLibraryManger().getCommandLibrary(aKey);
 }

 protected static CmdLibraryManager getCommandLibraryManger()
 {
```

```
  return CmdLibraryManager.getInstance();
}

public static void setValue(String aName,Object aObject,Object aValue)
{
  String mMethodName = modifyPrefix("set",aName);
  Class<?> mClass = null;
  if(aValue != null) mClass = aValue.getClass();
  Method mMethod = getMethod(aObject,mMethodName,mClass);
  Object[] mParams = new Object[1];
  mParams[0] = aValue;
  setValue(aObject,mMethod,mParams);
}

public static void setValue(Object aObject,Method aMethod,Object[] aArgs)
{
  try
  {
    aMethod.invoke(aObject, aArgs);
  }
  catch(Exception aException)
  {
    throw new ModelException(aException);
  }
}

public static String modifyPrefix(String aPrefix,String aName)
{
  StringBuilder mRtnValue = new StringBuilder();
  String mPrefix = "";
  if(aName.length()>aPrefix.length())
  {
    mPrefix = aName.substring(0,aPrefix.length());
  }
  if(mPrefix.equals(aPrefix))
  {
    mRtnValue.append(aName);
  }
  else
  {
    mRtnValue.append(aPrefix);
    mRtnValue.append(aName.substring(0,1).toUpperCase());
```

```
    mRtnValue.append(aName.substring(1));
  }
  return mRtnValue.toString();
 }

 public static Method getMethod(Object aObject,String aMethodName,Class<?>
aParamTypes)
 {
  Class<?>[] mParamTypes = new Class<?>[1];
  mParamTypes[0] = aParamTypes;
  return getMethod(aObject,aMethodName,mParamTypes);
 }

 public static Method getMethod(Object aObject,String aMethodName,Class<?>[]
aParamTypes)
 {
  Method mRtnValue = null;
  Class<?> mObjectClass = aObject.getClass();
  mRtnValue = getMethod(mObjectClass,aMethodName,aParamTypes);
  return mRtnValue;
 }
  public static void callBack(Object aObject,String aPostFix,Object... args) throws
IllegalArgumentException, IllegalAccessException, InvocationTargetException
 {
  Class<?>[] aParamTypes = new Class<?>[args.length];
  int mCount = 0;
  for(Object mObject: args)
  {
   aParamTypes[mCount++] = mObject.getClass();
  }
  Method mMethod = getCallBackMethod(aObject,aPostFix,aParamTypes);
  mMethod.invoke(aObject,args);
 }
  public static Method getCallBackMethod(Object aObject,String aPostFix,Class<?>[]
aParamTypes)
 {
  Method mRtnValue = null;
  StackTraceElement[] mElements = Thread.currentThread().getStackTrace();
  for(StackTraceElement mSTE: mElements)
  {
   String mMethodName = mSTE.getMethodName();
   if(mMethodName.endsWith(aPostFix))
```

```
    {
      mRtnValue = getMethod(aObject,mMethodName,aParamTypes);
    }
    if(mRtnValue != null) break;
  }
  return mRtnValue;
}

public static DTO createDTO(String aClassPath)
{
  DTO mRtnValue = null;
  try
  {
    Class<?> mClass = Class.forName(aClassPath);
    Object mObject = mClass.newInstance();
    if(mObject instanceof DTO)
    {
      mRtnValue = (DTO) mObject;
    }
  }
  catch (ClassNotFoundException aException)
  {
    aException.printStackTrace();
  }
  catch (InstantiationException aException)
  {
    aException.printStackTrace();
  }
  catch (IllegalAccessException aException)
  {
    aException.printStackTrace();
  }
  return mRtnValue;
}}
```

7.3 Model base class <abstract>

Overview:

An Abstract Class that the Components of the Model must all inherit; its main method is the execute method. The execute method wraps the execute call inside of a try catch block. In the event of an exception being thrown, the execute method will catch it and if it is the top of the call stack for that layer, it will call the Exception Handler Manager to process the exception. If no exception is caught, the execute method will call the following methods in order: pre-Process, process, and post-Process. The pre-process and post-Process methods are empty and are there in the event that any sub class should need them. The process method attempts to process the call using the command sent to the execute method. If the process method can determine which method to call using the command, it does so and then returns control back to the execute method. If it cannot determine what method to call, control is passed to the doWork method.

Objective:

The Objective of the Module abstract class is to provide a facade for all of the Model layer components. This allows each of the components to share common behaviors such as exception handling.

Responsibility:

The Model abstract class is responsible for providing a unformed look and feel for all Model layer components so they can share similar features.

Pattern Type:

The Model abstract base class uses the facade pattern to provide a similar interface to all other call components.

Structure:

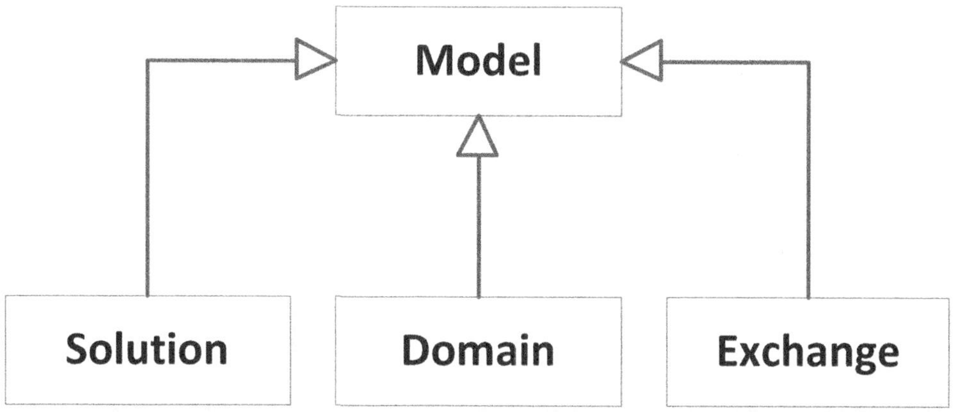

Code Sample:

```
public abstract class Model extends Module implements Component
{
 protected abstract ThreadLocal<Integer> getModelCount();
 protected abstract ExceptionHandlerManager getExceptionHandlerManager();
 protected abstract ComponentType getSubType();

 private List<CmdComponent> cmdComponents = null;;

 public void setCmdComponents(List<CmdComponent> aCmdComponent)
 {
  cmdComponents = Collections.unmodifiableList(aCmdComponent);
 }

 @Operation(action="runComponents")
 public void runComponents(Command aCommand,CmdMsg aCmdMsg)
 {
  runCmdComponents(aCmdMsg);
 }


 public void runCmdComponents(CmdMsg aCmdMsg)
 {
  if(cmdComponents != null)
  {
   for(CmdComponent mCmdComponent:cmdComponents)
   {

runCommand(mCmdComponent.getCommand(),mCmdComponent.getComponent(),aC
mdMsg);
   }
  }
 }

 public void runCmdComponents(CmdComponent aCmdComponent,CmdMsg
aCmdMsg)
 {
        runCommand(aCmdComponent.getCommand(),aCmdComponent.getCompone
nt(),aCmdMsg);
 }
```

```
protected int getComponentCount()
{
  int mRtnValue = 0;
  ThreadLocal<Integer> mModelCount = getModelCount();
  mRtnValue = mModelCount.get();
  return mRtnValue;
}

protected int incrementComponentCount()
{
        int mRtnValue = 0;
 ThreadLocal<Integer> mModelCount = getModelCount();
 mRtnValue = mModelCount.get();
 mRtnValue++;
 mModelCount.set(mRtnValue);
        return mRtnValue;
}

protected int decrementComponentCount()
{
 int mRtnValue = 0;
 ThreadLocal<Integer> mModelCount = getModelCount();
 mRtnValue = mModelCount.get();
 mRtnValue--;
 mModelCount.set(mRtnValue);
 return mRtnValue;
}

public void execute(Command aCommand,CmdMsg aCmdMsg)
{
 incrementComponentCount();
 try
 {
  preProcess(aCommand,aCmdMsg);
  process(aCommand,aCmdMsg);
  postProcess(aCommand,aCmdMsg);
 }
 catch(Throwable aThrowable)
 {
  if(getComponentCount() == 1)
  {
   try
```

```
      {
       abortProcess(aCommand, aCmdMsg);
       if(getExceptionHandlerManager() == null)
       {
        throw new ModelException(aThrowable);
       }
       else
       {
        getExceptionHandlerManager().handle(aCmdMsg,aThrowable);
       }

      }
      catch(Throwable aException)
      {
       throw new ModelException(aThrowable);
      }
     }
     else
     {
      if(aThrowable instanceof RuntimeException)
      {
       throw(RuntimeException)aThrowable;
      }
      else
      {
       throw new ModelException(aThrowable);
      }
     }
   }
   decrementComponentCount();
 }

 protected void preProcess(Command aCommand,CmdMsg aCmdMsg)
 {
  // Left Intentionally empty
 }

 protected void process(Command aCommand,CmdMsg aCmdMsg)
 {
  if(!CmdManager.doOperation(aCommand, this, aCmdMsg))
  {
   doWork(aCommand,aCmdMsg);
```

```
  }
 }

 protected void postProcess(Command aCommand,CmdMsg aCmdMsg)
 {
  // Left Intentionally empty
 }

 protected void abortProcess(Command aCommand,CmdMsg aCmdMsg)
 {
  // Left Intentionally empty
 }

 protected void doWork(Command aCommand,CmdMsg aCmdMsg)
 {
  // Left Intentionally empty
 }

 protected void runChildrenCommands(Command aCommand,CmdMsg aCmdMsg)
 {
  Collection<Command> mCommands = aCommand.getChildren();
  for(Command mCommand:mCommands)
  {
   CmdManager.runCommand(mCommand, aCmdMsg);
  }
 }
}
```

7.4 Solution Layer

Overview:

The Solution component is the top layer of the SoC and is used to run business logic. If the business logic can be contained in a single Domain object, then the Solution is mostly a pass-through. Logic that spans disjointed Domains/Business logic is always run in the Solution layer.

Objective:

The Object of the Solution component to provide a solution to a business problem; to solve a business problem, the solution will use one or more Domains to solve domain level logic problems. If there is logic that spans multiple domains or if there is any correlation to be done between domains, it is the responsibility of the Solution component to act as the coordinator of the business logic.

Responsibility:

The solution layer creates a cohesive interface between the outside word by way of the Service proxy and the internals of the Model. The Solution Layer is responsible for creating completed solution to a business problem.

Structure:

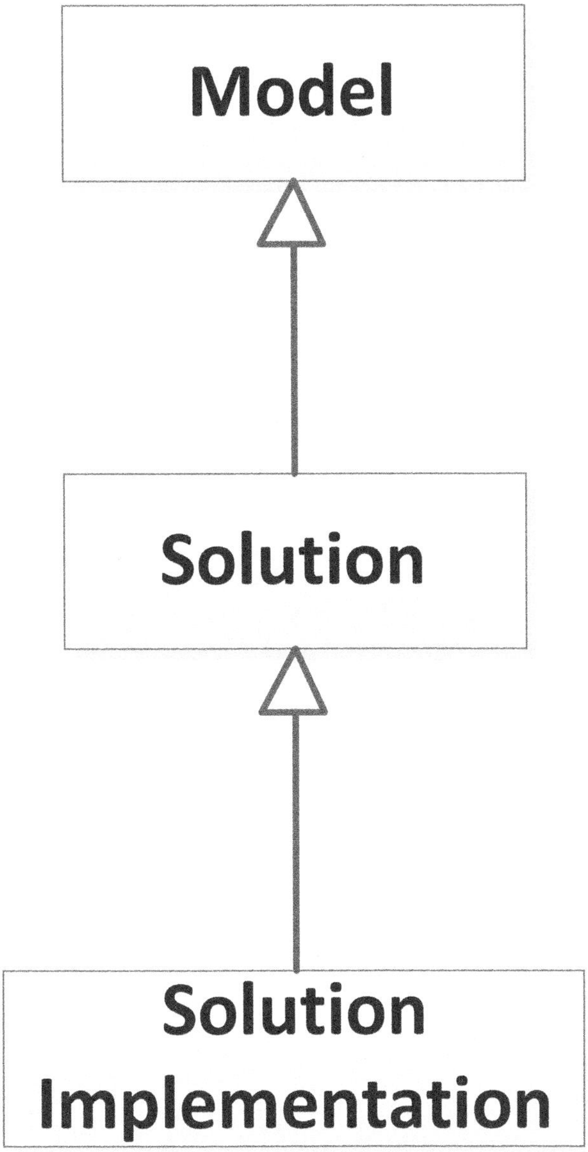

Work Flow:

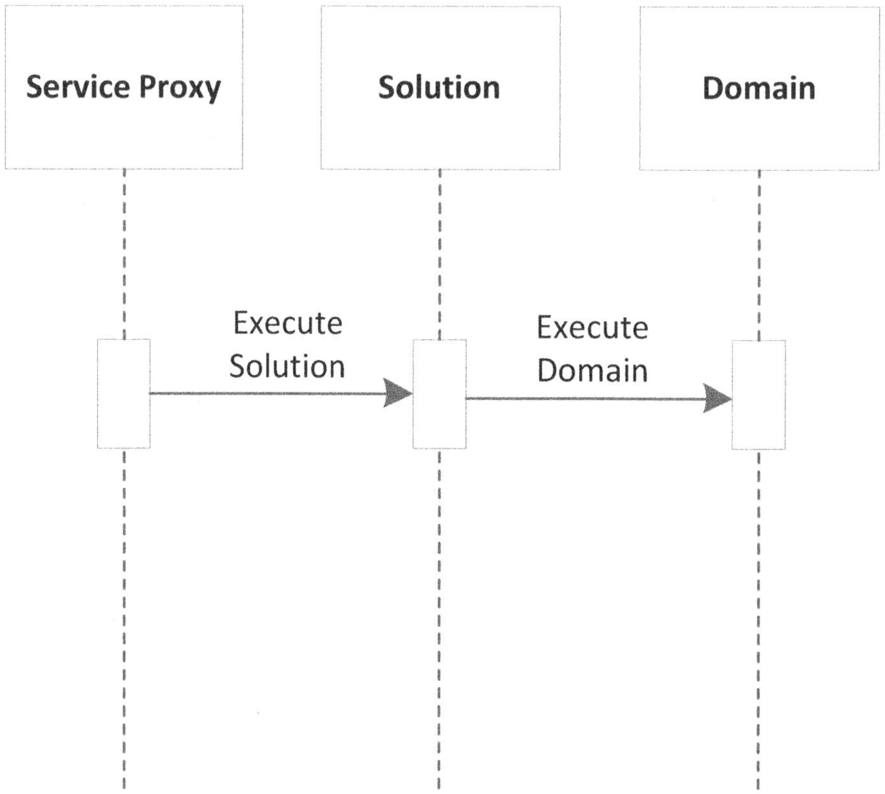
Service Proxy
Solution
Domain
Execute
Solution
Execute
Domain

Code Sample:

```
public abstract class Solution extends Model
{
 private static ExceptionHandlerManager exceptionHandlerManager;

 private static ThreadLocal<Integer> solutionCount = new ThreadLocal<Integer>();

 public ThreadLocal<Integer> getModelCount()
 {
  if(solutionCount.get() == null)
  {
   solutionCount.set(0);
  }
  return solutionCount;
 }

 protected ExceptionHandlerManager getExceptionHandlerManager()
 {
  return exceptionHandlerManager;
 }

 protected ComponentType getSubType()
 {
  return ComponentType.DOMAIN;
 }

 public void commit(CmdMsg aCmdMsg)
 {
  DTOSession mDTOSession = getSession(aCmdMsg);
  if(mDTOSession != null)
  {
   mDTOSession.commit();
   mDTOSession.close();
  }
 }

 public void commitNoClose(CmdMsg aCmdMsg)
 {
  DTOSession mDTOSession = getSession(aCmdMsg);
  if(mDTOSession != null)
  {
```

```
      mDTOSession.commit();
    }
  }

  public void rollback(CmdMsg aCmdMsg)
  {
    DTOSession mDTOSession = getSession(aCmdMsg);
    if(mDTOSession != null)
    {
      mDTOSession.rollback();
      mDTOSession.close();
    }
  }

  public DTOSession getSession(CmdMsg aCmdMsg)
  {
    DTOSession mRtnValue = null;
    DTO mDTO = aCmdMsg.getSession(DTOSession.key);
    if(mDTO instanceof DTOSession)
    {
      mRtnValue = (DTOSession)mDTO;
    }
    return mRtnValue;
  }

  public void postProcess(Command aCommand,CmdMsg aCmdMsg)
  {
    commit(aCmdMsg);
  }

  public void abortProcess(Command aCommand,CmdMsg aCmdMsg)
  {
    rollback(aCmdMsg);
  }

  @Override
  protected Class<?> getTheClass()
  {
    return Solution.class;
  }
}
```

```
public class SolutionGeneric extends Solution
{
 @Operation(action="generic")
 public void genericMethod(Command aCommand,CmdMsg aCmdMsg)
 {
  runCmdComponents(aCmdMsg);
 }
}
```

Dependency Injection:

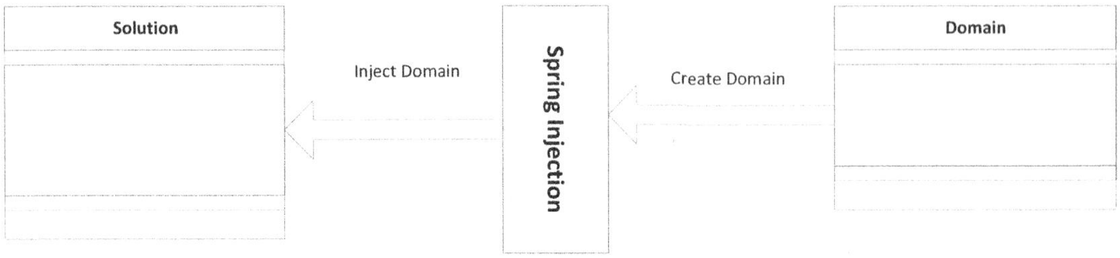

7.5 Domain Layer

Overview:

The Domain component contains related business logic. Such as User information Object and all of the methods associated directly with the object. Domain objects can be associate with other domain objects if there is a direct business relationship such as a manager to an employee.

Objective:

The Objective of the Domain component is to encapsulate business logic that is closely related such as employees in a group.

Responsibility:

The Domain component is responsible for providing concrete domain business logic that is logically group by related behavior.

Structure:

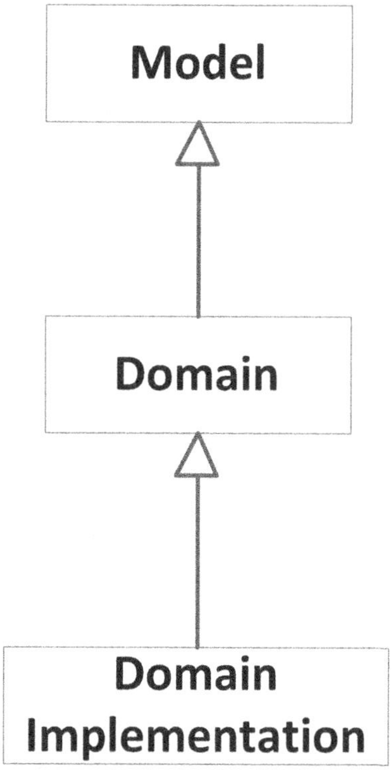

Work Flow:

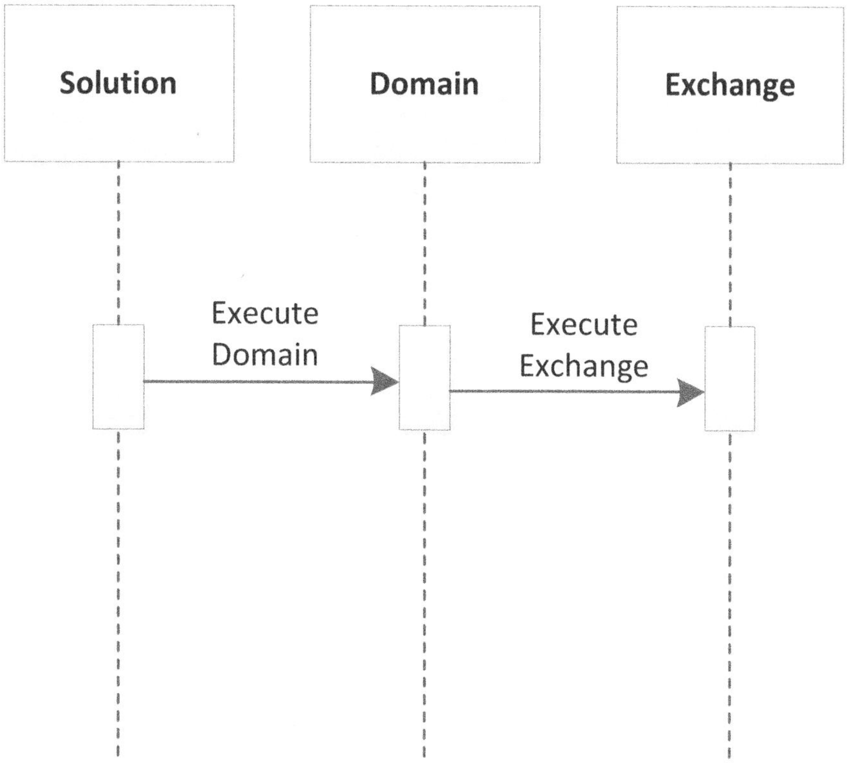
Solution
Domain
Exchange
Execute Domain
Execute Exchange

Code Sample:

```
public abstract class Domain extends Model
{
 private static ExceptionHandlerManager exceptionHandlerManager;

 private static ThreadLocal<Integer> domainCount = new ThreadLocal<Integer>();

 public ThreadLocal<Integer> getModelCount()
 {
  if(domainCount.get() == null)
  {
   domainCount.set(0);
  }
  return domainCount;
 }

 protected ExceptionHandlerManager getExceptionHandlerManager()
 {
  return exceptionHandlerManager;
 }

 protected ComponentType getSubType()
 {
  return ComponentType.EXCHANGE;
 }

 @Override
 protected Class<?> getTheClass()
 {
  return Domain.class;
 }
}


public class DomainGeneric extends Domain
{
 @Operation(action="generic")
 public void genericMethod(Command aCommand,CmdMsg aCmdMsg)
 {
  runCmdComponents(aCmdMsg);
 }
```

```
}

public class ExampleDomain extends Domain
{
 private CmdComponent storeDTOExampleCmdComponent;

 @Operation(action="copyRecordExample")
 public void copyRecordExample(Command aCommand,CmdMsg aCmdMsg)
 {
  DataTransfer mDTO = aCmdMsg.getRequest("exampleDTO);
  if(mDTO instanceof DTOExample)
  {
   DTOExample mDTOExample1 = (DTOExample)mDTO;
   DTOExample mDTOExample2 = copyDTOExample(mDTOExample1);
   mDTOExample2.setId(null); //force new insert
   storeRecord(aCmdMsg,mDTOExample2);
  }
 }

 private DTOExample copyDTOExample(DTOExample aInputRec)
 {
  DTOExample mRtnValue = new DTOExample();
  if(aInputRec != null)
  {
   MetaProcess.copy(aInputRec,mRtnValue);
  }
  return mRtnValue;
 }

 private void storeRecord(CmdMsg aCmdMsg,DTOExample aDTOExample)
 {
  Cmd mCommand = new Cmd();
  mCommand.setOperation("generic");
  aCmdMsg.setRequest("DTOExampleToCopy",aDTOExample);
  runCmdComponents(storeDTOExampleCmdComponent, aCmdMsg);
 }


        public CmdComponent
getStoreDTOExampleCmdComponentCmdComponent()
        {
                return storeDTOExampleCmdComponent;
```

```
        }

        public void
setStoreDTOExampleCmdComponentCmdComponent(CmdComponent
storeDTOExampleCmdComponent)
        {
                this.storeDTOExampleCmdComponent =
storeDTOExampleCmdComponent;
        }
}
```

Dependency Injection:

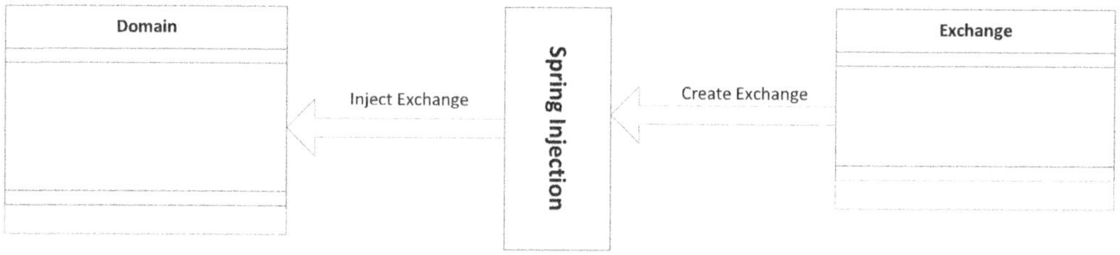

7.6 Exchange Layer

Overview:

The Exchange Component works in conjunction with the DAO. The Exchange Component wraps a DAO in order to separate the DAO technology from the Framework. The Exchange component receives a request from the Domain object using a Command Message Object and preps and the information for the DAO. The DAO is then called to do the real processing.

Objective:

The Objective of the Exchange is to act as a bridge between the technology used in the Framework and the Technology to access data from its repository (usually a database). This allows the DAO to utilize any technology that the project considers important such as a ORM like Hibernate.

Responsibility:

It is the responsibility of the Exchange to isolate the framework implementation code from the implementation of the data access and its underlying technology. This way, the data access technology can be changed without effecting the rest of the system.

Pattern Type:

The Exchange uses the Adapter Pattern to change the interface of the Data Access Object to the Interface that the Framework implementation can understand, thus providing a consistent facade throughout the system.

Structure:

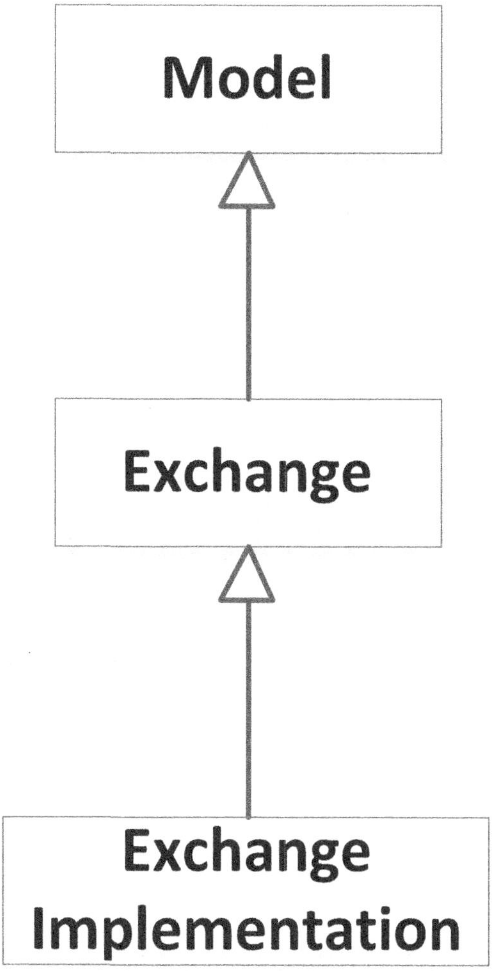

Work Flow:

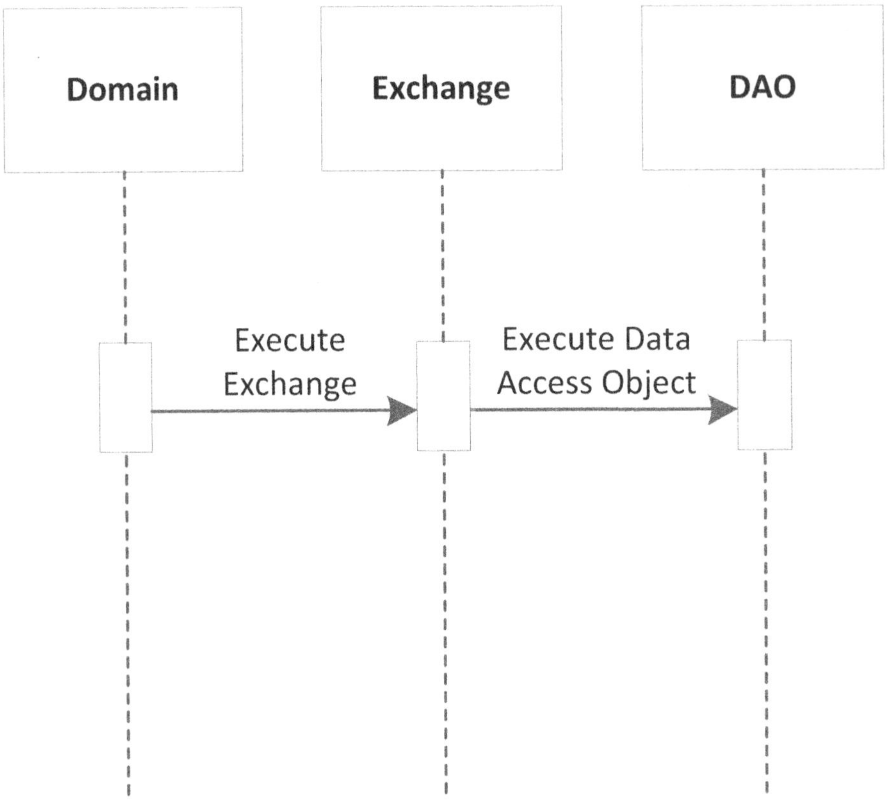
Domain
Exchange
DAO
Execute
Exchange
Execute Data
Access Object

Code Sample:

```
public abstract class Exchange extends Model
{
 private static ExceptionHandlerManager exceptionHandlerManager;

 private static ThreadLocal<Integer> exchangeCount = new ThreadLocal<Integer>();

 public ThreadLocal<Integer> getModelCount()
 {
  if(exchangeCount.get() == null)
  {
   exchangeCount.set(0);
  }
  return exchangeCount;
 }

 protected ExceptionHandlerManager getExceptionHandlerManager()
 {
  return exceptionHandlerManager;
 }

 protected ComponentType getSubType()
 {
  return ComponentType.UNKNOWN;
 }
}

public class ExchangeGeneric extends Exchange
{
 private DataAccess dataAccess;

 public void setDataAccess(DataAccess aDataAccess)
 {
  dataAccess = aDataAccess;
 }

 public void process(Command aCommand,CmdMsg aCmdMsg)
 {
  dataAccess.execute(aCommand,aCmdMsg);
 }
```

```
 @Operation(action="generic")
 public Object genericMethod(Command aCommand,CmdMsg aCmdMsg)
 {
  dataAccess.execute(aCommand,aCmdMsg);
  return null;
 }

 @Override
 protected Class<?> getTheClass()
 {
  return ExchangeGeneric.class;
 }
}


public class ExchangeGenericUsingCmd extends Exchange
{
 private DataAccess dataAccess;
 private Command command;

 public void setDao(DataAccess aDao)
 {
  dataAccess = aDao;
 }

 public void setCommand(Command aCommand)
 {
  command = aCommand;
 }

 @Operation(action="generic")
 public void genericMethod(Command aCommand,CmdMsg aCmdMsg)
 {
  dataAccess.execute(command, aCmdMsg);
 }

 @Override
 protected Class<?> getTheClass()
 {
  return ExchangeGenericUsingCmd.class;
 }
}
```

Dependency Injection:

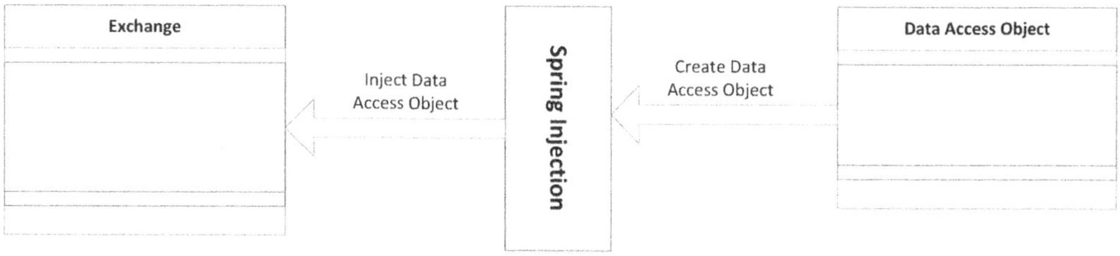

7.7 Data Access Objects

Overview:

The DAO Objects are a set of objects used to communicate with external systems such as databases using appropriate technology. In this system, we are using Hibernate to communicate with the database. The DAO encapsulates the Hibernate APIs isolating the developer from the underlying technology. Unlike the Solution, Domain, or the Exchange, the DAO does not necessarily need to follow any certain pattern. However, the system uses Hibernate Generic pattern to limit the amount of code the develop needs to generate. This pattern also predefines a set of methods.

Objective:

The Objective of the Data Access Object is to provide a way of injecting different types of technology for accessing data into the system. By implementing the DataAccess interface, the system can process almost any type of technology a development team desires.

Responsibility:

The Data Access Object (DAO) is responsible for accessing external data from the system such as a database. It can utilize such technology such as an Object Relationship Mapper (ORM) like hibernate, or it can use simple JDBC calls (not recommended). The DAO can be used to access flat files or they can be used to send JMS messages.

Pattern Type:

While the DAO does not require the use of the DAOGeneric Object, it is recommended that it be used. The DAOGeneric Object follows the Generic DAO Pattern.

Structure:

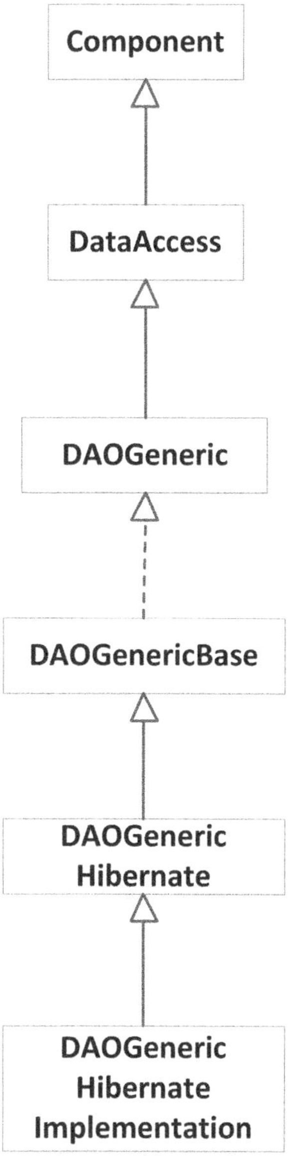
Component
DataAccess
DAOGeneric
DAOGenericBase
DAOGeneric Hibernate
DAOGeneric Hibernate Implementation

Work Flow:

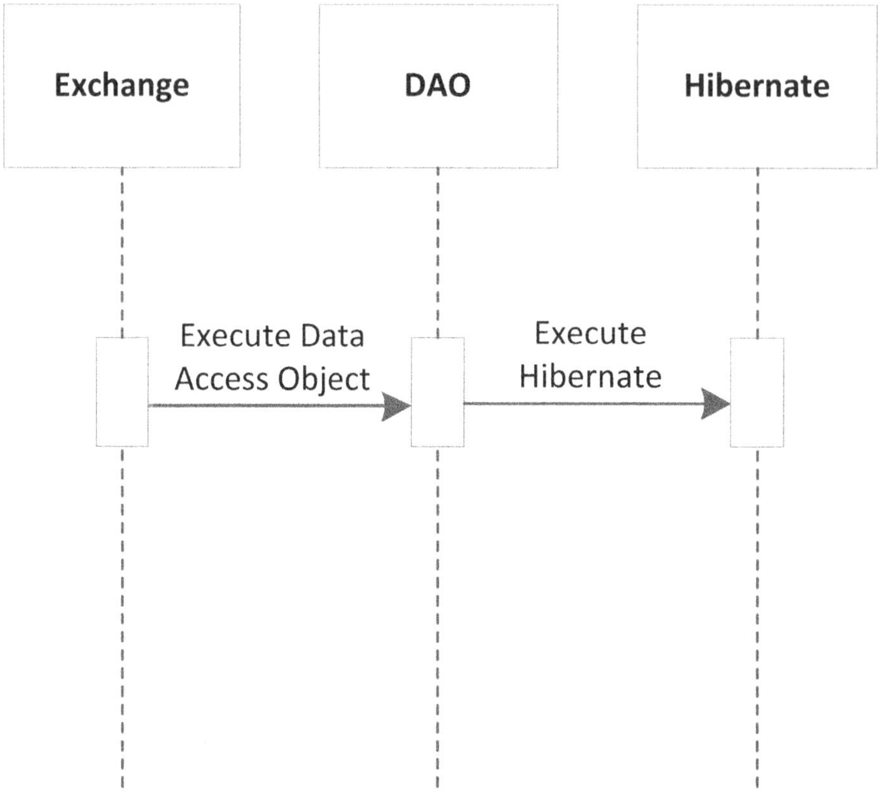
Exchange
DAO
Hibernate
Execute Data Access Object
Execute Hibernate

Code Sample:

```
public interface DataAccess extends Component
{
 //Intentionally left blank
}

public interface DAOGeneric<VO, KEY extends Serializable> extends DataAccess
{
 public VO findByKey(KEY aKey,CmdMsg aCmdMsg);

 public Collection<VO> findAll(CmdMsg aCmdMsg);

 public Collection<VO> findByQuery(CmdQuery aCmdQuery,CmdMsg aCmdMsg);

 public Collection<VO> findByQuery(CmdMsg aCmdMsg,String
aName,KeyValue<Object>... aKeyValue);

 public Collection<VO> findByExample(VO aExample,CmdMsg aCmdMsg);

 public VO makePersistent(VO aValueObject,CmdMsg aCmdMsg);

 public void makeTransient(VO aValueObject,CmdMsg aCmdMsg);

}

public abstract class DAOGenericBase <VO, KEY extends Serializable> extends Validate
implements DAOGeneric<VO, KEY>
{
 protected Object getRequestObject(String aKey,CmdMsg aCmdMsg)
 {
  Object mRtnValue = null;
  String mProcessValue = aKey;
  boolean mContinue = true;
  while(mContinue)
  {
   String mKey = getPrefixKey(mProcessValue);
   DTO mDTO = aCmdMsg.getRequest(mKey);
   if(mDTO instanceof DTOValues)
   {
    mProcessValue = getPostfixKey(mProcessValue);
    String mValueKey = getPrefixKey(mProcessValue);
```

```
      DTOValues mDTOValues = (DTOValues)mDTO;
      mRtnValue = mDTOValues.getValue(mValueKey);
    }
    else if(mDTO != null)
    {
      mProcessValue = getPostfixKey(mProcessValue);
      String mValueKey = getPrefixKey(mProcessValue);
      mRtnValue = MetaProcess.getData(mValueKey, mDTO);
    }
    else
    {
      mContinue = false;
    }
  }
  return mRtnValue;
}

private String getPrefixKey(String aKey)
{
  String mRtnValue = aKey;
  int mIndex = aKey.indexOf('.');
  if(mIndex>-1)
  {
    mRtnValue = aKey.substring(0,mIndex);
  }
  return mRtnValue;
}

private String getPostfixKey(String aKey)
{
  String mRtnValue = null;
  int mIndex = aKey.indexOf('.');
  if(mIndex > -1)
  {
    mRtnValue = aKey.substring(mIndex+1);
  }
  return mRtnValue;
}
}

public class DAOGenericHibernate<VO, KEY extends Serializable> extends
DAOGenericBase<VO,KEY>
```

```
{
 private Class<VO> persistentClass;
 private SessionFactory sessionFactory;
 private DTO dtoPrototype;
 private Map<String,DeclaredQueryColumn> columnMap = null;

 private class DeclaredQueryColumn
 {
  private String fieldName = null;
  private String columnName = null;
  private Class<?> fieldType = null;

  public String getFieldName()
  {
   return fieldName;
  }
 }


 public void setSessionFactory(SessionFactory aSessionFactory)
 {
  sessionFactory = aSessionFactory;
 }

 protected DTOHibernateSession getSession(CmdMsg aCmdMsg)
 {
  DTOHibernateSession mSession = null;
  DTO mDTO = aCmdMsg.getSession(DTOSession.key);
  if(mDTO instanceof DTOHibernateSession)
  {
   mSession = (DTOHibernateSession)mDTO;
  }
  else
  {
   mSession = new DTOHibernateSession();
   aCmdMsg.setSession(DTOSession.key, mSession);
  }
  return mSession;
 }

 private void startTransaction(CmdMsg aCmdMsg)
 {
```

```
  DTOHibernateSession mSession = getSession(aCmdMsg);
  mSession.startTransaction(sessionFactory);
}

public void setPersistentClass(Class<VO> aPersistentClass)
{
  persistentClass = aPersistentClass;
}

public Class<VO> getPersistentClass()
{
  return persistentClass;
}

@SuppressWarnings("unchecked")
public VO findByKey(KEY aKey,CmdMsg aCmdMsg)
{
  DTOHibernateSession mDTOHibernateSession = getSession(aCmdMsg);
  Session mSession = mDTOHibernateSession.getSession(sessionFactory);
  Class<VO> mPersistentClass = getPersistentClass();
  return (VO)mSession.load(mPersistentClass,aKey);
}

public List<VO> findAll(CmdMsg aCmdMsg)
{
  return findByCriteria(aCmdMsg);
}

@SuppressWarnings("unchecked")
public List<VO> findByExample(VO aExample,CmdMsg aCmdMsg)
{
  DTOHibernateSession mDTOHibernateSession = getSession(aCmdMsg);
  Session mSession = mDTOHibernateSession.getSession(sessionFactory);
  Criteria mCritiera = mSession.createCriteria(getPersistentClass());
  return mCritiera.list();
}

@SuppressWarnings("unchecked")
public List<VO> findByExample(VO aValueObject,String[]
aExcludeProperites,CmdMsg aCmdMsg)
{
  DTOHibernateSession mDTOHibernateSession = getSession(aCmdMsg);
```

```
  Session mSession = mDTOHibernateSession.getSession(sessionFactory);
  Criteria mCritiera = mSession.createCriteria(getPersistentClass());
  Example mExample = Example.create(aValueObject);
  for(String mExcludeProperty:aExcludeProperites)
  {
   mExample.excludeProperty(mExcludeProperty);
  }
  mCritiera.add(mExample);
  return mCritiera.list();
}

public VO makePersistent(VO aValueObject,CmdMsg aCmdMsg)
{
  DTOHibernateSession mDTOHibernateSession = getSession(aCmdMsg);
  Session mSession = mDTOHibernateSession.getSession(sessionFactory);
  startTransaction(aCmdMsg);
  mSession.saveOrUpdate(aValueObject);
  return aValueObject;
}

public VO save(VO aValueObject,CmdMsg aCmdMsg)
{
  DTOHibernateSession mDTOHibernateSession = getSession(aCmdMsg);
  Session mSession = mDTOHibernateSession.getSession(sessionFactory);
  startTransaction(aCmdMsg);
  mSession.save(aValueObject);
  return aValueObject;
}

public void makeTransient(VO aValueObject,CmdMsg aCmdMsg)
{
  DTOHibernateSession mDTOHibernateSession = getSession(aCmdMsg);
  Session mSession = mDTOHibernateSession.getSession(sessionFactory);
  startTransaction(aCmdMsg);
  mSession.delete(aValueObject);
}

public void flush(CmdMsg aCmdMsg)
{
  DTOHibernateSession mDTOHibernateSession = getSession(aCmdMsg);
  Session mSession = mDTOHibernateSession.getSession(sessionFactory);
  mSession.flush();
```

```
}

public void clear(CmdMsg aCmdMsg)
{
  DTOHibernateSession mDTOHibernateSession = getSession(aCmdMsg);
  Session mSession = mDTOHibernateSession.getSession(sessionFactory);
  mSession.clear();
}


@SuppressWarnings("unchecked")
public List<VO> findByQuery(CmdQuery aCmdQuery,CmdMsg aCmdMsg)
{
  DTOHibernateSession mDTOHibernateSession = getSession(aCmdMsg);
  Session mSession = mDTOHibernateSession.getSession(sessionFactory);
  Query mQuery = mSession.getNamedQuery(aCmdQuery.getNamedQueryName());
  for(KeyValue<String> mKeyValue: aCmdQuery.getKeys())
  {
    String mName = mKeyValue.getId();
    Object mRequestObject = getRequestObject(mKeyValue.getValue(),aCmdMsg);
    if(mRequestObject instanceof KeyValue)
    {
      mRequestObject = ((KeyValue<Object>)mRequestObject).getValue();
    }
    mQuery.setParameter(mName, mRequestObject);
  }
  List<VO> mResults = (List<VO>)mQuery.list();
  return mResults;
}

@SuppressWarnings("unchecked")
public List<VO> findByQuery(CmdDeclaredQuery aCmdDeclaredQuery,CmdMsg
aCmdMsg)
{
  DTOHibernateSession mDTOHibernateSession = getSession(aCmdMsg);
  Session mSession = mDTOHibernateSession.getSession(sessionFactory);
  String mSQL = "";
  StringBuilder mSQLBuilder = null;
  String mKey = aCmdDeclaredQuery.getDeclaredQueryName();
  String mDeclaredQueryString = Declarations.getQuery(mKey);
  mSQLBuilder = new StringBuilder(mDeclaredQueryString);
  for(KeyValue<String> mKeyValue: aCmdDeclaredQuery.getKeys())
```

```
{
 Object mRequestObject = getRequestObject(mKeyValue.getValue(),aCmdMsg);
 setNativeParameters(mSQLBuilder,mKeyValue.getId(), mRequestObject);
}
mSQL = mSQLBuilder.toString();
List<VO> mResults = new ArrayList<VO>();
try
{
 //Query query = mSession.createSQLQuery(mSQLBuilder.toString());
 Query query = mSession.createSQLQuery(mSQL);
 List<Object[]> mResultList = query.list();
 int mStart = mSQL.toUpperCase().indexOf("SELECT ");
 int mEnd = mSQL.toUpperCase().indexOf("FROM");
 String mColumnString = mSQL.substring(mStart+7, mEnd);
 List<String> mColumnRawList = MetaProcess.parseComma(mColumnString);
 List<String> mColumnList = new ArrayList<String>();
 for(String mColumnToken:mColumnRawList)
 {
  String mColumnTemp = mColumnToken;
  int mIndex = -1;
  while((mIndex = mColumnTemp.toUpperCase().indexOf(" AS ")) > -1)
  {
   mColumnTemp = mColumnTemp.substring(mIndex+4);
  }
  mColumnList.add(mColumnTemp.trim());
 }
 if(columnMap == null)
 {
  columnMap = getColumns();
 }
 for(Object[] row:mResultList)
 {
  int mIndex = 0;
  VO mValueObject = persistentClass.newInstance();
  mResults.add(mValueObject);
  for(Object mColumnData:row)
  {
   String mColumnName = mColumnList.get(mIndex++);
   DeclaredQueryColumn mDQColumn = columnMap.get(mColumnName);
   if(mDQColumn != null)
   {
    String mPropertyName = mDQColumn.getFieldName();
```

```
        Class<?> mParamType = mDQColumn.fieldType;
        MetaProcess.setData(mPropertyName, mValueObject, mParamType,
mColumnData, false);
       }
      }
     }
    }
    catch(Throwable aThrowable)
    {
     throw new ModelException(aThrowable);
    }
    return mResults;
  }

  private Map<String,DeclaredQueryColumn> getColumns()
  {
    Map<String,DeclaredQueryColumn> mRtnValue = new
HashMap<String,DeclaredQueryColumn>();
    Field[] mFields = persistentClass.getDeclaredFields();
    for(Field mField:mFields)
    {
     Annotation[] mAnnotations = mField.getAnnotations();
     for(Annotation mAnnotation:mAnnotations)
     {
      if(mAnnotation instanceof DeclaredColumn)
      {
       DeclaredQueryColumn mDeclaredQueryColumn = new DeclaredQueryColumn();
       DeclaredColumn mDeclaredColumn = (DeclaredColumn)mAnnotation;
       mDeclaredQueryColumn.columnName = mDeclaredColumn.name();
       mDeclaredQueryColumn.fieldType = mField.getType();
       mDeclaredQueryColumn.fieldName = mField.getName();
       mRtnValue.put(mDeclaredQueryColumn.columnName,
mDeclaredQueryColumn);
      }
     }
    }
    return mRtnValue;
  }



  @SuppressWarnings("unchecked")
```

```
 public List<VO> findByQuery(CmdMsg aCmdMsg,String aName,KeyValue<Object>...
aKeyValues)
 {
  DTOHibernateSession mDTOHibernateSession = getSession(aCmdMsg);
  Session mSession = mDTOHibernateSession.getSession(sessionFactory);
  Query mQuery = mSession.getNamedQuery(aName);
  for(KeyValue<Object> mKeyValue: aKeyValues)
  {
   mQuery.setParameter(mKeyValue.getId(), mKeyValue.getValue());
  }
  List<VO>  mResults = (List<VO>)mQuery.list();
  return mResults;
 }

 public List<VO> findByNativeSQL(CmdMsg aCmdMsg,CmdDynamicQuery
aCmdDynamicQuery)
 {
  DTOHibernateSession mDTOHibernateSession = getSession(aCmdMsg);
  Session mSession = mDTOHibernateSession.getSession(sessionFactory);
  String mSQL = "";
  StringBuilder mSQLBuilder = null;
  mSQLBuilder = new StringBuilder(aCmdDynamicQuery.getQueryString());
  for(KeyValue<String> mKeyValue: aCmdDynamicQuery.getKeys())
  {
   Object mRequestObject = getRequestObject(mKeyValue.getValue(),aCmdMsg);
   setNativeParameters(mSQLBuilder,mKeyValue.getId(), mRequestObject);
  }
  List<?> mMetaData = null;
  if(persistentClass == DTOValues.class)
  {
   String mSQLAppend = mSQLBuilder.toString();
   mSQLBuilder = new StringBuilder("SELECT ");
   DTOString mTableName = (DTOString)aCmdMsg.getRequest("table_name");
   String mMetaSQL = "SELECT COLUMN_NAME FROM ALL_TAB_COLUMNS
WHERE TABLE_NAME='"+mTableName.getValue()+"'";
   Query metaQuery = mSession.createSQLQuery(mMetaSQL);
   mMetaData = metaQuery.list();
   boolean mFirst = true;
   for(Object mObjectColumn:mMetaData)
   {
    String mColumn = (String)mObjectColumn;
    if(!mFirst) mSQLBuilder.append(",");
```

```
    mFirst = false;
    mSQLBuilder.append(mColumn);
  }
  mSQLBuilder.append(" from "+mTableName.getValue()+" "+mSQLAppend);
}
mSQL = mSQLBuilder.toString();
Query query = mSession.createSQLQuery(mSQL.toString());

List<?> mList = query.list();
List<VO> mRtnValue = new ArrayList<VO>();
for(Object mResultObjects:mList)
{
  Object[] mObjects = (Object[])mResultObjects;
  int mSize = 0;
  if(mObjects != null) mSize = mObjects.length;
  try
  {
    VO mObject = persistentClass.newInstance();
    if (mObject instanceof DataValueObject)
    {
      DataValueObject mValueObject = (DataValueObject)mObject;
      for(int Lp0=0;Lp0<mSize;Lp0++)
      {
        mValueObject.setValueNo(Lp0, mObjects[Lp0]);
      }
      mRtnValue.add(mObject);
    }
    if(mObject instanceof DTOValues)
    {
      DTOValues mValueObject = (DTOValues)mObject;
      for(int Lp0=0;Lp0<mSize;Lp0++)
      {
        mValueObject.setValue((String)mMetaData.get(Lp0),mObjects[Lp0]);
      }
      mRtnValue.add(mObject);
    }
  } catch (Exception aException)
  {
    throw new ModelException(aException);
  }
}
return mRtnValue;
```

```
}

public List<VO> findBySmartSQL(CmdMsg aCmdMsg, CmdSmartQuery
aCmdSmartQuery)
{
  List<VO> mRtnValue = new ArrayList<VO>();
  DTOHibernateSession mDTOHibernateSession = getSession(aCmdMsg);
  Session mSession = mDTOHibernateSession.getSession(sessionFactory);
  String mXmlQueryId = aCmdSmartQuery.getXmlQueryId();
  DTO mDTO = aCmdMsg.getRequest(mXmlQueryId);
  if (mDTO instanceof DTOXmlValue)
  {
    DTOXmlValue mDTOXmlValue = (DTOXmlValue) mDTO;
    SqlStmt mSqlStatement = SqlQueryBuilder.buildQuery(mDTOXmlValue);
    int mMaxRows = 10000;
    int mMaxBufferSize = 10000000;
    XMLTag mXMLTag = mDTOXmlValue.getXmlTag();
    if (mXMLTag != null)
    {
      XMLTag mParameters = mXMLTag.getXMLTagIgnoreCase("Parameters");
      if (mParameters != null)
      {
        XMLTag mTagMaxRecords = mParameters.getXMLTagIgnoreCase("MaxRecords");
        if (mTagMaxRecords != null)
        {
          String mValue = mTagMaxRecords.getValue();
          try
          {
            mMaxRows = Integer.valueOf(mValue);
          }
          catch (NumberFormatException aNumberFormatException)
          {
            // do nothing....
          }
        }
        XMLTag mTagMaxBufferSize =
mParameters.getXMLTagIgnoreCase("MaxBufferSize");
        if (mTagMaxBufferSize != null)
        {
          String mValue = mTagMaxBufferSize.getValue();
          try
          {
```

```
        mMaxBufferSize = Integer.valueOf(mValue);
      }
      catch (NumberFormatException aNumberFormatException)
      {
        // do nothing....
      }
    }
  }
}
if (mSqlStatement instanceof SqlSelect)
{
  SqlSelect mSelect = (SqlSelect) mSqlStatement;
  // String mSQL = mSelect.toSqlString(aCmdMsg);
  String mSQL = "SELECT *  FROM (" + mSelect.toSqlString(aCmdMsg) + ") WHERE
ROWNUM <= " + mMaxRows;
  List<String> columnNames = mSelect.getColumnNames(aCmdMsg);
  List<String> columnTypes = mSelect.getColumnTypes();
  int mSize = columnNames.size();
  HibernateWork mHibernateWork = new HibernateWork();
  mSession.doWork(mHibernateWork);
  Connection mConnection = mHibernateWork.getConnection();
  Statement mStatement = null;
  int mBufferCount = 0;
  try
  {
    mStatement = mConnection.createStatement();
    ResultSet mResultSet = mStatement.executeQuery(mSQL.toString());
    while (mBufferCount <=  mMaxBufferSize && mResultSet.next())
    {
      VO mObject = persistentClass.newInstance();
      if (mObject instanceof DTOValues)
      {
        DTOValues mValueObject = (DTOValues) mObject;
        for (int Lp0 = 0; Lp0 < mSize; Lp0++)
        {
          String mColumnType = columnTypes.get(Lp0);
          if (mColumnType.equals("String"))
          {
            String mValue = mResultSet.getString(Lp0 + 1);
            if (mValue != null)
            {
              mBufferCount += mValue.length();
```

```
          }
          mValueObject.setValue(columnNames.get(Lp0), mValue);
        }
        else if (mColumnType.equals("clob"))
        {
          Clob mClob = mResultSet.getClob(Lp0 + 1);
          char[] mBuffer = new char[1000];
          StringBuilder mBuilder = new StringBuilder();
          Reader mReader = mClob.getCharacterStream();
          int mCharRead;
          do
          {
            mCharRead = mReader.read(mBuffer, 0, 1000);
            if (mCharRead > 0)
            {
              mBuilder.append(mBuffer, 0, mCharRead);
              mBufferCount += mCharRead;
            }
          }
          while (mCharRead >= 0);
          mValueObject.setValue(columnNames.get(Lp0), mBuilder.toString());
        }
      }
      mRtnValue.add(mObject);
    }
  }
}
catch (Exception aException)
{
  throw new ModelException(aException);
}
finally
{
  if (mStatement != null)
  {
    try
    {
      mStatement.close();
    }
    catch (SQLException e)
    {
      e.printStackTrace();
```

```
          }
        }
      }
    }
  }
  return mRtnValue;
}

private StringBuilder setNativeParameters(StringBuilder aSql,String aKey,Object
aValue)
{
  String mKey = ":"+aKey;
  int mIndex = aSql.indexOf(mKey);
  if(mIndex > -1)
  {
    aSql.replace(mIndex, mIndex+mKey.length(), aValue.toString());
  }
  return aSql;
}

@SuppressWarnings("unchecked")
protected List<VO> findByCriteria(CmdMsg aCmdMsg,Criterion... aCriterions)
{
  DTOHibernateSession mDTOHibernateSession = getSession(aCmdMsg);
  Session mSession = mDTOHibernateSession.getSession(sessionFactory);
  Criteria mRtnValue = mSession.createCriteria(getPersistentClass());
  for(Criterion mCriterion: aCriterions)
  {
    mRtnValue.add(mCriterion);
  }
  return mRtnValue.list();
}

public static <VO,Key extends Serializable> DAOGenericHibernate<VO,Key>
create(SessionFactory aSessionFactory)
{
  DAOGenericHibernate<VO,Key> mDAO = new DAOGenericHibernate<VO,Key>();
  mDAO.setSessionFactory(aSessionFactory);
  return mDAO;
}

@SuppressWarnings("unchecked")
```

```
public void execute(Command aCommand,CmdMsg aCmdMsg)
{
 if(aCommand instanceof CmdQuery)
 {
  CmdQuery mCmdQuery = (CmdQuery)aCommand;
  List<VO> mResults = findByQuery(mCmdQuery,aCmdMsg);
  DTOList<DTO> mDTOList = new DTOList<DTO>();
  for(VO mValueObject: mResults)
  {
   DTO mDTO = copy(mValueObject);
   mDTOList.add(mDTO);
  }
  aCmdMsg.setResponse(mCmdQuery.getResponseId(), mDTOList);
 }
 if(aCommand instanceof CmdDeclaredQuery)
 {
  CmdDeclaredQuery mCmdDeclaredQuery = (CmdDeclaredQuery)aCommand;
  List<VO> mResults = findByQuery(mCmdDeclaredQuery,aCmdMsg);
  DTOList<DTO> mDTOList = new DTOList<DTO>();
  for(VO mValueObject: mResults)
  {
   DTO mDTO = copy(mValueObject);
   mDTOList.add(mDTO);
  }
  aCmdMsg.setResponse(mCmdDeclaredQuery.getResponseId(), mDTOList);
 }
 else if(aCommand instanceof CmdQryUpdate)
 {
  CmdQryUpdate mCmdQryUpdate = (CmdQryUpdate)aCommand;
  DTO mDTO = aCmdMsg.getRequest(mCmdQryUpdate.getRequestId());
  if(mDTO instanceof DTOList<?>)
  {
   DTOList<DTO> mDTOList = (DTOList<DTO>)mDTO;
   DTOList<DTO> mRtnList = new DTOList<DTO>();
   aCmdMsg.setResponse(mCmdQryUpdate.getResponseId(), mRtnList);
   for(DTO mDataTransfer:mDTOList)
   {
    VO mValueObject = copy(mDataTransfer);
    if(mCmdQryUpdate instanceof CmdQrySave)
    {
     VO mPersitedObject = save(mValueObject,aCmdMsg);
     DTO mDTOPersisted = copy(mPersitedObject);
```

```
      mRtnList.add(mDTOPersisted);
    }
    else
    {
      VO mPersitedObject = makePersistent(mValueObject,aCmdMsg);
      DTO mDTOPersisted = copy(mPersitedObject);
      mRtnList.add(mDTOPersisted);
    }
   }
  }
  else
  {
   VO mValueObject = copy(mDTO);
   if(mCmdQryUpdate instanceof CmdQrySave)
   {
    VO mPersitedObject = save(mValueObject,aCmdMsg);
    DTO mDTOPersisted = copy(mPersitedObject);
    aCmdMsg.setResponse(mCmdQryUpdate.getResponseId(), mDTOPersisted);
   }
   else
   {
    VO mPersitedObject = makePersistent(mValueObject,aCmdMsg);
    DTO mDTOPersisted = copy(mPersitedObject);
    aCmdMsg.setResponse(mCmdQryUpdate.getResponseId(), mDTOPersisted);
   }
  }
 }
 else if(aCommand instanceof CmdDynamicQuery)
 {
  CmdDynamicQuery mCmdDynamicQuery = (CmdDynamicQuery)aCommand;
  List<VO> mResults = findByNativeSQL(aCmdMsg,mCmdDynamicQuery);
  DTOList<DTO> mDTOList = new DTOList<DTO>();
  for(VO mValueObject: mResults)
  {
   if(mValueObject instanceof DTOValues)
   {
    mDTOList.add((DTOValues)mValueObject);
   }
   else
   {
    DTO mDTO = copy(mValueObject);
    mDTOList.add(mDTO);
```

```
    }

   }
   aCmdMsg.setResponse(mCmdDynamicQuery.getResponseId(), mDTOList);
  }
  else if(aCommand instanceof CmdSmartQuery)
  {
   CmdSmartQuery mCmdSmartQuery = (CmdSmartQuery)aCommand;
   List<VO> mResults = findBySmartSQL(aCmdMsg,mCmdSmartQuery);
   DTOList<DTO> mDTOList = new DTOList<DTO>();
   for(VO mValueObject: mResults)
   {
    if(mValueObject instanceof DTOValues)
    {
     mDTOList.add((DTOValues)mValueObject);
    }
    else
    {
     DTO mDTO = copy(mValueObject);
     mDTOList.add(mDTO);
    }

   }
   aCmdMsg.setResponse(mCmdSmartQuery.getResponseId(), mDTOList);
  }
  else if(aCommand instanceof CmdHibernateDoWork)
  {
   CmdHibernateDoWork mCmdHibernateDoWork =
(CmdHibernateDoWork)aCommand;
   DTOHibernateSession mDTOHibernateSession = getSession(aCmdMsg);
   Session mSession = mDTOHibernateSession.getSession(sessionFactory);
   HibernateWork mHibernateWork = new HibernateWork();
   mSession.doWork(mHibernateWork);
   mCmdHibernateDoWork.doWork(mHibernateWork.getConnection(), aCmdMsg);
  }
 }

 public DTO copy(VO aValueObject)
 {
  DTO mRtnValue = null;
  try
  {
```

```
      mRtnValue = dtoPrototype.getClass().newInstance();
      MetaProcess.copy(aValueObject, mRtnValue);
    }
    catch (Exception aException)
    {
      throw new ModelException(aException);
    }
    return mRtnValue;
  }

  public VO copy(DTO aValueObject)
  {
    VO mRtnValue = null;
    try
    {
      mRtnValue = persistentClass.newInstance();
      MetaProcess.copy(aValueObject,mRtnValue);
    }
    catch (Exception aException)
    {
      throw new ModelException(aException);
    }
    return mRtnValue;
  }

  public void setDTOClass(DTO aDTOPrototype)
  {
    dtoPrototype = aDTOPrototype;
  }
}
```

Chapter 8 Data Transfer Objects

8.1 Data Transfer Object

Overview:

All Data Transfer Objects must implement the interface DataTransfer. All DTOs must maintain some basic information (such as status of object, such as clean, dirty, and persisted). Otherwise, DTOs are basic java beans with getters and setters.

Objective:

It is the object of the Data Transfer Objects (DTO) to transfer data between layers and methods of the applications.

Responsibility:

The Responsibility of the DTO is to provide a transportation mechinism for passing data.

Pattern Type:

A Data Transfer Object is a Design pattern used to transport information in an application. DTOs have no behavior, only properties and should be serializable.

Structure:

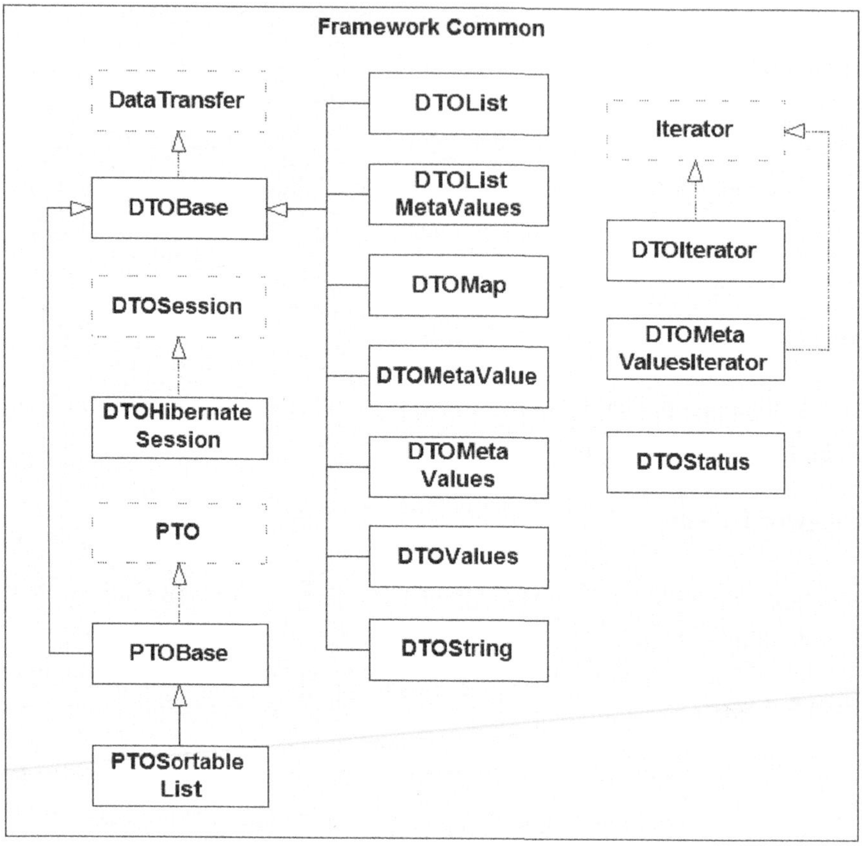
Framework Common
DataTransfer
DTOBase
DTOSession
DTOHibernate Session
PTO
PTOBase
PTOSortable List
DTOList
DTOList MetaValues
DTOMap
DTOMetaValue
DTOMeta Values
DTOValues
DTOString
Iterator
DTOIterator
DTOMeta ValuesIterator
DTOStatus

Code Sample:

```
public interface DTO extends Serializable
{
  public void dirty();
  public void persisted();
  public void clean();

  public boolean isDirty();
  public boolean isPersisted();
  public boolean isClean();

  public boolean isValid();
}

public abstract class DTOBase implements DTO
{
  private static final long serialVersionUID = 1L;
  private DTOStatus status = DTOStatus.CLEAN;

  @Override
  public void clean()
  {
    status = DTOStatus.CLEAN;
  }

  @Override
  public void dirty()
  {
    status = DTOStatus.DIRTY;
  }

  @Override
  public boolean isClean()
  {
    return status == DTOStatus.CLEAN;
  }

  @Override
  public boolean isDirty()
  {
    return status == DTOStatus.DIRTY;
```

```
  }

  @Override
  public boolean isPersisted()
  {
   return status == DTOStatus.PERSISTED;
  }

  @Override
  public boolean isValid()
  {
   return true;
  }

  @Override
  public void persisted()
  {
   status = DTOStatus.PERSISTED;
  }

  protected String stringSet(String aValue)
  {
   String mRtnValue = aValue;
   if(mRtnValue == null) mRtnValue = "";
   return mRtnValue;
  }
}
```

8.2 Basic DTOs

Overview:

A Basic DTO inherits the class DTOBase and creates a set of properties (based on setters and getters). Generally, speaking, other than inheriting DTOBase, a basic DTO is a basic java bean.

Objective:

Basic DTO are simple POJOs with basic elements such as a name or address.

Responsibility:

The basic DTO are responsible for providing basic properities for a set of data.

Structure:

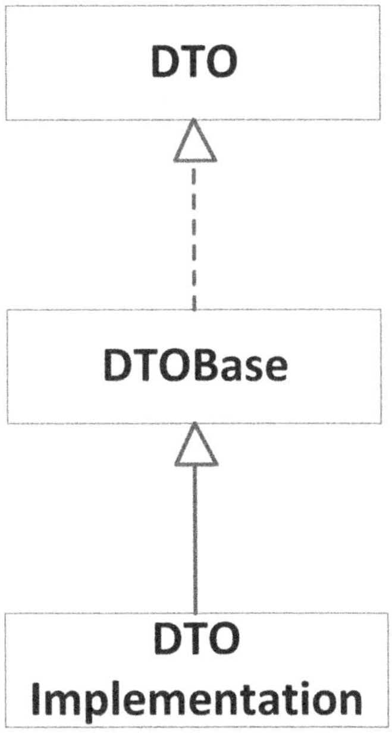

Code Sample:

```
public class DTOCustomer extends DTOBase
{

 private static final long serialVersionUID = 1L;

 private String firstName;
 private String lastName;
 private String address;
 private String city;
 private String state;
 private String zip;

 public String getFirstName()
 {
  return firstName;
 }

 public void setFirstName(String firstName)
 {
  this.firstName = firstName;
 }

 public String getLastName()
 {
  return lastName;
 }

 public void setLastName(String lastName)
 {
  this.lastName = lastName;
 }

 public String getAddress()
 {
  return address;
 }

 public void setAddress(String address)
 {
  this.address = address;
```

```
}

public String getCity()
{
 return city;
}

public void setCity(String city)
{
 this.city = city;
}

public String getState()
{
 return state;
}

public void setState(String state)
{
 this.state = state;
}

public String getZip()
{
 return zip;
}

public void setZip(String zip)
{
 this.zip = zip;
}

}
```

8.3 DTO List

Overview:

A DTOList is a DTO that wraps a list of DTO's. This allows a collection of DTOs to be passed around like a DTO. An example of a DTOList might be the results of a query where lists of DTOs representing rows in a database are returned.

Objective:

The Objective of the DTO List is to have a type that is a DataTransfer Object that contains a collection of other DTOs regardless of the DTO type as long as they implement the DTO interface.

Responsibility:

It is the responsibility of the DTOList to pass as a collection a set of DTOs like any other DTO. This allows the DTOList to be stored just as if it where basic DTO.

Structure:

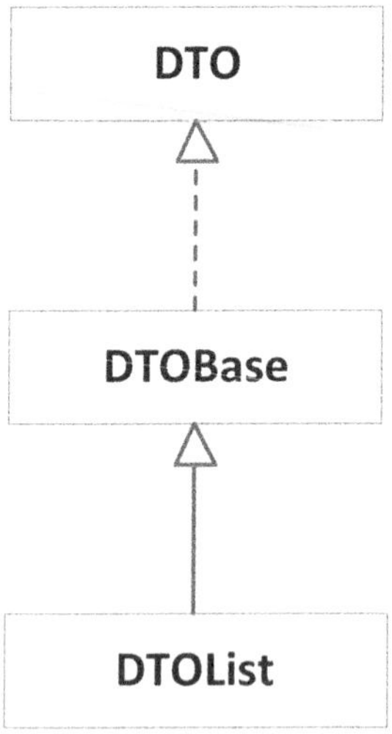

Code Sample:

```
public class DTOList<DataTransferObject extends DTO> extends DTOBase implements
Collection<DataTransferObject>
{
 private static final long serialVersionUID = 1L;
 private List<DataTransferObject> listOfDTOs = new ArrayList<DataTransferObject>();

 public boolean add(DataTransferObject aDTO)
 {
  return listOfDTOs.add(aDTO);
 }

 public Collection<DataTransferObject> getList()
 {
  return Collections.unmodifiableList(listOfDTOs);
 }

 public int size()
 {
  return listOfDTOs.size();
 }


 @Override
 public void clear()
 {
  listOfDTOs.clear();
 }

 @Override
 public boolean contains(Object aObject)
 {
  return listOfDTOs.contains(aObject);
 }

 @Override
 public boolean containsAll(Collection<?> aCollection)
 {
  return listOfDTOs.containsAll(aCollection);
 }
```

```
@Override
public boolean isEmpty()
{
  return listOfDTOs.isEmpty();
}

@Override
public Iterator<DataTransferObject> iterator()
{
  return (Iterator<DataTransferObject>)new DTOIterator<DataTransferObject>(this);
}

@Override
public boolean remove(Object aObject)
{
  return listOfDTOs.remove(aObject);
}

@Override
public boolean removeAll(Collection<?> aCollection)
{
  return listOfDTOs.removeAll(aCollection);
}

@Override
public boolean retainAll(Collection<?> aCollection)
{
  return listOfDTOs.retainAll(aCollection);
}

@Override
public Object[] toArray()
{
  return listOfDTOs.toArray();
}

@Override
public <T> T[] toArray(T[] aArray)
{
  return listOfDTOs.toArray(aArray);
}
```

```
  @Override
  public boolean addAll(Collection<? extends DataTransferObject> aCollection)
  {
   return listOfDTOs.addAll(aCollection);
  }

  public DataTransferObject get(int aIndex)
  {
   return listOfDTOs.get(aIndex);
  }

}
```

8.4 DTO Maps

Overview:

DTOMaps is similar to a DTOList except that DTOs are stored based on a key value pair.

Objective:

The object of the DTOMap is to combine the behavior of a map with that of a DTO. DTOMaps only store types of DTO.

Responsibility:

It is the responsibility of the DTOMap to pass as a map of DTOs like any other DTO. This allows the DTOMap to be stored just as if it where basic DTO.

Structure:

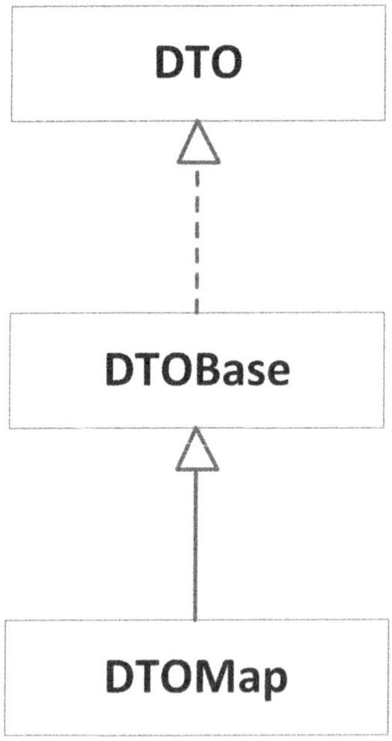

Code Sample:

```
public class DTOMap extends DTOBase
{
 private static final long serialVersionUID = 1L;
 private Map<String,DTO> mapOfDTOs = new HashMap<String, DTO>();

 public void setDTO(String aKey,DTO aDTO)
 {
  mapOfDTOs.put(aKey,aDTO);
 }

 public DTO getDTO(String aKey)
 {
  return mapOfDTOs.get(aKey);
 }
}
```

8.5 DTO Values

Overview:

DTOValues is like a basic DTO except for the properties are stored as a set of key, value pairs. The values don't need to be a DTO.

Objective:

The objective of the DTOValues objects is to provide a way of passing data with a loosely coupled structure. This way, the structure can be flexible to meet the needs of the business logic.

Responsibility:

It is the responsibility of the DTOValues object to transport loosely defined data structure that change to meet the needs of the business requirements. For example, an application might read a file that has a list of properity names and their values, which can then stored as a key value pair.

Structure:

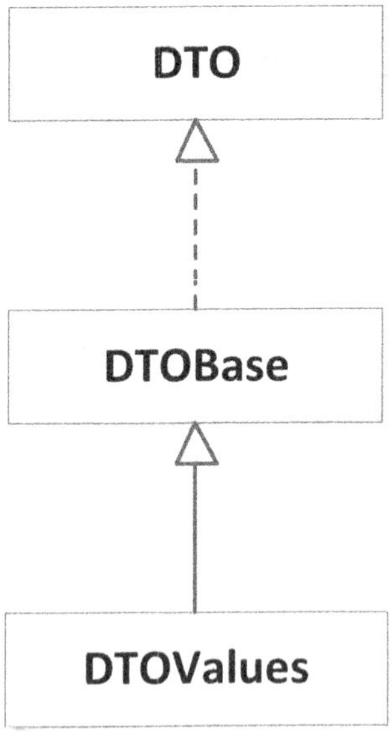

Code Sample:

```
public class DTOValues extends DTOBase
{

  private static final long serialVersionUID = 1L;

  private Map<String, Object> values = new HashMap<String, Object>();

  public void setValue(String aKey,Object aValue)
  {
   values.put(aKey, aValue);
  }

  public Object getValue(String aKey)
  {
   return values.get(aKey);
  }

  public Set<String> getKeys()
  {
        return values.keySet();
  }
}
```

8.6 DTO Strings

Overview:

A DTOString is a DTO that contains one element of a String.

Objective:

The objective of the DTOString is to be able to pass String data as a DTO.

Responsibility:

The responsibility of the DTOString is to provide a transportation object that passing string data.

Structure:

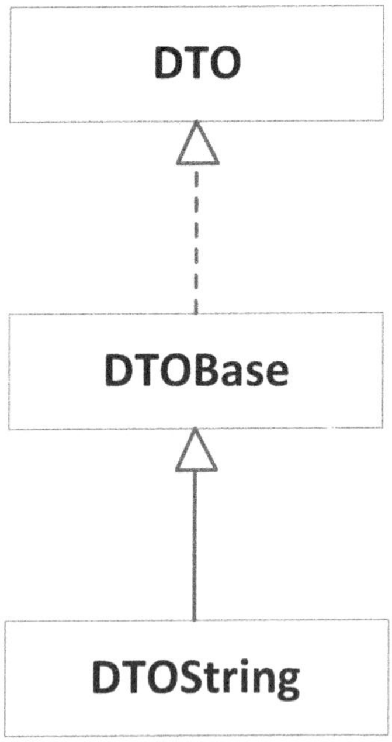

Code Sample:

```
public class DTOString extends DTOBase
{
 private static final long serialVersionUID = 1L;
 private String value;

 public DTOString()
 {
  //empty constructor
 }

 public DTOString(String aValue)
 {
  value = aValue;
 }

 public void setValue(String aValue)
 {
  value = aValue;
 }

 public String getValue()
 {
  return value;
 }
}
```

Chapter 9 Intra-Application Communications

9.1 Command Message Pattern

When attempting to write reusable, easy to maintain code, there are many challenges. In today's world, there are many challenges with common patterns to solve them. One of the most useful patterns is the Model-View-Control patterns. However, often the Controller and Model may or may not be part of the same code base. Often times, the Model might be in some type of service pattern. In addition, most well-designed Models have multiple layers which present multiple challenges. With modern development process, many systems use dependency injection, such as applications that use Spring. One of the values of dependency injection, is the ability to glue diverse components together without the need for the injector to know much about the type of the component. This encourages loose coupling which allows for greater maintainability, more robust designs, and provides for Rapid software development.

However, one of the problems encountered is how to write components with a common facade and without tight coupling. One of the solutions to this problem is the Command Message Pattern.

Consider the following architecture pattern:

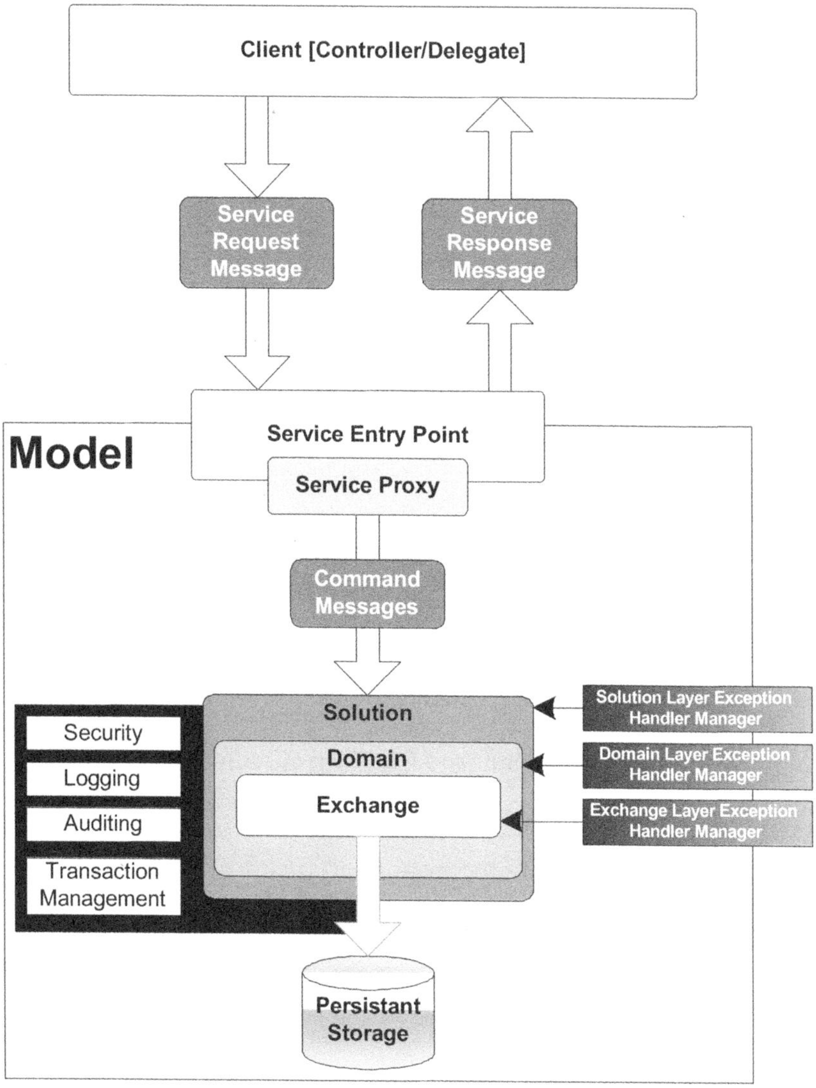

Consider the following class hierarchy.

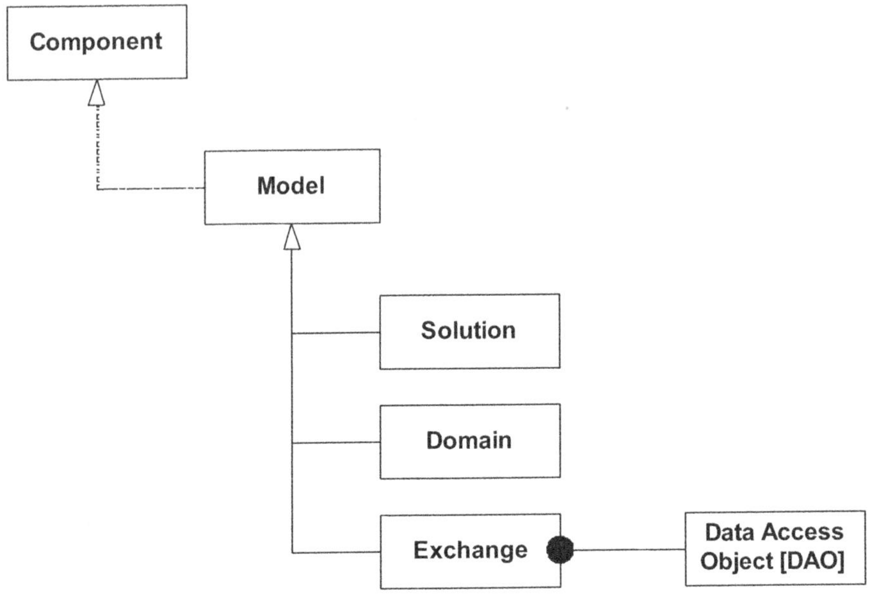


```
public interface Component
{
public void execute(Command aCommand,CmdMsg aCmdMsg);
}
```

With each tier implementing the Component interface, they implement the Component Facade which takes two arguments {Command, and the Command Message}.

Now, consider the Command Message Class [Pattern].

```
public interface CmdMsg
{
public void addCommand(Command aCommand);
public void setRequest(String aKey,DataTransfer aDTO);
public void setResponse(String aKey,DataTransfer aDTO);
public void addError(ErrorNode aErrorNode);
public Collection<ErrorNode> getErrors();
public Command getCommand(String aName);
public DataTransfer getRequest(String aKey);
public DataTransfer getResponse(String aKey);
```

```
public Set<String> getResponseKeys();
public void pushCommands();
public void popCommands();
}
```

As processing begins at the upper layer [Solution], information passed to the model is put into DTOs and then inserted into the list of Request DTOs. As processing continues, DTO's can be read, inserted, or Modified in either the Request or the Response list of DTO'S. Commands can be added or processed, and as errors are encountered, [or Exceptions] they can be added to the set of Errors.

When the execute method is called, the command can be examined and can be used to direct the flow of execution. However, it would be convenient to go directly to a well defined internal method. Using reflection patterns, this can be accomplished. Consider the following code snippet:

```
public @interface Operation
{
static final String defaultValue="<none>";
String action();
String requestKey() default defaultValue;
String responseKey() default defaultValue;
}
```

Now lets look at an implementation using the operation annotation.

```
public class User extends Domain
{
@Operation(action="readUser")
public void readUser(Command aCommand,CmdMsg aCmdMsg)
{
runCmdComponents(aCmdMsg); // Parent class has list of commands to be run
} // Which includes a command to call User Exchange.
}

public class UserExchange extends Exchange
{
private DataAccess dataAccess;
public void setDao(DataAccess aDao)
{
```

```
dataAccess = aDao;
}
@Operation(action="readUser")
public void readUser(Command aCommand,CmdMsg aCmdMsg)
{
KeyValue<String> mUserValue = new KeyValue("userName","userInfo.userName");
KeyValue<String> mPasswordValue = new KeyValue("password","userInfo.password");
CmdQuery mCmdQuery = new CmdQuery("Name",
ComponentType.EXCHANGE,"ComponentName",
"operation",null,null,"userInfo","userByUserNamePassword",mUserValue,mPasswordVa
lue);
dataAccess.execute(mCmdQuery, aCmdMsg);
}
}

public class DAOHibernateUser extends DAOGenericHibernate<HVOUser, Serializable>
{
public DAOHibernateUser()
{
setDTOClass(new DTOUser());
setDozerMapper(new DozerBeanMapper());
}
public DAOHibernateUser(SessionFactory aSessionFactory)
{
setDTOClass(new DTOUser());
setDozerMapper(new DozerBeanMapper());
setSessionFactory(aSessionFactory);
}
}
```

Using Reflection Java Patterns, the calling class can now call directly to the required method without having to go to the execute method.

These Patterns allow spring to inject components into other components [Such as a DAO injected into an Exchange Object]

Consider the following Spring configuration.

```
<beans>
<bean id="UserDAO" class="com.example.impl.model.access.user.DAOHibernateUser">
<property name="sessionFactory" ref="sessionFactoryExample"/>
</bean>
```

```
<bean id="UserExchange" class="com.impl.model.exchange.users.UserExchange">
<property name="dao" ref="UserDAO"/>
</bean>
<bean id="CmdUserExchange" class="com.fmw.model.cmd.Cmd">
  <property name="name" value="userExchangeReadRow"/>
  <property name="componentName" value="UserExchange"/>
  <property name="componentTypeName" value="EXCHANGE"/>
  <property name="operation" value="readUser"/>
</bean>
<bean id="CmdComponentUserExchange"
class="com.fmw.model.component.cmd.CmdComponent">
<property name="component" ref="UserExchange"/>
<property name="command" ref="CmdUserExchange"/>
</bean>
</beans>
<beans>
<bean id="UserDomain" class="com.impl.model.domain.users.User">
  <property name="cmdComponents">
    <list>
      <ref bean="CmdComponentUserExchange"/>
    </list>
  </property>
</bean>
<bean id="CmdUserDomain" class="com.fmw.model.cmd.Cmd">
  <property name="name" value="usersDomainReadTrans"/>
  <property name="componentName" value="UsersDomain"/>
  <property name="componentTypeName" value="DOMAIN"/>
  <property name="operation" value="readUser"/>
</bean>
<bean id="CmdComponentUser"
class="com.fmw.model.component.cmd.CmdComponent">
  <property name="component" ref="UserDomain"/>
  <property name="command" ref="CmdUserDomain"/>
</bean>
</beans>
```

In the configuration above, both the DAO and the Commands are injected into the Exchange. This allows Spring to control which DAO is called by the Exchange. At the same time, the Spring Configuration injects the Exchange and the command into the Domain Object. This allows Spring to control the execution pattern of the Domain.

When this pattern is followed, it allows for Rapid Development since every class follows a consistent pattern, which when implemented causes the execution flow to be consistent and controlled by the injection of the command object. Each component doesn't have to worry about passing and receiving information back and forth. Each component can simply insert or read from the Command Message Object.

This allows also for the system to inject various components into the system without worry about cascade method signature changes.

The Command Message Pattern also makes it easier to such advanced programming techniques such as Aspects since all of the classes use a consistent facade.

Command Message Wrap Up:

Using the Command Message Pattern along with Spring Inject provides a very powerful method of building applications which allows for adding or subtracting functionality by simply adding or change a a Spring configuration.

This provides lose coupling since all components have basically the same facade and/or method signatures that can be processed using Java Reflection patterns.

9.2 Command Message Inheritance

The Command Message implements the CmdMsg interface.

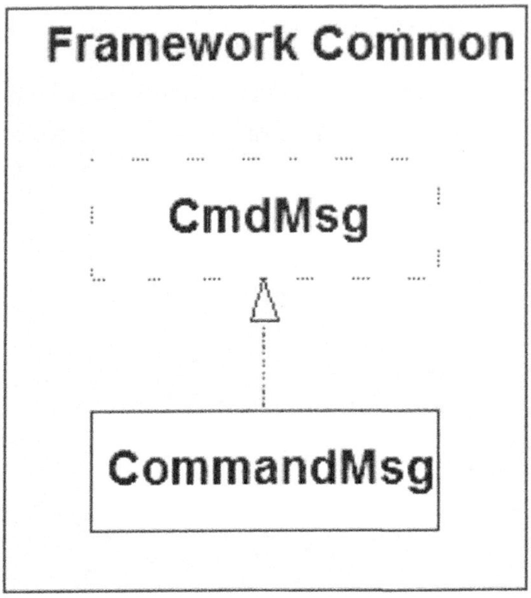


```
public interface CmdMsg
{
  public void addCommand(Command aCommand);
  public void setSession(String aKey,DTO aDTO);
  public void setRequest(String aKey,DTO aDTO);
  public void setResponse(String aKey,DTO aDTO);
  public void addError(ErrorNode aErrorNode);
  public Collection<ErrorNode> getErrors();

  public Command getCommand(String aName);
  public Collection<Command> getCommands();
  public DTO getSession(String aKey);
  public DTO getRequest(String aKey);
  public DTO getResponse(String aKey);
  public Set<String> getResponseKeys();
  public void pushCommands();
  public void popCommands();
```

```
    public String getUserId();
    public void setUserId(String userId);
    public String getApplicationId();
    public void setApplicationId(String applicationId);
    public String getConversationId();
    public void setConversationId(String conversationId);
    public String getMessageId();
    public void setMessageId(String messageId);
    public String getRouterId();
    public void setRouterId(String routerId);
    public Date getRequestTime();
    public void setRequestTime(Date requestTime);
    public String getUserRole();
    public void setUserRole(String userRole);
    public String getAlias();
    public void setAlias(String alias);
}
```

9.3 Command Message Contents

The Command Message is the heart and sole of the Agile Architecture. It allows Developers to create components without concerning themselves about what the other components data input or output requirement are. When a components data requirements change, it does not effect any other component directly. It allows for rapid refactoring as well.

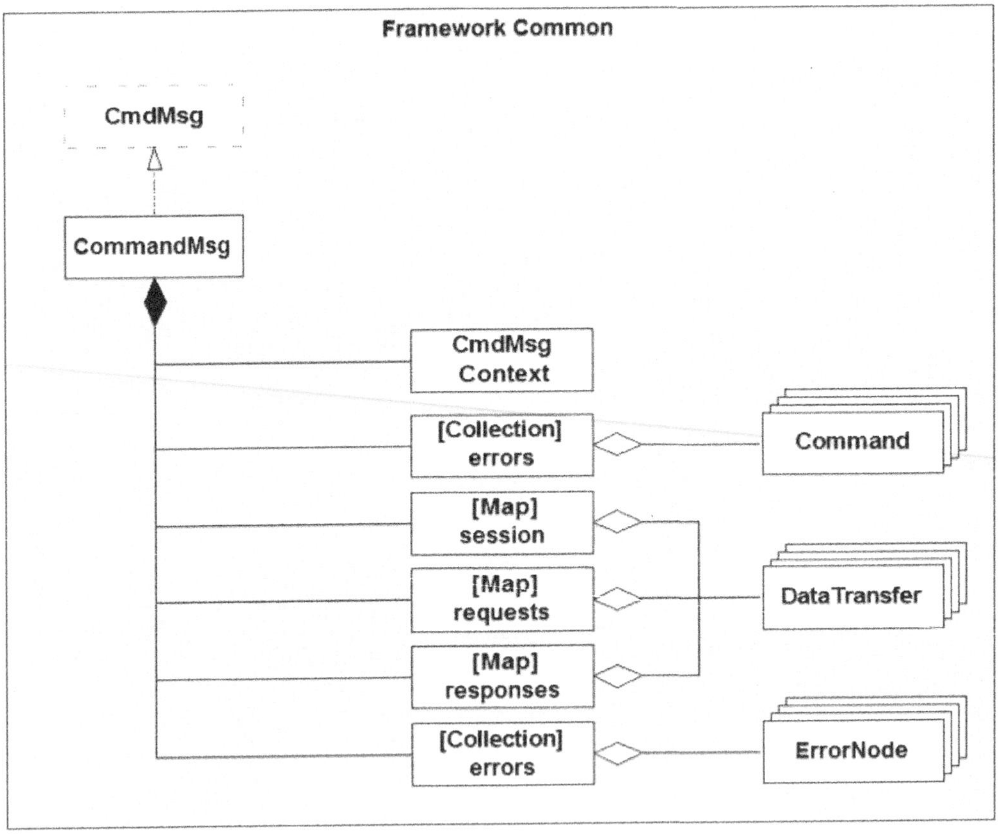

```
public class CommandMsg implements CmdMsg
{
 private CmdMsgContext messageContext = new CmdMsgCtx();
 private List<Command> commands = new ArrayList<Command>();
 private Map<String,DTO> session = new HashMap<String,DTO>();
 private Map<String,DTO> requests = new HashMap<String, DTO>();
 private Map<String,DTO> responses = new HashMap<String,DTO>();
 private Collection<ErrorNode> errors = new ArrayList<ErrorNode>();

 private Stack<List<Command>> commandStack = new Stack<List<Command>>();


 @Override
 public Collection<Command> getCommands()
 {
  return Collections.unmodifiableCollection(commands);
 }

 @Override
 public DTO getRequest(String aKey)
 {
  return requests.get(aKey);
 }

 @Override
 public DTO getResponse(String aKey)
 {
  return responses.get(aKey);
 }

 @Override
 public Set<String> getResponseKeys()
 {
  return responses.keySet();
 }

 @Override
 public DTO getSession(String aKey)
 {
  return session.get(aKey);
 }
```

```
@Override
public void popCommands()
{
 commands = commandStack.pop();
}

@Override
public void pushCommands()
{
 commandStack.push(commands);
 commands = new ArrayList<Command>();
}

@Override
public void setRequest(String aKey, DTO aDTO)
{
 requests.put(aKey,aDTO);
}

@Override
public void setResponse(String aKey, DTO aDTO)
{
 responses.put(aKey, aDTO);
}

@Override
public void setSession(String aKey, DTO aDTO)
{
 session.put(aKey, aDTO);
}

@Override
public void addCommand(Command aCommand)
{
 commands.add(aCommand);
}

@Override
public Command getCommand(String aName)
{
 Command mRtnValue = null;
 for(Command mCommand: commands)
```

```
 {
  if(mCommand.getName().equals(aName))
  {
   mRtnValue = mCommand;
   break;
  }
 }
 return mRtnValue;
}

@Override
public void addError(ErrorNode aErrorNode)
{
 errors.add(aErrorNode);
}

@Override
public Collection<ErrorNode> getErrors()
{
 return Collections.unmodifiableCollection(errors);
}

public void setMessageContext(CmdMsgContext aMessageContext)
{
 messageContext = aMessageContext;
}

@Override
public String getAlias()
{
        return messageContext.getAlias();
}

@Override
public String getApplicationId()
{
        return messageContext.getApplicationId();
}

@Override
public String getConversationId()
{
```

```
        return messageContext.getConversationId();
}

@Override
public String getMessageId()
{
        return messageContext.getMessageId();
}

@Override
public Date getRequestTime()
{
        return messageContext.getRequestTime();
}

@Override
public String getRouterId()
{
        return messageContext.getRouterId();
}

@Override
public String getUserId()
{
        return messageContext.getUserId();
}

@Override
public String getUserRole()
{
        return messageContext.getUserRole();
}

@Override
public void setAlias(String alias)
{
        messageContext.setAlias(alias);
}

@Override
public void setApplicationId(String applicationId)
{
```

```
        messageContext.setApplicationId(applicationId);
    }

    @Override
    public void setConversationId(String conversationId) {
    }

    @Override
    public void setMessageId(String messageId)
    {
        messageContext.setMessageId(messageId);
    }

    @Override
    public void setRequestTime(Date requestTime)
    {
        messageContext.setRequestTime(requestTime);
    }

    @Override
    public void setRouterId(String routerId)
    {
        messageContext.setRouterId(routerId);
    }

    @Override
    public void setUserId(String userId)
    {
        messageContext.setUserId(userId);
    }

    @Override
    public void setUserRole(String userRole)
    {
        messageContext.setUserRole(userRole);
    }

}
```

9.4

9.5 Message Context

The purpose of the Message Context is to allow the passing information about the user and the application information.

User Id : User Id that the execution is using

Application Id : The Id of the Application making the request

Conversation Id: The Conversation Id passed from the calling application

Message Id : An Id assigned for each incoming messages

Router Id : An Id assigned by the calling application

Request Time : Time that the request was made

User Role : Roles

Alias : The actual id of the caller

9.6 Commands

The Commands are a set of execution orders. A typical Command might be the name of a Solution to run and the operation (method) to call. There are number of predefined command types including a basic command, a Command Query Object, and a Command Query Native Object.

9.7 Session Objects

Session Objects are a set of DTO's that are stored for a session. These are passed in by the calling process.

9.8 Request Objects

Request objects is a set of DTOs that are sent to the Service Proxy which are needed to run the logic.

9.9 Response Objects

Response Objects are a set of DTOs that are to be returned to the calling application.

9.10 Errors

Errors are a collection of errors that were detected by the service. If there are no errors, then the service executed without errors or exceptions that were not recoverable. Exceptions are never returned to the calling application, instead errors are.

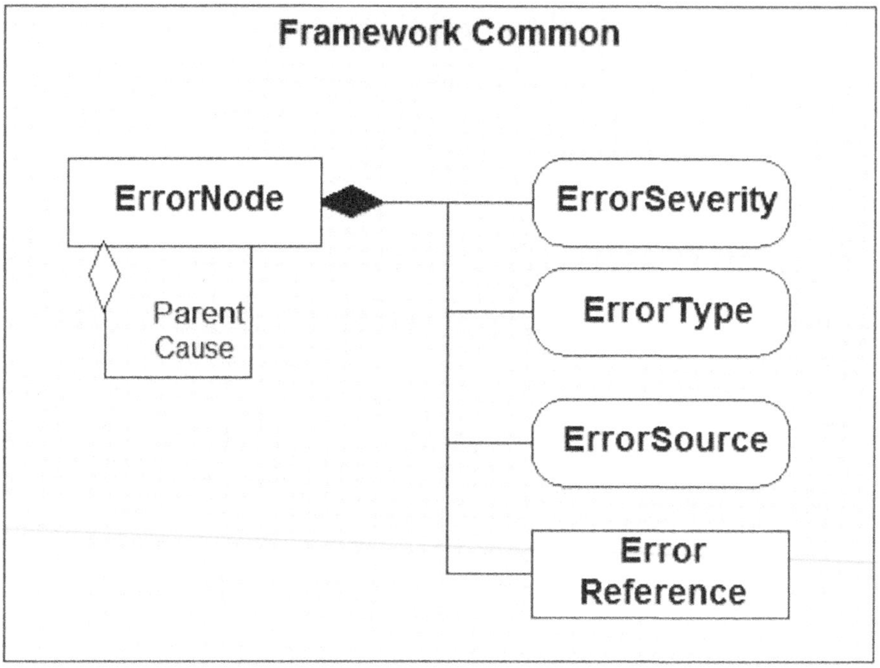

Chapter 10 Errors and Exceptions

10.1 The need for common exception and error handling

Exception and error handling can one of the most important aspects of an agile architecture. There are many issues that are associated with exception and error processing including:

- When and how often to log the event.
- Transformation of the meaning of the event as it bubbles up the stack of layers and tiers of the system.
- Identification of the event with the current processing flow.
- Presentation of the event to the user into human readable format including multiple languages.
- Potential for recovery from an exception or error event.
- Alternate Path processing.
- Reduce redundant implementation of exception or error handling.
- Transaction processing and determining if to roll back or not.
- Clean up processing of allocated resources.

10.2 Encapsulating Rules for Exception and Exceptions

In an Agile Architecture, checked exceptions are discouraged and should never be used unless a component can catch the exception and do something meaningful. Whenever a check exception is expected, it should be caught and wrapped into a runtime exception.

All run time exceptions should be ignored by the developer as the system has built in exception handling mechanism. Whenever the processing passes into a layer (Solution, Domain, Exchange), the software creates an exception handler in the execute method where exceptions are caught. This exception handler is only created by the first instance of logic hitting the particular layer. Sub sequential cross layer calls do not create an exception handler, but uses the initial entry point of the layer. For instance, if the initial Solution A is called, and that Solution calls Solution B, then Solution A will handle all exceptions thrown and Solution B will ignore them.

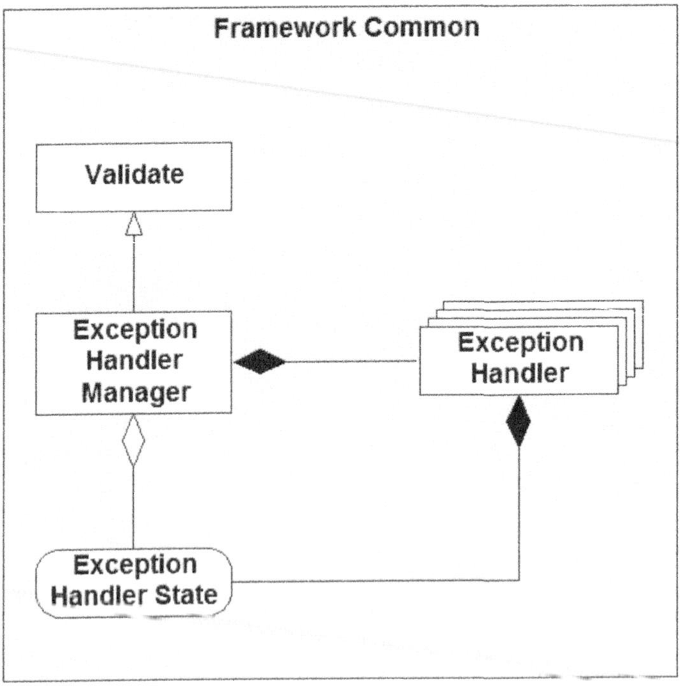

10.3 Component Exceptions

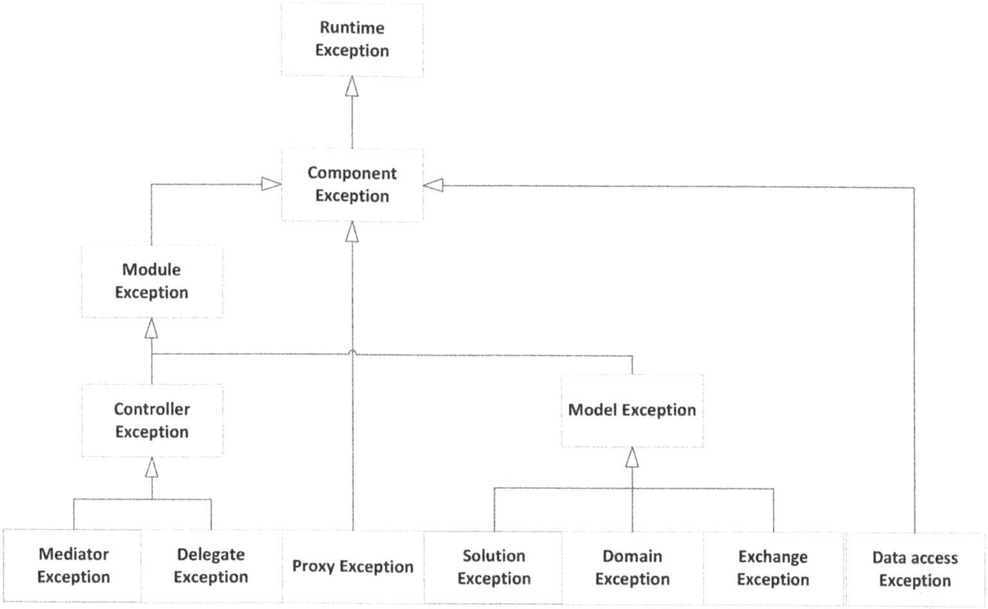

10.4 Exception classes

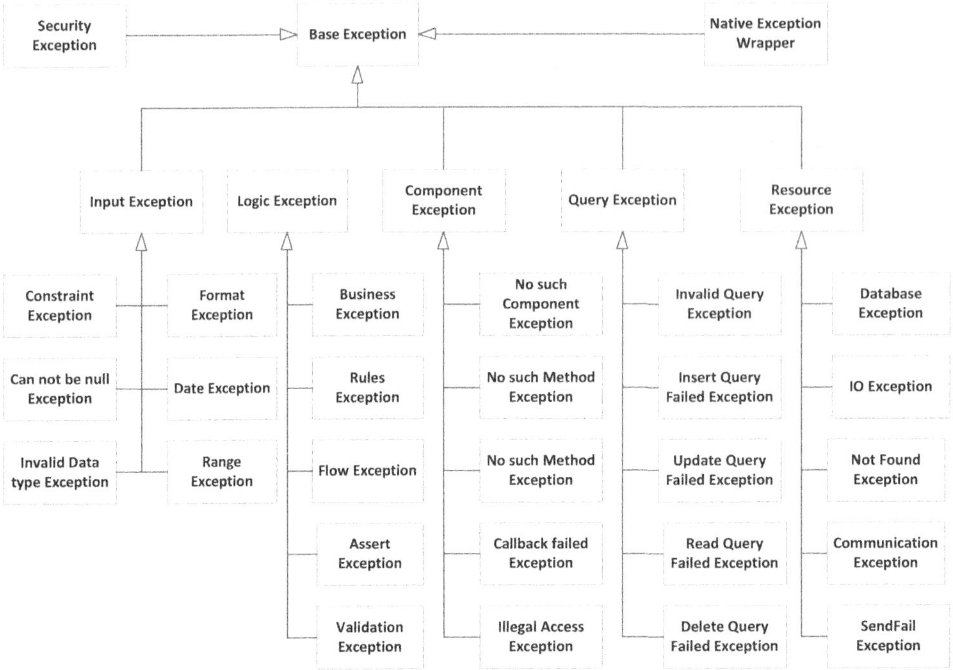

10.5 Activity Monitoring

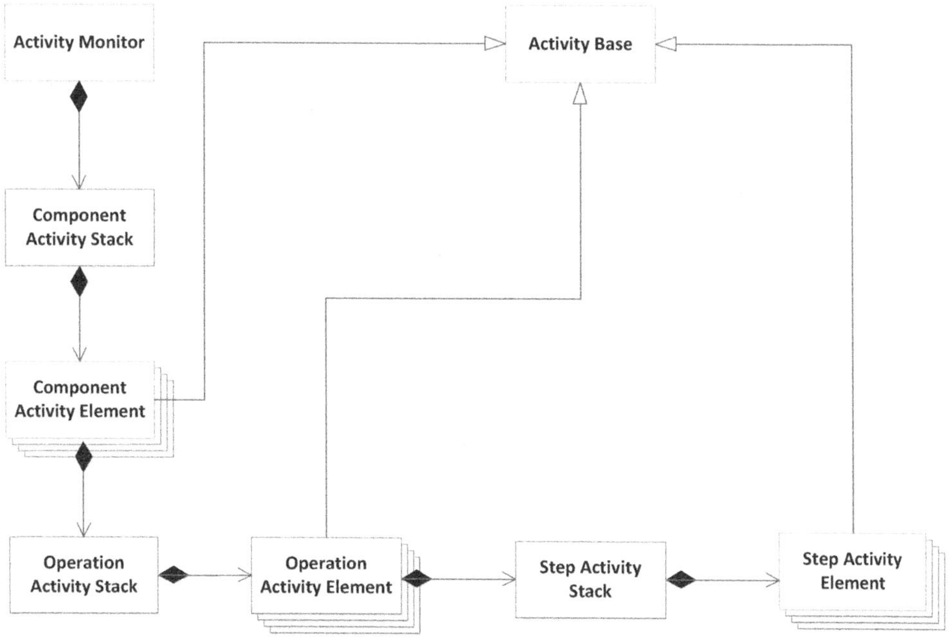

10.6 Exception Translation

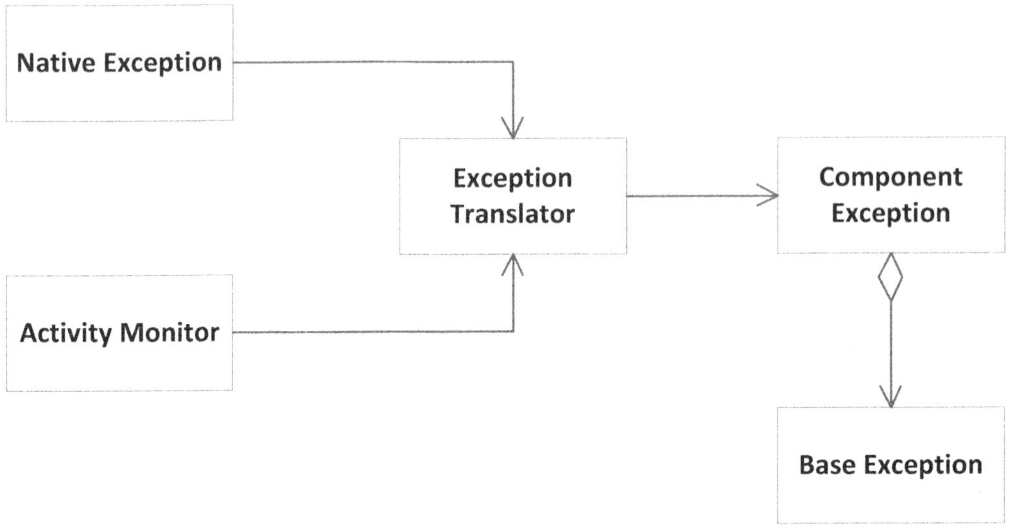

10.7 Exception Handlers

As previously stated, each layer has a set of Exception Handlers that are loaded at start up time. These Exception Handlers are called on by one. Each Exception Handler determines if they can handle the exception. If they can, the exception is processed and control is continued to the next Exception Handler. If none of the Exception Handlers handle the exception, the exception is wrapped in a Wrapped Exception and then thrown so that an upper layer exception handler will take care of the exception.

10.8 Exception Handler Manager

At the top of each layer is an Exception Handler Manger. The system is designed to automatically deal with Runtime Exceptions alleviating the Developer from Exception Handling Concerns. The only time a Developer should concern themselves with exceptions is when they are either forced to catch a checked exception (which they can simple convert it to a runtime exception and throw it), or in the rare cases where it is possible to recover from an exception, they can catch it and throw it.

The Exception Handler Manager contains a set of Exception Handlers. Each Handler determines if it can handle an exception and what to do with the exception. Some possibilities are to convert the exception to a different kind of exception that the upper layers/tiers can understand, or to convert them to an error and store them in the Command Message Object.

If an Exception Handler Manager can not handle an exception, it is thrown up to the pervious component. While it is acceptable for the Domain and Exchange Layers to re-throw Exception, the Solution Layer default should be to convert the exception to an error object and return the results to the caller.

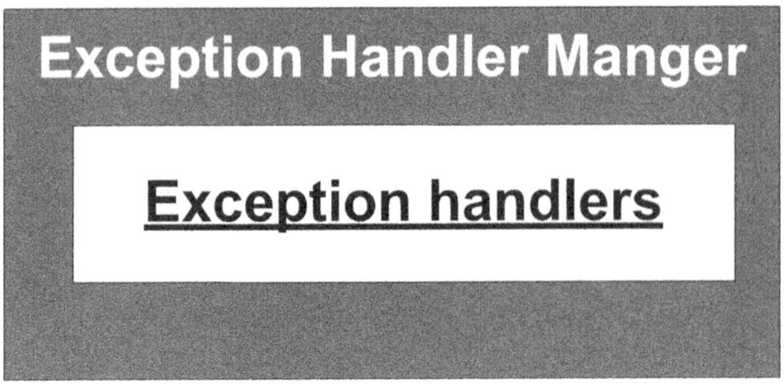

Code Sample:

```
public class ExceptionHandlerManager extends Validate
{
  public static final String title = "ExceptionHandlerManager";

  private Map<ErrorPriority, List<ExceptionHandler>> exceptionHandlers = new
HashMap<ErrorPriority, List<ExceptionHandler>>();

  public void handle(CmdMsg aCmdMsg,Throwable aRuntimeException)
  {
    ExceptionHandlerState mRtnValue =
handle(aCmdMsg,ErrorPriority.HIGH,aRuntimeException);
    if(mRtnValue == ExceptionHandlerState.CONTINUE || mRtnValue ==
ExceptionHandlerState.NOT_PROCESSED)
    {
      ExceptionHandlerState mResult =
handle(aCmdMsg,ErrorPriority.MEDIUM,aRuntimeException);
      if(!(mResult==ExceptionHandlerState.NOT_PROCESSED)) mRtnValue = mResult;
    }
    if(mRtnValue == ExceptionHandlerState.CONTINUE || mRtnValue ==
ExceptionHandlerState.NOT_PROCESSED)
    {
      ExceptionHandlerState mResult =
handle(aCmdMsg,ErrorPriority.LOW,aRuntimeException);
```

```
    if(!(mResult==ExceptionHandlerState.NOT_PROCESSED)) mRtnValue = mResult;
   }
   if(mRtnValue == ExceptionHandlerState.CONTINUE || mRtnValue ==
ExceptionHandlerState.NOT_PROCESSED)
   {
    ExceptionHandlerState mResult =
handle(aCmdMsg,ErrorPriority.INFORMATIONAL,aRuntimeException);
    if(!(mResult==ExceptionHandlerState.NOT_PROCESSED)) mRtnValue = mResult;
   }
  }

 private ExceptionHandlerState handle(CmdMsg aCmdMsg,ErrorPriority
aPriority,Throwable aException)
 {
  ExceptionHandlerState mRtnValue = ExceptionHandlerState.NOT_PROCESSED;
  List<ExceptionHandler> mPriorityList = exceptionHandlers.get(aPriority);
  if(mPriorityList != null)
  {
   for(ExceptionHandler mHandler:mPriorityList)
   {
    if(mHandler.canHandle(aException))
    {
     boolean mResults = mHandler.handle(aCmdMsg, aException);
     if(mResults)
     {
      mRtnValue = ExceptionHandlerState.CONTINUE;
      ExceptionHandlerState mState = mHandler.state(aException);
      if(mState.equals(ExceptionHandlerState.END))
      {
       break;
      }
      if(mState.equals(ExceptionHandlerState.RETHROW))
      {
       if(aException instanceof RuntimeException)
       {
        throw(RuntimeException)aException;
       }
       else
       {
        exception("caught exception", title, "ExceptionHandlerState
handle(CmdMsg,ErrorPriority,Throwable)", "", "", ErrorType.FRAMEWORK,
aException);
```

```
          }
        }
      }
    }
  }
 }
 return mRtnValue;
}

public void addExceptionHandler(ErrorPriority aPriority,ExceptionHandler aHandler)
{
 List<ExceptionHandler> mPriorityList = exceptionHandlers.get(aPriority);
 if(mPriorityList == null)
 {
  mPriorityList = new ArrayList<ExceptionHandler>();
  exceptionHandlers.put(aPriority,mPriorityList);
 }
 mPriorityList.add(aHandler);
}

public void addExceptionHandler(String aPriorityValue,ExceptionHandler aHandler)
{
 for(ErrorPriority mPriority:ErrorPriority.values())
 {
  if(mPriority.getName().equals(aPriorityValue))
  {
   addExceptionHandler(mPriority,aHandler);
  }
 }
}
}
```

10.9 Predefined Exceptions

There is a set of predefined Exceptions.

Check Exception: Used to send an exception when parameters passed do not match expectations.

Error Exception: Base class for some other exceptions.

Model Exception: Used by the framework whenever an unexpected exception occurs during the execution of the framework.

Wrapped Exception: Used to wrap an exception thrown from logic outside of the framework such as an SQL Exception.

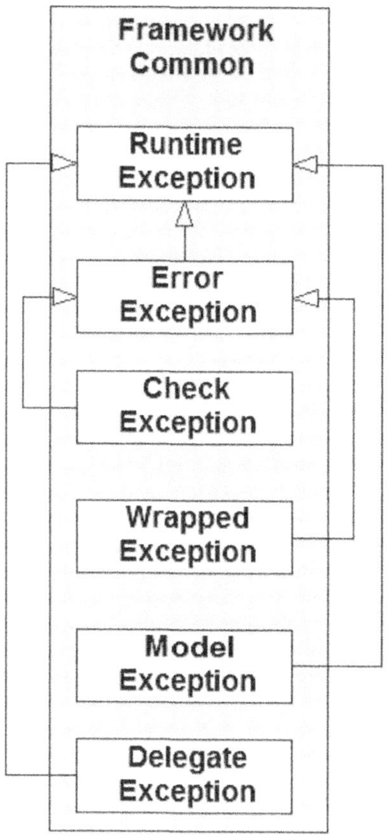

Chapter 11 Loader

Loaders are used to load initial context into the system. The usual context is the Spring Application Context. Loaders run once at start up time and are never run again.

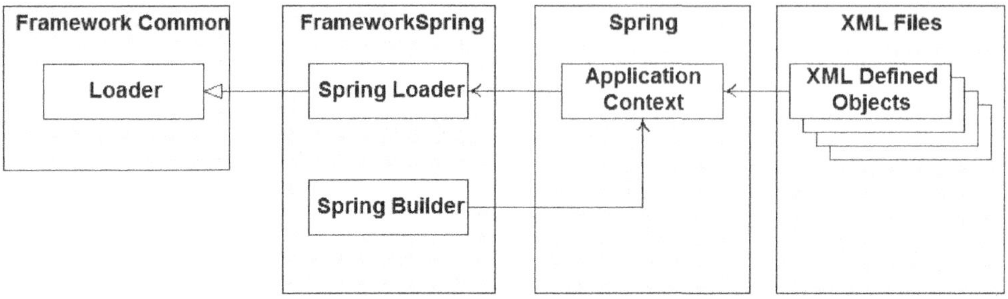

Chapter 12 Transaction Management Session

Overview:

Transaction Management is one the least understood principle in frameworks and is rarely written about. While Transaction can start at any point in the excution of a Data Access Object, they must be completed at the top of the Model execution path. In order to do this, the Transaction Session must be either initiated at the beginning of the Solution stack or at the first time a change to the database is processed in the Data Access Object. The problem with starting a Transaction Session on the Solution Layer, it requires the Solution to have knowledge of the type of Transaction Sessions required.

To overcome this, in the Framework presented here, a Transaction Session object is created and stored in the Command Message and held there the first time an update to the database occurrs.

Objective:

The Object of the Transaction Management is to control the start and end of a Transaction Session. The Transaction Session can end either with a commit if everything went well, or a rollback if it did not. The Transaction Management objective is to provide a procedure to start Transaction Session and the first time required and to execute a commit or a rollback at the end of processing of the Solution top layer.

Responsibility:

The Transaction Management Session is responsible for mainting control of the starting and stop of transactions and determining if a transaction should be rollbacked or committed. Generally speaking Transactions are always committed unless either they are explicitly rollbacked or and exception is caught by the Exception Handler.

Pattern Type:

The Transaction Management Session uses the abstract session pattern to perform its processing.

Structure:

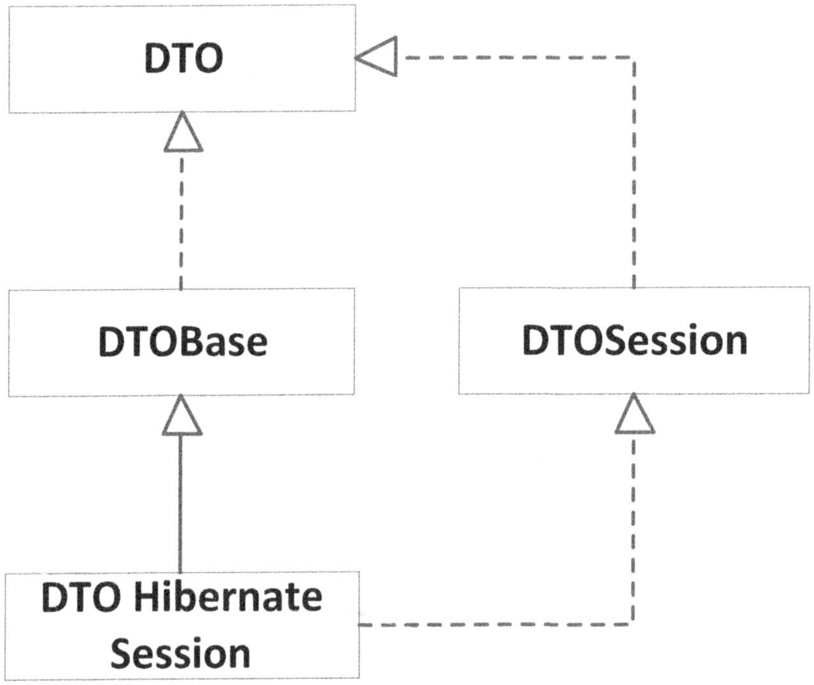

Code Sample:

```
public interface DTOSession extends DTO
{
 public static final String key = "persistence session";
 public boolean commit();
 public boolean rollback();
 public boolean close();
}

public class DTOHibernateSession extends DTOBase implements DTOSession
{

 private static final long serialVersionUID = 1L;

 public Map<SessionFactory,SessionNode> sessionMap = new HashMap<SessionFactory,
SessionNode>();

 public class SessionNode
 {
  private SessionFactory sessionFactory;
  private Session session;
  private Transaction transaction;

  public SessionFactory getSessionFactor()
  {
   return sessionFactory;
  }

  public void setSessionFactor(SessionFactory aSessionFactory)
  {
   sessionFactory = aSessionFactory;
  }

  public Session getSession()
  {
   return session;
  }

  public void setSession(Session aSession)
  {
   session = aSession;
```

```
  }

  public Transaction getTransaction()
  {
   return transaction;
  }

  public void setTransaction(Transaction aTransaction)
  {
   transaction = aTransaction;
  }
}

public SessionNode getSessionNode(SessionFactory aSessionFactory)
{
 SessionNode mRtnValue =null;
 mRtnValue = sessionMap.get(aSessionFactory);
 return mRtnValue;
}

 public void setSession(SessionFactory aSessionFactory,Session aSession)
 {
  SessionNode mNode = getSessionNode(aSessionFactory);
  if(mNode == null)
  {
   mNode = new SessionNode();
   sessionMap.put(aSessionFactory, mNode);
  }
  mNode.setSession(aSession);
 }

 public Session getSession(SessionFactory aSessionFactory)
 {
  Session mRtnValue = null;
  SessionNode mNode = sessionMap.get(aSessionFactory);
  if(mNode != null)
  {
   mRtnValue = mNode.getSession();
  }
  else
  {
   mNode = new SessionNode();
```

```
    mRtnValue = aSessionFactory.openSession();
    mNode.setSession(mRtnValue);
    sessionMap.put(aSessionFactory, mNode);
  }
  return mRtnValue;
}

public boolean startTransaction(SessionFactory aSessionFactory)
{
  boolean mRtnValue = false;
  SessionNode mNode = sessionMap.get(aSessionFactory);
  if(mNode != null)
  {
    Session mSession = mNode.getSession();
    Transaction mTransaction = mNode.getTransaction();
    if(mTransaction == null)
    {
      mTransaction = mSession.beginTransaction();
      mNode.setTransaction(mTransaction);
    }
    mRtnValue = true;
  }
  return mRtnValue;
}

public boolean commit()
{
  boolean mRtnValue = false;
  Collection<SessionNode> mNodes = sessionMap.values();
  for(SessionNode mNode:mNodes)
  {
    Transaction mTransaction = mNode.getTransaction();
    if(mTransaction != null)
    {
      mTransaction.commit();
      mTransaction = null;
      mNode.setTransaction(mTransaction);
      mRtnValue = true;
    }
  }
  return mRtnValue;
}
```

```
public boolean rollback()
{
 boolean mRtnValue = false;
 Collection<SessionNode> mNodes = sessionMap.values();
 for(SessionNode mNode:mNodes)
 {
  Transaction mTransaction = mNode.getTransaction();
  if(mTransaction != null)
  {
   mTransaction.commit();
   mTransaction = null;
   mNode.setTransaction(mTransaction);
   mRtnValue = true;
  }
 }
 return mRtnValue;
}

public boolean currentSession(SessionFactory aSessionFactory)
{
 boolean mRtnValue = false;
 SessionNode mNode = sessionMap.get(aSessionFactory);
 if(mNode.getSession() != null) mRtnValue = true;
 return mRtnValue;
}

public boolean currentTransaction(SessionFactory aSessionFactory)
{
 boolean mRtnValue = false;
 SessionNode mNode = sessionMap.get(aSessionFactory);
 if(mNode.getTransaction() != null) mRtnValue = true;
 return mRtnValue;
}

public boolean close()
{
 boolean mRtnValue = false;
 Collection<SessionNode> mNodes = sessionMap.values();
 for(SessionNode mNode:mNodes)
 {
  Session mSession = mNode.getSession();
```

```
      if(mSession != null)
      {
        mSession.close();
        mSession = null;
        mNode.setSession(mSession);
        mRtnValue = true;
      }
    }
    sessionMap = new HashMap<SessionFactory, SessionNode>();
    return mRtnValue;
  }
}
```

Chapter 13 Meta Programming

13.1 Meta/Reflection

The Introspector class is used to call methods and query objects. The Framework uses this for a number of reasons. One of the main reason is so that when a component is called using the execute method, the execute method will look at the operation in the command and will find an annotation that matches the operation and the required parameters. If it finds a match, the method inside of the component is called to for further processing.

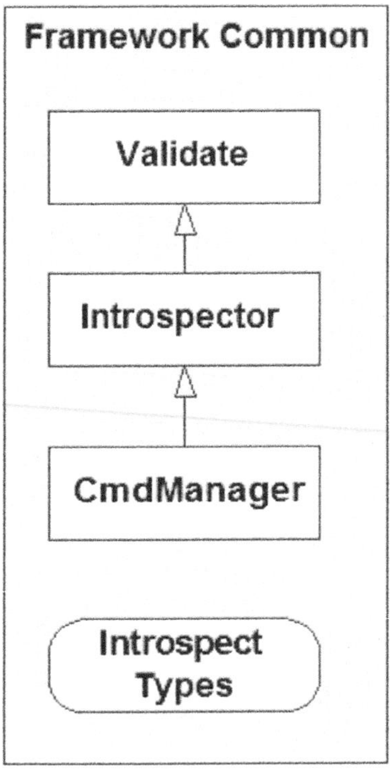

13.2 Factory Manager and Factories

When the Loader object loads the Spring Configuration, the factory manager is loaded with callable components (usually Solutions, but may be Domains or Exchanges). Additionally, initial commands are also stored in the Factory Manager by Command Id. Whenever a Service Proxy is called with the id for the command and the name of the Solution, the framework uses the factory manager to lookup both the Command Objects as well as the Solution Component.

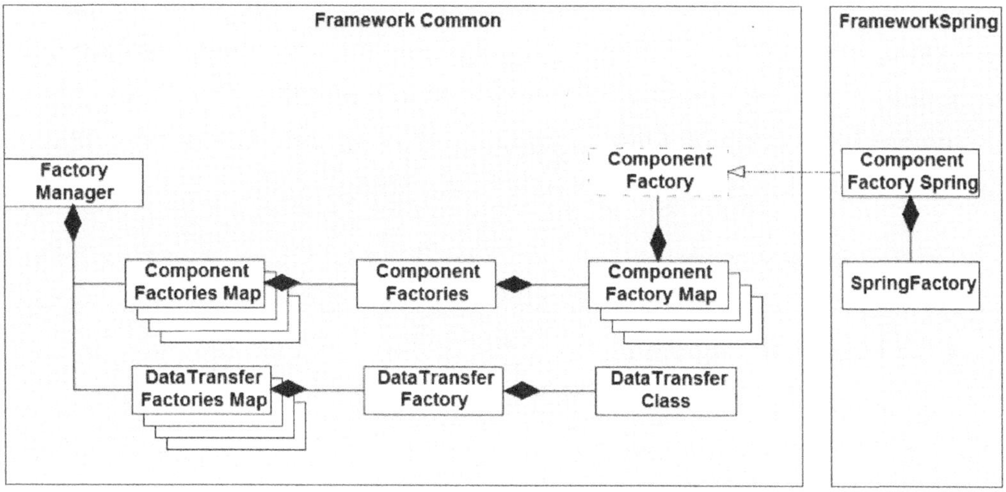

13.3 Working with XML Data

Often in todays world, application software must deal with XML data. This data may be stored in a clob in the database or received from a Message Queue or read from a file. In order to work with XML data, it can be helpful to build a tree structure to not only hold the data but to also allow for XML data manipulation and Searching. To accomplish this, a set of XML classes can be designed and built to handle all of the XML work.

The XML Class/Object is an object relationship that represents an XML Hierarchy. The XMLType is an interface that represents all possible types of XML Data. The XMLBase class is an abstract class that provide shared processing for the other classes. The XMLTag represents a set of XML Structures and is a container for other XMLTypes. The XMLTag main purpose is to capture the name of the XML Tag and hold representation of other XML Structures. The XMLValue holds the value of a tag (a String). XML Tags can contain both XML Tags and XMLValues. XMLValues can only hold a string.

In addition to holding a set of XML Types, XML Tags also have other functions such as building a XML String and searching for an XML Tag name and returning the value of the tag.

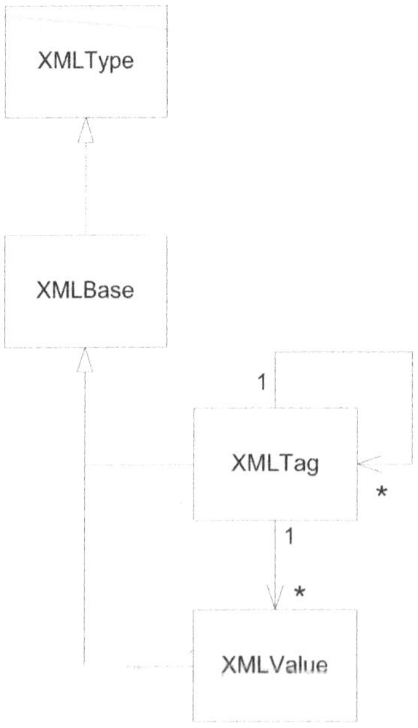

Chapter 14 Framework Spring Project

14.1 Introduction

The Framework Spring project isolates the specific code that uses Spring from the rest of the framework. In the framework itself there are two types of Spring packages. The first package is for the spring factory and the second is for the Spring loader.

14.2 Spring Factories

ComponentFactorySpring: Uses spring to create a Component. This class calls Spring and receives and Object back. The code checks the object type to ensure it is a component. If it is a component, it is cast to the Component type and returned.

```
public class ComponentFactorySpring extends Validate implements ComponentFactory
{
 private static final SpringFactory springFactory = new SpringFactory();
 private String beanName;

 private static final String TITLE = "Component Factory Spring";
 private static final String BEAN_NOT_FOUND = "Bean not found!";

 public ComponentFactorySpring()
 {
        //empty constructor
 }

 public ComponentFactorySpring(String aBeanName)
 {
  beanName = aBeanName;
 }

 public void setBeanName(String aBeanName)
```

```
  {
    beanName = aBeanName;
  }

  public String getBeanName()
  {
    return beanName;
  }


  @Override
  public Component create(CmdMsg aCmdMsg)
  {
    Component mRtnValue = null;
    Object mObject = springFactory.getBean(getBeanName());
    if(mObject instanceof Component)
    {
      mRtnValue = (Component)mObject;
    }
    check("Param
Error",TITLE,"setValue","",BEAN_NOT_FOUND,ErrorType.FRAMEWORK,mRtnValue);
    return mRtnValue;
  }

}
```

SpringFactory: Is the direct connections between the framework and Spring. This class calls the SpringContext to get the Spring Application Context and uses it to create an Object using Spring.

```
public class SpringFactory
{
  public Object getBean(String aName)
  {
    ApplicationContext mContext = SpringContext.getContext();
    return mContext.getBean(aName);
  }
}
```

SpringContext: Stores the Spring Application Context as well as the configuration locations. During the initial start up of the system, the configuration contexts are stored in the SpringContext. Once the first call to the SpringContext is called to get the ApplicationContext, the object checks to see if one has been created, if not it will create the Spring Application Context, otherwise, it will re-use the existing context.

```
public class SpringContext extends Validate
{
 private static final String TITLE = "SpringContext";
 private static final String ILLEGAL_PATH = "Context Path can not be null!";
 private static Collection<String> configLocations = new ArrayList<String>();
 private static ApplicationContext context = null;

 public static ApplicationContext getContext()
 {
  if(context == null)
  {
   synchronized(SpringFactory.class)
   {
    if(context == null)
    {
     String[] mConfigurations = getConfigurationArray();
     context = new ClassPathXmlApplicationContext(mConfigurations);
    }
   }
  }
  return context;
 }

 private static String[] getConfigurationArray()
 {
  int mSize = configLocations.size();
  String[] mRtnValue = new String[mSize];
  configLocations.toArray(mRtnValue);
  return mRtnValue;
 }

 public static void addContextPath(String aPath)
 {
```

```
  check("Param
Error",TITLE,"setValue","",ILLEGAL_PATH,ErrorType.FRAMEWORK,aPath);
  synchronized(SpringFactory.class)
  {
   if(!configLocations.contains(aPath))
   {
    configLocations.add(aPath);
    context = null;
   }
  }
 }
}
```

14.3 Spring Loader

Spring Loader: The Spring Loader is an abstract class that uses the getContextPath to retrieve the context path from the implementing object(s). The loader should be called when a proxy class is loaded using a static block constructor. This starts the Spring Loader and in turn uses the SpringBuilder to build the Components and the Component Factories in the system as well as load other definitions from the Spring Configuration Files.

```
public abstract class SpringLoader extends Loader
{
 protected SpringLoader()
 {
  //empty constructor
 }

 protected void loadConfigurations()
 {
  for(String mContextPath: getContextPath())
  {
   addContextPath(mContextPath);
  }
 }

 protected abstract String[] getContextPath();

 protected static void addContextPath(String aPath)
 {
  SpringContext.addContextPath(aPath);
 }

 public boolean loadBuilder()
 {
  boolean mRtnValue = false;
  ApplicationContext mContext = SpringContext.getContext();
  Object mObject = mContext.getBean("SpringBuilder");
  if(mObject instanceof SpringBuilder)
  {
   mRtnValue = true;
  }
  return mRtnValue;
```

```
 }
}
```

SpringBuilder: When the Spring Configuration files are loaded, they create a SpringBuilder object and call the setLibraryEntries and the setComponentEntries to load the definitions of the Command Libraries and the Components.

```
public class SpringBuilder
{
 public void setLibraryEntries(ArrayList<CmdEntry> aListOfCommandEntries)
 {
  CmdLibraryManager mCmdLibraryManager = CmdLibraryManager.getInstance();
  for(CmdEntry mCmdEntry: aListOfCommandEntries)
  {
   CmdLibrary mLibrary =
mCmdLibraryManager.getCommandLibrary(mCmdEntry.getType());
   if(mLibrary == null)
   {
    mLibrary = new CmdLibrary();
    mCmdLibraryManager.loadCommandLibrary(mCmdEntry.getType(), mLibrary);
   }
   mLibrary.addLibraryEntry(mCmdEntry.getName(), mCmdEntry.getCommand());
  }
 }

 public void setComponentEntries(ArrayList<ComponentEntry>
aListOfComponentEntries)
 {
  FactoryComponentManager mFactoryManger =
FactoryComponentManager.getInstance();
  for(ComponentEntry mComponentEntry: aListOfComponentEntries)
  {
   ComponentType mType =
ComponentType.getComponentType(mComponentEntry.getType());
   String mName = mComponentEntry.getName();
   String mBeanName = mComponentEntry.getBeanName();
   ComponentFactory mFactory = new ComponentFactorySpring(mBeanName);
   mFactoryManger.loadComponentFactory(mType, mName, mFactory);
  }
 }
}
```

Chapter 15 Framework Hibernate

15.1 Introduction

The Framework Hibernate contains all the Hibernate Specific classes for the Framework.

15.2 The Hibernate Generic DAO

The Hibernate Generic DAO defines and process the GenericDAO Pattern methods. These include:

- findByKey
- findAll
- findByExample
- makePersistent
- save
- makeTransient
- findByQuery
- findByNativeQuery
- findByCriteria
- execute (by Command Object)

Chapter 16 Wiring using Spring

16.1 Introduction

Generally speaking, the Spring Configuration files can be divided into a number sub configuration files.

- Spring.cfg.xml
- *.builder.spring.cfg.xml
- *.solution.cfg.xml
- *.domain.cfg.xml
- *.exchange.cfg.xml
- *.exchange.cfg.cmd.xml
- *.dao.cfg.xml
- *.keyvalue.cfg.xml
- *datasource.cfg.xml

16.2 Master Spring Configuration file

This xml file is used only to import the other xml files. It is xml file that the software system must load to start the Spring configuration.

Example:

File Name: example.spring.cfg.xml

```
<?xml version="1.0" encoding="UTF-8"?>
<!DOCTYPE beans PUBLIC "-//SPRING//DTD BEAN//EN"
"http://www.springframework.org/dtd/spring-beans.dtd">
<beans>
 <import resource="classpath:example.datasource.cfg.xml"/>
 <import resource="classpath:example.exchange.cfg.xml"/>
 <import resource="classpath:example.domain.cfg.xml"/>
 <import resource="classpath:example.solution.cfg.xml"/>
 <import resource="classpath:example.builder.spring.cfg.xml"/>
</beans>
```

In the above example, five xml files are included into the processing

16.3 Spring Builder Configuration File

This xml file is used to build the Spring Objects and control the dependency injection controlled by Spring. This allows an object to function without having to have a deep understanding of how the underlying object works.

When Spring is started, it creates a java object (spring bean) called SpringBuilder. This Spring Builder has two sets of operations: Set Command Library entries and set Component Entries. These entries are used to build the Component factories as well as build the underlying components and their commands.

Example:

File Name: example.builder.spring.cfg.xml

```
<?xml version="1.0" encoding="UTF-8"?>
<!DOCTYPE beans PUBLIC "-//SPRING//DTD BEAN//EN"
"http://www.springframework.org/dtd/spring-beans.dtd">
<beans>

 <import resource="example.builder.entry.spring.cfg.xml"/>

 <bean id="SpringBuilder" class="com.dth.fmw.model.spring.loader.SpringBuilder">
  <property name="libraryEntries">
   <list>
    <ref bean="CmdEntryExample1Entry"/>
    <ref bean="CmdEntryExample2Entry"/>
    <ref bean="CmdEntryExample3Entry"/>
    <ref bean="CmdEntryExample4Entry"/>
   </list>
  </property>
  <property name="componentEntries">
   <list>
    <ref bean="example1"/>
    <ref bean="example2"/>
    <ref bean="example3"/>
    <ref bean="example4"/>
   </list>
  </property>
 </bean>
</beans>
```

File Name: example.builder.entry.spring.cfg.xml

```
<?xml version="1.0" encoding="UTF-8"?>
<!DOCTYPE beans PUBLIC "-//SPRING//DTD BEAN//EN"
"http://www.springframework.org/dtd/spring-beans.dtd">
<beans>
  <bean id="CmdEntryExampl1Entry"
class="com.dth.fmw.common.component.library.CmdEntry">
    <property name="type" value="Solution"/>
    <!-- This is the type of the entry, usually Solution unless used for testing -->
    <property name="name" value="CmdExample1Solution"/>
    <property name="command" ref="CmdExample1Solution"/>
  </bean>
<bean id="example1" class="com.dth.fmw.common.component.ComponentEntry">
     <property name="type" value="SOLUTION"/>
     <property name="name" value="Example1Solution"/>
     <property name="beanName" value="Example1Solution"/>
  </bean>
</beans>
```

16.4 Spring Solution Configuration File

These xml files define the Solution Components and inject them with their underlying Domain objects and the Commands to call the Domain Object.

Example:

File Name: example.solution.cfg.xml

```
<?xml version="1.0" encoding="UTF-8"?>
<!DOCTYPE beans PUBLIC "-//SPRING//DTD BEAN//EN"
"http://www.springframework.org/dtd/spring-beans.dtd">
<beans>


  <bean id="Example1Solution"
class="com.dth.fmw.model.component.solution.SolutionGeneric">
    <property name="cmdComponents">
      <list>
        <ref bean="CmdComponentExample1Domain"/>
      </list>
    </property>
  </bean>

  <bean id="CmdExample1Solution" class="com.dth.fmw.common.cmd.Cmd">
    <property name="name" value="Example1Solution"/>
    <property name="componentName" value="Example1Solution"/>
    <property name="componentTypeName" value="SOLUTION"/>
    <property name="operation" value="generic"/>
  </bean>

  <bean id="CmdComponentExample1Solution"
class="com.dth.fmw.model.component.cmd.CmdComponent">
    <property name="component" ref="Example1Solution"/>
    <property name="command" ref="CmdExample1Solution"/>
  </bean>
```

16.5 Spring Domain Configuration File

These xml files define the Domain Components and inject them with their underlying Exchange Objects and the Commands to call the Exchange Object.

Example:

File Name: example.domain.cfg.xml

```
<?xml version="1.0" encoding="UTF-8"?>
<!DOCTYPE beans PUBLIC "-//SPRING//DTD BEAN//EN"
"http://www.springframework.org/dtd/spring-beans.dtd">
<beans>
 <bean id="Example1Domain"
class="com.dth.fmw.model.component.domain.DomainGeneric">
  <property name="cmdComponents">
   <list>
    <ref bean="CmdComponentExample1Exchange"/>
   </list>
  </property>
 </bean>

 <bean id="CmdExample1Domain" class="com.dth.fmw.common.cmd.Cmd">
  <property name="name" value="Example1Domain"/>
  <property name="componentName" value="Example1Domain"/>
  <property name="componentTypeName" value="DOMAIN"/>
  <property name="operation" value="generic"/>
 </bean>

 <bean id="CmdComponentExample1Domain"
class="com.dth.fmw.model.component.cmd.CmdComponent">
  <property name="component" ref="Example1Domain"/>
  <property name="command" ref="CmdExample1Domain"/>
 </bean>
```

16.6 Spring Exchange Configuration File

These xml files define the Exchange Components and inject them with their underlying DAOs and the Commands to call send to the DAOs.

Example:

Filename: example.exchange.cfg.xml

```
<?xml version="1.0" encoding="UTF-8"?>
<!DOCTYPE beans PUBLIC "-//SPRING//DTD BEAN//EN"
"http://www.springframework.org/dtd/spring-beans.dtd">
<beans>
  <import resource="classpath:example.keyvalue.cfg.xml"/>
  <import resource="classpath:example.exchange.cmd.cfg.xml"/>
  <import resource="classpath:example.dao.cfg.xml"/>
  <bean id="Example1Exchange"
 class="com.dth.fmw.model.component.exchange.ExchangeGenericUsingCmd">
    <property name="dao" ref="Example1DAO"/>
    <property name="command" ref="Example1ExchangeCmdQuery"/>
  </bean>
  <bean id="CmdExample1Exchange" class="com.dth.fmw.common.cmd.Cmd">
    <property name="name" value="Example1Exchange"/>
    <property name="componentName" value="Example1Exchange"/>
    <property name="componentTypeName" value="EXCHANGE"/>
    <property name="operation" value="generic"/>
  </bean>
  <bean id="CmdComponentExample1Exchange"
 class="com.dth.fmw.model.component.cmd.CmdComponent">
    <property name="component" ref="Example1Exchange"/>
    <property name="command" ref="CmdExample1Exchange"/>
  </bean>
    <bean id="CmdExample1Exchange" class="com.dth.fmw.common.cmd.Cmd">
    <property name="name" value="Example1Exchange"/>
    <property name="componentName" value="Example1Exchange"/>
    <property name="componentTypeName" value="EXCHANGE"/>
    <property name="operation" value="generic"/>
  </bean></beans>
```

16.7 Spring Exchange Command Configuration File

These xml files define the query commands used by the Exchanged and passed to the DAOs for processing. They also contain the name of the query or if a dynamic query is used then the query string itself.

Example:

File Name: example.exchange.cmd.cfg.xml

```
<?xml version="1.0" encoding="UTF-8"?>
<!DOCTYPE beans PUBLIC "-//SPRING//DTD BEAN//EN"
"http://www.springframework.org/dtd/spring-beans.dtd">
<beans>
 <bean id="Example1ExchangeCmdQuery" class="com.dth.fmw.common.cmd.CmdQuery">
<!-- Name -->
   <constructor-arg value="Example1ExchangeCmdQuery"/>
<!-- Component Type -->
   <constructor-arg value="EXCHANGE"/>
<!-- Component Name -->
   <constructor-arg value="Example1DAO"/>
<!-- operation -->
   <constructor-arg value="findByQuery"/>
<!-- Command Parent -->
   <constructor-arg><null/></constructor-arg>
<!-- Command Children -->
   <constructor-arg><null/></constructor-arg>         <!-- Response ID -->
   <constructor-arg value="example1ResponseInfo"/>   <!-- Named Query Name -->
   <constructor-arg value="exmple1ByPrimaryKey"/>
<!-- Key Values -->
   <constructor-arg>
     <list>
      <ref bean="Example1Id"/>
     </list>
   </constructor-arg>
 </bean>
</beans>
```

16.8 Spring DAO Configuration File

These xml files define the DAOs and inject them with the session Factory for Hibernate/Spring.

Example:

File Name: example.dao.cfg.xml

```
<?xml version="1.0" encoding="UTF-8"?>
<!DOCTYPE beans PUBLIC "-//SPRING//DTD BEAN//EN"
"http://www.springframework.org/dtd/spring-beans.dtd">
<beans>
  <bean id="Example1RunDAO"
class="com.dth.example.access.DAOHibernateExample1">
    <property name="sessionFactory" ref="sessionFactoryExample"/>
  </bean>
</beans>
```

16.9 Spring Key Value Configuration File

These xml files are used to replace arguments in the SQL with real data.

Example:

File Name: example.keyvalue.cfg.xml

```
<?xml version="1.0" encoding="UTF-8"?>
<!DOCTYPE beans PUBLIC "-//SPRING//DTD BEAN//EN"
"http://www.springframework.org/dtd/spring-beans.dtd">
<beans>
 <bean id="Exampl1Id" class="com.dth.fmw.common.util.KeyValue">
  <constructor-arg value="id"/>
  <constructor-arg value="example1Info.id"/>
 </bean></beans>
```

16.10 Spring Data Source Configuration File

This xml file defines the data sources and configures them. They also contain the list of annotated Packages and annotated classes.

Example:

File Name: example.datasource.cfg.xml

```
<?xml version="1.0" encoding="UTF-8"?>
<!DOCTYPE beans PUBLIC "-//SPRING//DTD BEAN//EN"
"http://www.springframework.org/dtd/spring-beans.dtd">
<beans>

  <bean id="ExampleDataSource"
class="org.springframework.jdbc.datasource.DriverManagerDataSource">
     <property name="driverClassName" value="oracle.jdbc.driver.OracleDriver"/>
     <property name="url" value="jdbc:oracle:thin:@example.dth.com:1526 "/>
     <property name="username" value="userName"/>
     <property name="password" value="password"/>
  </bean>

 <bean id="sessionFactoryExample"
class="org.springframework.orm.hibernate3.annotation.AnnotationSessionFactoryBean">
  <property name="dataSource" ref="ExampleDataSource"/>
  <property name="annotatedClasses">
   <list>
    <value>com.dth.example.access.HVOExample1</value>
    <value>com.dth.example.access.HVOExample2</value>
    <value>com.dth.example.access.HVOExample3</value>
   </list>
  </property>
  <property name="annotatedPackages">
   <list>
    <value>com.dth.example.access</value>
   </list>
  </property>
  <property name="hibernateProperties">
   <props>
    <prop key="hibernate.dialect">org.hibernate.dialect.OracleDialect</prop>
    <prop key="hibernate.bytecode.provider">javassist</prop>
    <prop key="hibernate.show_sql">true</prop>
```

```
      <prop key="hibernate.format_sql">true</prop>
      <prop key="hibernate.use_sql_comments">true</prop>
      <prop key="hibernate.cache.use_second_level_cache">false</prop>
      <prop key="hibernate.hbm2ddl.auto">update</prop>
      <prop key="hibernate.connection.pool_size">10</prop>
      <prop key="hibernate.query.factory_class">
       org.hibernate.hql.classic.ClassicQueryTranslatorFactory
      </prop>
      <prop key="hibernate.c3p0.min_size">5</prop>
      <prop key="hibernate.c3p0.max_size">20</prop>
      <prop key="hibernate.c3p0.timeout">300</prop>
      <prop key="hibernate.c3p0.max_statements">50</prop>
      <prop key="hibernate.c3p0.idle_test_period">300</prop>
    </props>
   </property>
  </bean>
</beans>
```

Chapter 17 Generic Components

17.1 Concept

The basic concept of Generic Components is to push all repeated code into a single class that can be configured using either Generic Java type or configured using Spring. In the framework, there are 3 Generic Components configured using Spring (SolutionGeneric, DomanGeneric, Exchange Generic) and one abstract class using the Generic Java Type (DAOGenericBase).

In cases where the Component is configured by Spring, when every the Component does nothing but call a Component below it or there is a repeatable pattern, Generic Component can be used to handle this situations.

Bibliography

Architecting and Designing J2EE Applications, Sun Microsystem publication, 2003

Architecture Patterns for Enterprise-wide SOA, Borjan Cace, www.via-nova-architectura.org, 2008

Building Application Frameworks, Mohamed E. Fayad, Doublas C. Schmidt, and Ralph E. Johnson, Wiley Computer Publishing, 1990

Component Based Architecture Suppliementing Service Oriented Architectures, Badri Sriraman, Rakesh Radhakrishman, Sun Microsystem Publishing, 2005

Component-based Software Engineering, Wikipedia

Core JavaServer Faces, Third Edition, David Geary and Cay Horstmann, Prentice Hall, 2010

Core J2EE Patterns, Second Edition, Deepak Alur, John Crupi, and Dan Malks, Sun Microsystem Press Publication, 2003

Dependency Injection, Griffin Caprio, MSDN Magazine, 2005

Dependency Injection Benefits, Jakob Jenkov, Jenkov.com, 2011

Dont Repeat Yourself, http://c2.com/cgi/wiki?DontRepeatYourself

Enterprise Integration Patterns, Gregor Hohpe and Bobby Woof, Anderson-Wesley, 2009

Exception management and error tracking in J2EE, Kåre Kjelstrøm and Jens Schjærff Byager, JavaWorld.com, 07/11/05

Hibernate in Action, Christian Bauer and Gavin King, Maning publications, 2004

How to Build Better Software, Oren Eini, 2006

Implementing Application Frameworks, Mohamed E. Fayad, Doublas C. Schmidt, and Ralph E. Johnson, Wiley Computer Publishing, 1999

Inversion of Control (IoC), Daniel Rinehart, BFPUG, Jun 6, 2007

Inversion of Control Containers and the Dependency Injection Pattern, Martin Fowler, martinfowler.com, 2011

Maser Data Integration and the Single Source of Truth, Published in B-Eye-Network, March 2005

Orthogonality and the DRY Principle, Bill Venners, Artima Developer, March 10, 2003

Patterns of Enterprise Application Architecture, Martin Fowler, Addision-Wesley, 2005

Rapid Development, Steve McConnell, Microsoft Press, 1996

Service Component-Based Architecture, Version 2.0, Architecture and Infrastructure Committee, Federal Chief Information Officers Council, 2004

Service-oriented agility, Pal Kroghdahl, Gottried Luef, Christoph Steindl, developer works, 2005

Service-Oriented Architecture (SOA) vs. Compnent Based Architecture, Helmut Petritsch

SOA, Principles of Service Design, Thomas Erl, Prentice Hall, 2008

Software Components: Course-grained versus fine-grained, Michael Beisiegel, Dave Booz, Mike Edwards, Eric Herness, Stephen Kinder, developerWorks, IBM, 2007

Spring in Action, Second Edition, Craig Walls, Manning Publications, 2008

Succeeding with Component-Based Architecture in e-Government, John C. Butler, David R. Mayo, and John Weiler, Industry Advisory Council (IAC), 2003

Sun Certified Enterprise Architect for J2EE Technology, Mark Cade and Simon Roberts, Sun Microsystem Press, 2002

The Art of Speration of Concerns, derekgreer, http://www.aspiringcraftsman.com/2008/01/03/art-of-separation-of-concerns/, 2008

Understanding separation of concerns, Hafedh Mili, Amel Elkharraz and Hamid Mcheick, Laboratoire de recherché sur les Technologies du Commerce Electronique, 2004

Index

Made in the USA
Middletown, DE
05 November 2026

36612684R00205